Tour de Provence

Tour de
PROVENCE

Julian More

Photographs by John Miller

PAVILION

For Sheila
with special thanks for sharing Provence and helping
with the book at all stages of its creation.

First published in Great Britain in 2001 by
PAVILION BOOKS

A member of **Chrysalis** Books plc

64 Brewery Road, London, N7 9NT

This paperback edition published in Great Britain
in 2003 by Pavilion Books

Text © Julian More 2001
Photographs © John Miller 2001
Design and layout © Pavilion Books Ltd.

The moral right of the author has been asserted

Designed by Bernard Higton
Illustrations by Michael Munday
Maps by David Williams

A CIP catalogue record for this book is available from the
British Library.

Text set in Simoncini Garamond
Printed in Spain by JCG

ISBN 1 86205 429 0

10 9 8 7 6 5 4 3 2 1

This book can be ordered direct from the publisher. Please contact
the Marketing Department. But try your bookshop first.

3 1907 00140 9274

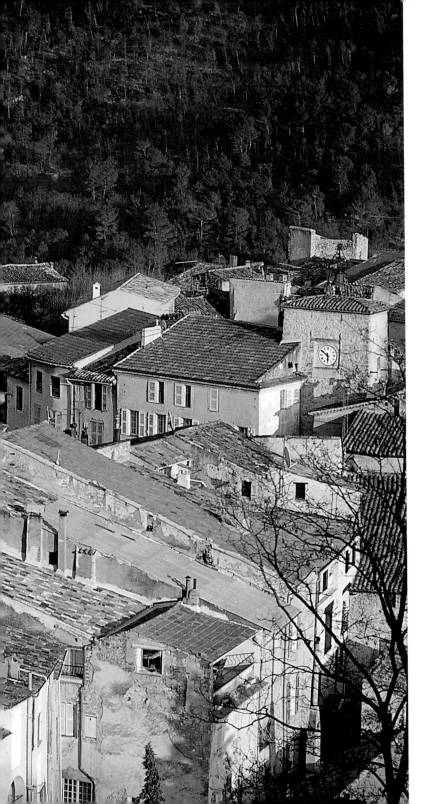

Contents

Chapter 1

MY PROVENCE

Even the longest lasting love affairs need a booster from time to time. And mine with Provence, which was already forty years old, called for more than the traveller's equivalent of a dozen oysters or ginseng; nothing but a complete second honeymoon would do.

This book is that second honeymoon, the chronicle of a sentimental journey undertaken in a blissfully sunny March. I found much to reactivate my juices; if not exactly new things, things with a new slant, the constantly changing scene since the years I had first known it. Provence reinvents itself as unpredictably as the wine's new year.

Upper Vaucluse, Provence of the Popes

The author, about to set off on his travels

It all began a long, long time ago, entirely unoriginally, in St-Tropez. An unexpected windfall meant that my wife Sheila and I could afford to flash out a bit, parking our convertible on the waterfront of Bardotville and hoping to catch a glimpse of the great BB herself. We did. Later, during a family holiday at Grimaud I learned to play *pétanque*, bowling small metal balls with a fisherman, a mason and a garage mechanic. From other happy stays at La Garde-Freinet and Bargemon, where our ten-year-old-daughters attended the village school, I took back to the London smog the singular aroma of hot pine needles and wild thyme; at home in Camden Town we chucked more garlic and herbs into our casseroles and made *daubes* with Argentinian wine, the cheapest available at the time.

It was almost inevitable that we should land up here some

day. A precarious but full life writing musicals in London and New York included adaptation of a French one, *Irma La Douce*, and translating French song lyrics. This further whetted my Gallic appetite and after 25 years based in London, we up-sticked to Paris in 1976. Two years later we bought our patch of Provence and, after frequent visits, moved here permanently in the early nineties. Between doing nothing as elegantly as possible, I still managed to write musicals and books, including two on Provence with photographs by our daughter, Carey. Grandchildren visit every summer and, for them, Provence has become a place where childhood memories are born. Twenty years? Is that really how long we'd nurtured our appetite like our trees? A lot less hair and a lot more garden proved it.

Where once a much-loved wilderness greeted us in the first winter of our content, now roses rambled and grapes burgeoned. The cypresses that Sheila and I had planted together as 2 feet (60cm) tall saplings now formed a 15 feet (4.6m) hedge, providing the lawn with a necessary wind-break against the savage north-easterly mistral. The lawn, though it would disgrace a Home Counties village cricket pitch, was not doing badly considering; a distinctly Provençal British lawn with bald patches but how good to siesta on our own green grass in the shade of our own olive trees. We can give guests our own olives with their drinks, not to mention our own figs and grapes for dessert. Roses bloom among the santolina and oleander. For a *daube provençale*, a slow-cooking aromatic beef stew, I can pick our own herbs, scattered about the garden in casual clumps – thyme, savoury, mint, fennel, sage, tarragon, bay-leaves, and a long hedge of rosemary overgrown with clematis.

Below us our village, its bell tower ghostly in the morning mist or silhouetted by dying sun, may be on a main road but somehow remains pleasantly off the beaten track. When winter's grip mysteriously loosens and hurtling rooftiles no longer threaten our skulls, wafts of woodsmoke down gusty alleys change to encouraging smells of new-baked bread. A burgeoning baker's wife talks suddenly of births and lottery wins instead of arthritis and funerals. Once again we become aware of the fountain's tinkle, the click of those little metal balls as veterans of the game uncreak to do battle in the shade of plane trees. Towards March, with winter behind us, the sap begins to rise and new passions stir the blood.

That spring, I became restless. Twenty years was a long time. I was in danger of becoming a smug recluse, doing nothing just a little *too* elegantly. I needed the outside world. I needed ...

A holiday? Visitors think we're permanently on holiday. But home is not just anywhere you hang your Camargue sombrero; it is also where you pay your taxes, face misunderstandings with neighbours, repair roofs, and try to stay out of the bankruptcy courts. To make visitors less envious, I reassure them: there's no pleasure without pain. Only pick up *La Provençe*, *Nice-Matin*, *Le Meridional* or turn on the regional news on France's Channel 3 and you're in very different country: a land not of goat's milk and lavender honey but corruption, floods, racism, and the crasser aspects of mass tourism.

In twenty years, the rose-tinted spectacles get a lens change. We see more clearly. Eyes are opened to a darker side of the Provençal character, secret duplicity and chauvinistic reserve, a mercurial moodswing as violent as the sudden blowing-up of a mistral, described so poignantly by Marcel Pagnol in *Jean de Florette*. We foreigners (Parisians are as foreign as we are!) compound the downside in an entirely different but no less insidious way, corrupting the natural order with our Style Provençale pretentiousness.

Decentralization has given the region (Provence Alpes – Côte-d'Azur, as it's been known officially since 1974) more control over its own affairs. The benefits: superb regional nature parks, excellent communications, high technology know-how. The downside: a conflict between an energetic attraction of outsiders and a paradoxal attempt to preserve the Provençal identity. The Côte d'Azur and Riviera suffer from property development overkill, while remote hill villages are dying on their feet. In high-density tourist areas such as the Lubéron and Les Alpilles, sophisticated promotion tends to create a theme park ambience, a sort of Disneyland-en-Provence.

What changes for better or worse would I see? Would affection become anger? It was time, I decided, to redefine my Provence. Time to make a voyage of rediscovery – and discovery. Much of the vast region I had never visited. I spent days pouring over the essential Michelin Road Atlas of France.

Geographically, Provence is the Romans' Provincia, the origin of the name. Although it stretched as far as Narbonne to the west, today's approximate parameters are: from Nîmes 190 miles (145 km) east to the Italian border, from the Mediterranean 130 miles (210 km) north to Drôme Provençale and the High Alps. From my home in north-western Provence, I took enchantingly traffic-free *routes départmentales* (D roads) all the way south-east to Nice, from one end of Provence to the other without a single Autoroute (motorway or freeway) and only touching *routes nationales* (N roads) where short links were necessary. The itinerary covered five *départments* (French administrative areas), each with its distinct character, different terrain, culture, wine and gastronomic specialities.

The journey started in Vaucluse, heartland of Côtes du Rhône wine where many a pope, exiled to Avignon in the fourteenth century, quaffed Châteauneuf-du-Pape by the litre. From Vaison-la-Romaine I drove through the spiky Dentelles hills and Beaumes-de-Venise, Carpentras the truffle capital, to the touristy Lubéron and *still* found secret places to hike and bike with no one around but a chirring cricket and a few bell-tinkling goats.

Across the Durance River, I arrived in my next *départment* Bouches-du-Rhône where the two mighty rivers combine and flow to the Mediterranean. In the hallucegenic light of fertile flatlands and craggy hills, I went in search of van Gogh at Arles and St-Rémy, Cézanne at Aix-en-Provence and Montagne-Ste-Victoire, and Picasso's burial place at Vauvenargues.

Var is the louche *départment*, with the longest stretch of Mediterranean coast where crooked politicians and political mafiosi racketeer most lucratively among the bronzing beach bums. Profane and sacred, Var also contains Mary Magdelene's Cave and Le Thoronet Abbey (arguably the finest site in Provence), hinterland perched villages, pristine swimming on the enchanted island of Port-Cros and herb-scented walks among the red rocks of the Esterel hills.

I drove through a mimosa forest soon after entering the *départment* of Alpes-Maritimes to find an astonishingly unspoiled village, Auribeau-sur-Siagne, only a few miles inland from the fleshpots of Cannes. Then, onwards and upwards from Grasse's heady perfumes, via my favourite Provençal city Nice, to the Mercantour National Park. In the deceptive simplicity of alpine villages like Roure, young sheepfarmers confront the menace of wolves wiping out their livelihood – to the outcry of Greens proclaiming The Rights of Wolf.

My fifth *départment*, Alpes de Haute-Provence, known for its dramatic gorges like Verdon and wide open spaces like the Montagne de Lure, took me to Manosque, home-town of Provence's most evocative writer, Jean Giono, orginator of *La Femme du Boulanger* (The Baker's Wife) adapted and directed by Marcel Pagnol to become one of France's all-time movie hits. No writer more powerfully

and wittily than Giono evokes the tough peasant life of the hills and plateaux, the once grindingly poor up-country villages now saved by second-home owners. This new prosperity is evident in market towns like Forcalquier, Banon and Sault.

Nearing home, I reached my last and wildest *départment*, Drôme. Its amiable hills, between Rhône Valley and High Alps are perfect trekking country where eagles plane overhead and clearly-marked paths provide endless vistas of enchantment. Apricots, lime blossom, and olives abound in the valleys, herb-fed lambs on hillside meadows. Among the world's many Last Shangri La's, the wine-making Ste-Jalle Valley rates high on the list of contenders for the title.

My own tailor-made Tour de Provence took in this incredible variety of terrain, people and things to do and see. Each chapter covers a *départment*. Apart from describing the journey, I eleborate on certain aspects in sidebars – cultural, gastronomic, viticultural, where to stay and eat along the way. Reservations, by the way, are really only necessary in July and August, at Christmas, Easter and French school holidays.

As it was March, I needed no reservation, never planned where I would dine and sleep that night. I winged it, in the freewheeling, leisurely kind of travel that engenders love. Slow caresses of countryside, foreplay among the narrow streets or country lanes before the ecstasy of viewing some great *monument historique* or view round a corner. Selective and personal in its choices, the itinerary in no way pretends to be comprehensive. Those who have never experienced Provence's infinite pleasures – and, hopefully others – may be encouraged to follow my itinerary. Old Provence hands will, I'm sure, have fun finding fault with my choice of restaurants, hotels, and places visited. You can't please everyone. Quite unashamedly, however, I did please myself.

JULIAN MORE'S ITINERARY

- - - - - ALTERNATIVE ROUTE

Dieulefit
Valréas
LA COSTE
Buis-les-Baronnies
Vaison-la-Romaine
MT. VENTOUX
Sault
Château-Arnoux
Digne
NAT. PARK OF MERCANTOUR
Valberg
St.Martin Vésubie
Carpentras
Forcalquier
Luis
Les Mées
St.André-les-Alpes
Annot
RHÔNE
Gordes
LUBERON
Manosque
Moustiers
Castellane
GORGES DU LOUP
Vence
Nice
St. Rémy
Les Baux
DURANCE
GORGES DU VERDON
Grasse
Fayence
Arles
Salon-de-Provence
Aix-en-Provence
Lorgues
ESTEREL
La Napoule
Antibes
MT. STE. VICTOIRE
Trets
Fréjus
La Ste Baume
Bormes-les-Mimosas
Île de Port-Cros

LA COSTE

Vaison-la-Romaine

Gordes

Chapter 2

POPE'S PARADISE

VAUCLUSE

Upper Vaucluse, Provence des Papes, was ruled by Popes until the French Revolution. Hence its most famous wine, Châteauneuf-du-Pape. Côtes du Rhône vineyards, like those on the Digi near Visan (above right) benefit from the Rhône valley's sunshine, pebbles, clay, chalk, and sand. Further south, Côtes du Lubéron produces a good spicy red near Roussillon (below right and far right), the 'rose-red' village with its ochre, pine-topped cliffs.

LA COSTE TO VAISON-LA-ROMAINE

The sun rose, an aura of golden light behind Mont Ventoux, gradually creeping out from behind the mountain to spread its light wide into clear blue sky. The air was brisk and clean. A miraculous day for March. And what a day to be starting a journey!

Provence is constantly surprising. Even the lane where I set forth can pull a surprise or two. Badgers, baby rabbits and doe scuttle across it unexpectedly. A backroad so far back it doesn't even rate a number on the map. It runs between the Côtes du Rhône vineyards of our neighbours, Pierrot and Yves, and is blessed with its fair share of Midi sun. Honeysuckle, poppies, yellow Genista, and dog-roses flourish in the hedgerows. Come December, however, a freak snowstorm can make chains necessary. Almond blossom in February is delicate as a Japanese print. Puddles after diluvian April showers dry up before our eyes in a mistral's fury, and La Coste, as our home is known because of its position on vineyards slopes (*coste* or *coteaux*), becomes Les Hauts de l'Hurlevent (Wuthering Heights).

At journey's beginning, our lane basked in this extraordinary March sunshine, windless and warm. Running along a panoramic hogsback, more than 1,000 feet (305m) above sea level, it is where we take our daily walk. Always the same walk, though it seldom looks or smells the same. The year's cycle, or 'the roundness of days' as that great chronicler of Provence Jean Giono calls it, is nowhere more evident than on this ridge. Days, according to Giono, are not long: 'They are shaped round, in the manner of things eternal and stable – sun, world, God.' On summer's dog days, an evening stroll is redolent with the scent of pine and patches of purple lavender among the green woods. Autumn's damp, earthy smells surround mushroomers, trying in vain to protect their secret places for the best

sanguines and *chanterelles,* as they appear furtively from the holm-oaks with bulging plastic bags. As late as March, russet oak leaves stay on the branches. Then finally they fall, as spring's young buds push through. Hawthorn and juniper bloom. Bleak, patterned vineyards exchange their wintry ochres and umbers for a rich, green mantle. The year, in the roundness of its days, will inevitably come full circle. It is a comforting certainty in uncertain times.

I was in no hurry. Not five minutes from home, I found another neighbour, Marianne, at work in her vineyard which dates from medieval times. When I told her I was off on a one-man rally in a Fiat Panda, her eyes widened. '*C'est pahhh vraiyyy!*' she exclaimed in her singsong Swiss accent. Though winemaking is said to be a recipe for turning a large fortune into a small one, former Geneva sculptress Marianne is profitably integrated into our macho wine fraternity, and even Pierrot admits: 'She doesn't make a bad wine, *La Suissesse!*'

The panorama from Marianne's Domaine de Coste Chaude was my yardstick for the journey. What Provençal view could beat this? West across the rich flatlands of the Rhône Valley to the hills of the Cevennes; south to a distant glimpse of van Gogh's Alpilles; east, a circus of Drôme Provençale hills with hardly a building of any kind; and, dominating the landscape, our lone magic mountain, Mont Ventoux, with its white cap (snow in winter, shale in summer), our Mount Fuji that never found its Hokusai.

After passing a rare field of Provençal polyculture, olives harmoniously cohabiting with apricot trees, I turned right on to the D191 and wound down into the Aigues valley. I made another stop at the village fountain of St-Maurice-sur-Aigues. Not the prettiest fountain, but I'd forgotten to fill my water bottle. It was a little early in the day for stronger stuff but, shortly after a right on to the D94 along the vineyard valley, the St-Maurice Wine Cooperative

Villedieu, the friendliest village in the area

TH = Table d'Hôtes (guest house with dinner)
CH = Chambre d'Hôtes (bed and breakfast only)

Apart from the Parsons B&B (see p.17), Villedieu has Ferme Templière de la Baude (TH), an ancient Crusader farm where the Monins welcome you like private guests. It's quite a surprise to get the bill.

In Vaison-la-Romaine, head for the Hostellerie Le Beffroi. Pretty garden, antique-filled rooms, medieval spendour. Great for exploring the cobbled streets of the Old Town. A mile or so from Entrechaux's Roman Bridge (off the D20 to Faucon) is a delightful small country hotel, La Manascale, surrounded by vineyards. At Malucène, L'Origan in the town centre is a simple, comfortable pub with terrace overlooking Mont Ventoux. Not far off the route at Le Barroux (D938), there's country house comfort at Mas de La Lause (TH). La Treille (TH) is simply furnished and is perfectly situated for Dentelles walkers and Beaumes-de-Venise sippers.

For city centre quiet and comfort, Hôtel du Fiacre at Carpentras occupies a romantic seventeenth-century convent. Nine miles (14km) from Carpentras at Crillon-le-Brave (D974, D138) are the luxurious Hostellerie with all-round hill views, or the less expensive Clos St-Vincent (TH) charmingly situated in the ramparts.

An honest country pub, Trois Colombes, has a swimming pool at St-Didier-les-Bains. And the Auberge de la Fontaine at Venasque gets top marks for a village hotel in a notably beautiful village. The enterprising Soehlkes provide five suites with open fires in the living-room – and off-season cookery classes.

Venasque's Auberge de Fontaine gets top marks

already had imbibers filling their plastic wine containers. We are notoriously promiscuous about where we buy wine, and *cartes de fidélité* (a wine co-operative's equivalent of Air Miles) are of little use. 'I've found a terrific new red at Cairanne!' a friend will confide, lowering their voice as if imparting a closely guarded secret. 'Rocher – biodynamically produced!' And excitedly we hurry to Cairanne to try Rocher.

A left on to the D20 towards Vaison-la-Romaine took me across the Aigues river, where a sign announced that I was in Upper Vaucluse, Provence of the Popes. That gives us Upper Vauclusians, ruled as we were by Popes till the French Revolution, a historical edge on the rest of the region. This is a wealthy wine-making, agricultural area which does not depend on outsiders; Marianne is the exception that proves the rule.

Those in search of big *bastides* (fortified farmhouses built around courtyards) or substantial land for sale, have always found them thin on the ground in Upper Vaucluse. Others content with more modest real estate tend to settle in villages – like the friendliest in our area, Villedieu. Left off the D20, the narrow D75 passes the comfortable B&B of a popular Anglo-French couple in the antique business, Monique and John Parsons. After a right at La Vigneronne, Villedieu's excellent Wine Cooperative, the D7 climbs to two medieval gateways. Its church's crenellated bell tower sits eccentrically askew the Romanesque nave. Fortifications face north, and rues des Remparts and du Mistral are well named; against a mistral (three, six, or nine days, traditionally) there is no defence, but it does get rid of microbes and was once considered attenuating circumstances if you threw a loved one down the well after more than nine days of it. Villedieu's bracing position may account for its inhabitants' sociability. On summer Sunday evenings there's an open-house at the Café du Centre

for wine and pizza. You can order your pizza in advance from proprietor Jean-Marc Mussier. Those that don't know anyone may begin a holiday romance around the pretty square's cooling fountain; those that know everyone check out who's sleeping with whom. Gérard Depardieu once lived here, but Villedieu has managed to remain singularly unstarry.

From Villedieu, the D94 winds down through more vineyards and joins the D51 to Vaison. In the 14 miles (22km) between home and Vaison, I hardly saw another car. Now, approaching the town through this bucolic back door, I suddenly caught a glimpse of its fortress ruins atop a bluff on the other side of the Ouvèze River. I was reminded of ruins more recent.

AFTER THE FLOOD

On 22 September 1992, Vaison-la-Romaine experienced the catastrophe of a flash flood. An Atlantic cold front moving eastward caused three violent storms: 8⅜ inches (21cm) of rain fell, *one-third of the average annual rainfall in three hours*. Rainwater gushing off comparatively low-lying vineyards like those behind our house had shown me the force of it; gushing off Mont Ventoux from 6,261 feet (1,908m) into the narrow Toulourenc river, or from other high hills into the Lauzon, Groseau and Ouvèze was disastrous. These rivers converge just upstream of Vaison-la-Romaine.

The roaring torrent first hit a camping site. Debris of logs and ripped-up trees took caravans and tents and people with it. At Vaison's Roman bridge, it was funnelled into a deep, narrow defile, causing it to rise 55 feet (17m) in a matter of seconds. Who will ever forget the terrible news footage of a flood-borne caravan slamming into the bridge?

Thirty-five people lost their lives, a heavy count for a small town of 5,660 inhabitants. Some are still missing –

The Market Show can be fun any time

the exact number will probably never be known. Damage to businesses, homes and public monuments was catastrophic. And over the years since the flood, Vaison has had to battle for every franc of insurance claims and public funding. If it hadn't been for private donations from lovers of Vaison from all over the world, the ancient sandstone floor of the St-Nazareth cathedral, which stands less than 100 yards (91m) from the river, might never have been restored; the church was closed from November 1995 to March 1996 for the work to be done. A fine Garden of Remembrance where the worst flood damage took place reminds us of the shameful negligence of certain authorities – before and after the flood.

Rising above it, the people of Vaison are resilient; solidarity through suffering had the town quickly on its feet. Sightseers who once came ghoulishly to see flood remains have now returned to Roman remains. And the Tuesday market is one of the great spectacles of Vaucluse.

At the height of the summer season, market crowds take

on World Cup Final proportions; for serious shopping, I like to arrive at eight before the crowds, be gone by nine before the heat, and head only for the regular stalls I have come to know and love. The Market Show, however, with no shopping list, just picking up maybe a sausage or cheese I've never tried, can be fun any time. The whole town is *en fête*, as though celebrating its survival, its will to live another Tuesday.

The Farmer's Market is my favourite. A small 'off' section between the Cave Cooperative and Roman Theatre has a few home producers, from not more than a few miles away, selling whatever is fresh that very morning from their gardens or goats or chickens. It was chilly. Madame Garnier of Puymeras had nothing but a few goat's cheeses on the stall in front of her – from her six goats. 'They don't mind the cold,' she laughed, rubbing and blowing on her mittened hands. 'They're from the mountains. Not me, I was slipping about on the ice this morning.' Madame Joubert from Violès was there with quince jelly, chestnut cream and blackberry jams, *frisée* salad, sorrel and a couple of tomato plants. The dashing Monsieur Benedetti from Rasteau, his cap rakish as Jean Gabin's, proudly displayed camomile, celery, thyme, glistening little *rougette* salads, sage, bay leaf, fresh and dried mint. And found time to tell me, 'My father came here from Tuscany, aged twenty. We Italians fit in around here. In Nice there were *de* Benedettis – from the old Tuscan nobility. By the way, I have an old wine press for sale. Want to buy it?' The old charmer could have sold me a whole winery!

I moved on to the market proper where *placements* were taking place. A tough ritual, this. An official from the Mairie, accompanied by *gendarmes*, followed by an anxious group of unplaced stall holders, bustled through the market assigning places. Already well-placed in their usual strategic position up front of the colourful Market Garden

ROMAN VAISON

Vaison-la-Romaine is very much alive and well again

Thanks to archaeologist Canon Sautel and philanthropist Maurice Burrus, who were behind excavations that began with the 6,000-seat Roman theatre in 1907, Vaison became the second most important Roman site for urban architecture after Pompeii.

Following the Celto-Ligurians and Greeks, the *pax romana* established itself (bringing with it bread and circuses) all over southern Gaul in the first century. Where the rural Vocontii tribe were thus pacified, today's July Arts Festival graces the twilit Roman theatre with such *divertissements* as a Pagnol or Marivaux play, jazz on a summer's night, or a dance group from Russia. Less monolithic than Orange's more renowned theatre, it provides no grand opera; Vaison is a friendly, intimate festival.

The two Roman sites are on either side of Avenue Générale de Gaulle. To the west, La Villasse reveals a Roman shopping street with colonnaded remains, the *thermae* and *palaestyra* for baths and physical exercise, and two villas (Dolphin and Silver Bust) with rooms indicated (admission is free). To the east, Puymin is a delightful wooded hill to stroll around, with two houses (Arbour and Laurelled Apollo), a religious sanctuary with portico remains, and the theatre (entry fee payable). There is also the well-laid-out modern Théo-Desplans Museum which contains artefacts from all these sites.

section, Nicole and Jean-Marie Cochet from Carpentras had a dazzling display of baby palms, orange-trees, arbutus and pomegranate by 8.30a.m. 'We load the van the night before, get here at 7.30a.m.,' said Nicole, very down-to-earth and dynamic. 'Nobody works nights any more.'

Early tomatoes, aubergines, peppers and courgettes come from more southerly sun: Morocco, southern Italy, Spain. 'The Spanish wholesalers give us 45 days' credit,' a stall holder told me with an air of regret. 'I have to deal with them to make a living.' All is not lost to foreign fiends, however. As spring turns to summer, inevitably local cherries, peaches, apricots, melons, grapes will be piled in abundance on the gleaming stalls.

Tasting is never taboo. Pick a cherry yourself, no one will complain, just be careful where you spit the stone. You can nibble dried sausage made with herbs, hazelnut, pure pork, beef, garlic, goat, wild boar, and even donkey; or Corsican liver sausage, *lonzo* and *coppa.* Work your way through the olives: the tiny, tasty ones from Nice, crinkly-skinned from Nyons, Greek, Italian, Moroccan, and green *picholines* for apéritifs from Le Gard. There's a stall with a choice of black and green tapenade, anchovy relish, *olivade de poivron.* Madame Kijarra took me through her ewe's milk cheeses from Cevennes; *pastre,* she tells me, is the patois for 'shepherd' and she goes every year on the transhumance with a flock, up to the highlands on 15 June, back down again on 15 September. 'It takes five days,' she said. 'Not tiring, you go the pace of the ewes and the lambs.'

We get our meat from Alain Nicholas of Pré Rond high up near Séderon, whose stall always has a queue of faithful customers. Drômois lamb like velvet, succulent young pork, home-made *charcuterie* – enough to make a vegetarian break their vows. From the ecological Ferme de Closonne, Frank Berthou brings stuffed pigeons, home-made pâtés and duck *confits.* La Fontaine d'Argent at

Gently wooded hills and lush orchards near Vaison

Malaucène to Beaumes-de-Venise, the most spectacular drive yet

up the flimsiest of female undergarments in a brisk wind.

It's tiring work. Time for coffee or pastis on Place Montfort, Vaison's main square. Terrace cafés line one side. Meeting friends on market day is a big social event. Our haunt is Chez Pascal, a relatively recent *boulangerie-patisserie-glacier* with wood-fired oven visible, baking the many kinds of bread. We relax, listening to 'Le Plus Beau Tango du Monde', the retro voice of Gardel rising above the market's hubbub. In July, singers from the tri-annual Choralie choir festival busk around the café tables. A New Orleans band beats it out in a corner of the square, making every Tuesday a mardi-gras.

Suze-la-Rousse send a van with home-smoked salmon and their own fresh trout tank. Bouzigue oysters, Marseilles fish soup, red mullet, monkfish and squid tempt us from many a fish stall, as do our friends at Le Regale d'Asie with their spit-roasted Vietnamese chicken in a citronella sauce. Our lime blossom, verbena, and green tea, and every conceivable dried herb or spice or pepper come from the stall next door, Vu Dinh Van from Eygalières.

There are rolls of pretty Provençal prints (first imported from India by Marseilles traders) – long skirts, short skirts, tablecloths and napkins; olive wood salad bowls and servers, pestle-and-mortars, butter pats, tongs and spoons. You can find anything at Vaison – from bead curtains to electric saws, from charcoal-oven pizzas to car batteries, from trainers to second-hand books. I even saw a fat man in a tartan cap, cigarette butt bouncing on lip, trying to hang

Vaison-la-Romaine is very much alive and well again. But when the summer heat builds up through August, and September storm clouds hang over the Ouvèze valley, faces at the Tuesday market show more than a hint of anxiety, and prayers in St-Nazareth Cathedral become more fervent. The people of Vaison know only too well: history does repeat itself.

VAISON-LA-ROMAINE TO CARPENTRAS

I headed out of town on the busy D938 to Malaucène but almost at once escaped on to the more peaceful D151 via St-Marcelin-Les-Vaison. It shrank to the modest C3 before reaching another sturdy Roman bridge where the Ouvèze river's shady banks tempt one to a lyrical summer bathing spot; its one ogival arch supports the narrowest of roads –

just the width of a smallish car. Scrape through, and a junction with the D13 brings you to Entrechaux.

Entrechaux has the prominent landmark of a ruined castle, eerily fairy-tale when floodlit, apparently floating in mid-air. It also has one of our most congenial restaurants, the St-Hubert, where the Mourets run an old-style, family show. Surrounded by gourmand grannies, beaming babies, and indulgent young couples, a winter's Sunday afternoon (12–5p.m.) is pleasantly whiled away with a shellfish-platter, wild boar *civet*, wild duck and never-ending fill-ups of house Châteauneuf-du-Pape. Later, beneath the shade of a great wisteria pergola, a truffle omelette is perfect when you're not hungry but longing for luxury.

From Entrechaux to Malaucène, the D13 and D938 run between low, gently wooded hills and lush orchards, roads to enchant the senses – sight, smell and sound. The French call it *le bien-être,* and no well-being could be sweeter, driving in such perfect surroundings.

From Malaucène's wide main boulevard, bristling with cafés and hotels, I took a walk through a sinuous medieval back street to Calvary hill, a short climb past cypress trees like hooded penitents. The panorama of Mont Ventoux (Windy Mountain) loomed large. The town, where Pope Clement V once had a summer residence, is its base camp. A comparatively easy climb to see the summer sunrise begins nearby. The Italian poet-priest Petrarch, who was attached to the Papal Court in Avignon, climbed the mountain in May 1336:

at first vividly struck by the unfamiliarity of the air I breathed and by the vastness of the panorama, I shifted my gaze: clouds floated at my feet. From there, I turned my eyes towards Italy, the direction of a longing heart. Spiked and snowy Alps appeared quite close to me, despite the great distance.

Malaucène to Beaumes-de-Venise on the D90 was the most spectacular drive yet. Climbing to the Col de La Chaine (1,548ft/472m), the whole southerly expanse spread out below: misty, forested hills, the surreal contours of Roque Alric monastery, and the fertile plain of Carpentras beyond. This was the Pays des Dentelles de Montmirail, a chain of eccentric hills like a set of extremely sharp, irregular teeth, with wonderful hikes and mountain-bike tracks. From the eagle's nest village of Suzette, you can see both the southern, gentler slopes of Ventoux and the Dentelles.

Beaumes-de-Venise's famous dessert wine comes into its own on Christmas Eve. Before Midnight Mass, the traditional meatless supper ends with thirteen Provençal desserts which represent Christ and the twelve Apostles. The fine sweet wine is a perfect accompaniment for *pompes à l'huile* (sweet, flat pastry), home-made nougat, *papillottes* (little sweet crackers for the children), mandarins, dates, dried fruit and nuts. My mouth watering at the mere thought, I asked a road-sweeper outside the church directions for Domaine de Durban: 'It's a good five kilometres into the hills,' he warned. In fact, it was two. Local directions in Provence can be erratic; exaggeration is not just a characteristic of Marseilles, and one should be prepared for arriving early or, more often, late. Domaine de Durban is stunningly situated, high on a clay-and-chalk plateau in the Dentelles with vineyards sloping south to Beaumes and north to Gigondas (a wine they also make). Its fine old *mas* (small country house) and winery sit conveniently between the two. Two Leydier sons and their mother run the family business. 'The Romans brought the muscat grape for sweet wine,' one of the sons told me. 'Not Good King René as everyone thinks.' Frankly, I was more interested in what the Leydiers made of it, even though it was only 9.30a.m. A heavy hit of sweet wine so soon after breakfast was a real test, and the bouquet of honey and apricots went perfectly with the hour.

Peaceful roads like the D21 from Beaumes to Caromb are not all chirping crickets; a jet fighter from Orange air base screeched overhead and disappeared behind cliffs honeycombed with caves. After a glimpse of Le Barroux's castle through pink and white fruit blossom, a Route des Vins sign announced Côtes du Ventoux country. The Route des Vins is to wine lovers what the Tour de France is to cyclists, a test of endurance. Going from *appellation* to *appellation*, winery to winery, they can taste and buy, and with luck avoid *le ballon* (breathalyzer). Côtes du Ventoux, a lighter but no less tasty wine than Côtes du Rhône, stretches south from the magic mountain as far as the Lubéron.

Down on the plain now, I explored Caromb. After a dull approach, pleasant surprises: an unusually elaborate wrought-iron cage on top of its campanile; a pleasantly quiet place for refreshment at Le Beffroy Hotel; and Haut Frères Olive Oil Mill. Continuing by the D13 to Carpentras, I merged with the fast and furious D974 into the city, passed an ancient aqueduct, and got snarled up in a chaotic system of one-ways. I was already unused to urban traffic.

LIVING WITH TROUBLE

One of the hassles of French travel is trying to get to a site before midday closing. The lunch break is sacred as an imprinted shroud. At Carpentras, I hastily parked in the narrow rue de la Porte de Mazan. No problem, I thought. There were other cars, mine was small and unobtrusive. At least it got me to the Synagogue on time.

First, a little history essential to the appreciation of Carpentras, capital of the Comtat Venaissin, and its famous Synagogue. During the Middle Ages, the Comtat Venaissin belonged to the mega-powerful Counts of Toulouse. Lesser barons could be controlled by the

Catholic Church which, not content with its spiritual role, proved adept at wheeling and dealing in affairs of power and property, acting as a cohesive force more powerful than a mere one-château baron. The Church met its match with the Counts of Toulouse who ruled Southern France more with a velvet glove than an iron fist. They encouraged chivalry, erudition, and the famous Courts of Love where troubadours wooed Countesses with impunity and song, while the Counts were off fighting a Crusade.

The Toulouses were religious liberals, supporting the reformist Cathars. The Cathars, like Saint Benedict, believed in purity, and campaigned against Catholics' high living, low loving, and corrupt power game. The Church led a crusade against the heretic Cathars. In 1229, beaten in battle, the Counts of Toulouse were forced to expiate their support of the Cathars by presenting the Papal Court with such prize possessions as Avignon (convenient for the Popes' exile from 1309 to 1377) and the Comtat Venassin of which Carpentras became the capital.

Now comes a curious paradox. Though intolerant of Christian reformists, the Catholic Church gave protection to Jews. When an insolvent Philip the Fair (a misnomer, if ever there was one) confiscated Jewish property to help fill the royal coffers and expelled them from France, many Jews found refuge in the Comtat Venaissin. What was France's loss was the Comtat's gain. From 1394, Carpentras developed a thriving Jewish community whose ghetto contained doctors, artisans, scholars, and above all translators. Later, refugees from the Sephardic Spanish community, victims of Isabella and Ferdinand's vicious ethnic cleansing, brought with them translations of Greek philosophy from Arabic into Hebrew. Their subsequent translations from Hebrew into Latin for the Catholic Church did much to prepare for the enlightenment of the French Renaissance.

First, a warning. Traditionally, Provençals eat best at home; when they go out, they mostly do not want the Provençal specialities we do. Something a bit fancier leads to gastronomic pretension. A tasty starter may be followed by a disappointing main dish, the meal retrieved by an inventive dessert – or variations on that theme!

Vaison-la-Romaine's Brin d'Olivier (olive branch), in a shady courtyard, lives up to its Provençal name with aubergine *millefeuille* and *loup de mer* (sea-perch) flambéed in pastis. A Marcel Pagnol ambience (his father was born in Vaison) makes Auberge de la Bartevelle a most convivial choice, serving hotpot of salmon with basil and shellfish, *méli-mélo* (stew) of young rabbit with onion conserve, and duck breast with preserved pears.

Don't miss the pleasures of the St-Hubert at Entrechaux (see p.23). Les Géraniums at Le Barroux, is a superior village café-restaurant with a warm welcome and excellent

country cooking: quail pâté with onion conserve, duck *foie gras* flavoured with Beaumes-de-Venise, rabbit scented with savory, kid with rosemary, *crème brulée* with liquorice, parfait with lavender.

To taste Gigondas, Vacqueyras and Beaumes-de-Venise close to the soil, go to Les Florets at Gigondas, a large country restaurant tucked away in the Dentelles hillside woods. On its bosky terrace, enjoy tomato-and-onion tart, roast duck flavoured with vanilla, and individal chocolate cakes.

Grand restaurants where the waitresses whip off the silver *cloches* in unison are rare in Upper Vaucluse. Near Carpentras, Hostellerie de Crillon Le Brave's candlelit terrace can be romantic with a full moon on Mont Ventoux and the herb garden perfumes at their most pungent. Home-made *gnoccis* are especially good. Budget travellers will appreciate Trappier in Carpentras: workman's food at its increasingly rare best.

Auberge la Fontaine at Venasque makes the most of local delicacies like truffles and foie gras. *Gigot d'Agneau de Venasque* and red fruit soup are star turns. At the cheaper bistro next door, under the same management, there's *daube de taureau* which goes to prove even a bull can be tender.

TRUFFLE CAPITAL

Watch people snuffle around for a deal at the truffle market, November-to-March on Saturday mornings, at the little village of Richerenches near Valréas. You'd think it was some ancient pagan rite until you learn that there's even a Truffle Mass in the church.

An extraordinary shopping arcade, Passage Boyer

Better still, go to Carpentras, truffle capital of Provence. No power game of the medieval Church could be played more craftily than the Friday morning truffle market outside the Hotel de l'Univers. The black diamond, changing hands with several cuts before reaching Paris at a vastly inflated price, grows mainly on the southern slopes of Mont Ventoux. In the humus-rich, chalky soil beloved of truffle oaks, mycelium activates the growth of the world's most expensive mushroom on the oak tree's roots. Seven years after planting, your dog or pig, attracted by the scent, can then start sniffing around the clear area round the tree and burrowing for black diamonds. Best eaten whole like potatoes, or slices under the skin of a chicken, in a plain lettuce salad, or in scambled eggs.

Carpentras has other delights: the arcaded rue des Halles with Librairie de l'Horloge, the best bookshop for miles; the secret, elegant mansions of rue Moricelly; a Jesuit college where the great Provençal

botanist Jean-Henri Fabre (The Homer of Insects) once taught; and an extraordinary nineteenth-century shopping arcade, Passage Boyer, with high glass-and-iron curved roof. A sweet tooth can be indulged at Jouvaud for patisserie, Bono for crystallized fruit, and Confiserie du Ventoux for *berlingots* (caramel candy). A peaceful stroll by the Auzon River provides a delicious cool balm when the July sun frazzles gateway, rampart, campanile, and the great Friday market. A city for all centuries and seasons.

So naturally I was in a hurry to get to the Synagogue, one of the oldest in France, before it closed at twelve. At the very centre of the Old Town, it stands in the Place de L'Hôtel de Ville, its modest eighteenth-century façade set back in a street where once the *juiverie provençale* contained more than a thousand people within a 240-yard (219m) stretch. As I arrived, a group of nearly that many schoolboys were pouring out of the Synagogue after a visit.

'I didn't have enough *yarmulkes* for them all,' said Madame Andrée, our humorous welcomer, handing me my skullcap. I was glad to share the comparatively small upstairs Prayer Room with just a scholarly Dutchman and his teenage son. It bears witness to the community's prosperity: two crystal chandeliers, three carved-wood menorahs, Ark containing the Torah scrolls, tabernacle where the Rabbi reads the Torah, and a tiny period chair for a young child's circumcision. 'Only a few seconds and it's over!' Madame Andrée assured us. 'And that gallery with the grille is where my female ancestors were finally allowed to come up and attend the service. Before, they had to stay downstairs!'

Downstairs was out of bounds to visitors ('Unfortunately some idiots have tried to damage it'). It is the oldest (fourteenth-century) part of the Synagogue, containing a Mikva pool for ritual baths, fed by spring water from Mont Ventoux, and a bakery for unleavened bread. The matza was baked there until the beginning of the century and exported to the States and North Africa.

Finally, I asked Madame Andrée a delicate question, which had been on my mind all through the visit and which I tried to phrase tactfully. 'Madame, what is the morale of the Jewish community after the sad event of 1990?'

Her reply was direct and to the point, given with a gentle, resigned smile. 'Oh, Monsieur, that's finished. It's all in the past.'

Outside, the scholarly Dutchman asked me what sad event I was referring to, and I was shocked that he had never heard of it. I imagined it to be as well-known as the Vaison flood.

'The desecration of Jewish graves,' I said.

Carpentras had the same tolerant traditions as the rest of Provence which has opened its doors to different races and practised the cohabitation of religions since the Phocean chief Protis married Ligurian Princess Gyptis in Massilia (Marseilles) around 600 BC. A close look at the magnificent Western portal of St-Siffrein cathedral casts a doubt. It is known as the Jewish gate, because converts to the Christian faith passed that way. The flamboyant Gothic stone carving is one of the finest in southern France; it contains a strange symbolic ball of stone, into which rats are burrowing. The 'rat ball' is the Catholic Church gnawed by heretics of all colour and creed – Cathars, Jews, Moors. So the protection of Jews by the Popes, we can safely assume, was more for their skills than for humanitarian reasons.

On the night of 9 May 1990, thirty-four graves in the Jewish cemetery had been vandalized. Three young male suspects were arrested, all members of the extreme right PNFE (Nationalist Party of France and Europe). They had connections in the right places, however, and were released. Silence. A Provençal version of Sicilian *omertà* (see no evil, hear no evil, speak no evil) descended over the city like a smoke screen. It was not until 1996 that the case and eventual trial were transferred to Marseilles where, bereft of a phoney alibi, the perpetrators faced the maximum penalty: two years' imprisonment.

National Front leader Jean-Marie Le Pen may have condemned the crime but will always be remembered for dismissing the Holocaust as 'a detail of history'. Of French Jewish patriotism Madame Andrée told us proudly: 'The Synagogue was the meeting place of French

Revolutionaries. After the Revolution, when the Church and State were separated, the ghetto was closed, and we Jews could live and work where we wanted'. Now sixty-four Jewish families in Carpentras are cohabiting peacefully with Islamic neighbours, France's largest marginalized ethnic group and principal target of the National Front.

When I got back to my car, a *flic* was writing out a parking ticket. 'I was in a hurry to get to the Synagogue before it closed,' I explained. 'I missed the no-parking sign.' The usual lame stuff.

The *flic* looked at me oddly. Listened to my accent. Inspected my papers. Saw I was a foreign resident. I had Vaucluse plates, which all begin with 84. He tore up the parking ticket. 'Go and park in Place Jean-Jaurès – like everyone else.'

CARPENTRAS TO THE LUBÉRON

From Carpentras to Mazan on the D942 you cross a fertile plain of cherry orchards and vineyards, in sight of the truffle-oak woods of Mont Ventoux where you poach at your peril. Mazan is a busy little crossroads market-and-wine town, bustling and brash on market day. The fattest woman I've ever seen in Provence – and that's saying something – waddled beaming from stall to stall. Joyfully, she filled a shopping basket with a whole field of asparagus. Beyond the fourteenth-century medieval gate, back street tranquillity pervaded an alley where delicious smells of garlicky roasts wafted from the houses and people greeted one another with the obligatory three kisses. *Danger Chute de Pierres* announced Mazan's vulnerability to Provence's thirty-odd winds and the risk of a stone falling on your head from the edge of the roof, where it holds down Roman tiles. At the end of the street, the

Penitents Noirs Museum, folkloric but not folksy, had a fine old stone kiln in the garden. Through a sturdy, beautifully carved wooden door, the silence was typical of small Provençal Gothic-and-Romansesque country churches. A perfect haven after a hot, noisy market.

Ugly black plastic strips covered vast fields of asparagus beside the network of little roads (D1, D5, D4a, D39) to St-Didier-les-Bains. This former watering-place revealed its best-kept secret, hidden away behind the main street: Château de Thézan, now a private clinic, an exquisite Renaissance building in a courtyard with a mossy fountain. After St-Didier, the D28 began to climb through the Forêt Domaniale de Venasque (forest belonging to the Venasque *commune*). On a slow drive like this, you're aware of features of the same landmark appearing from different angles: distant Mont Ventoux, for instance, now framed in blossom-covered fruit-trees, more Fuji-like than ever.

Venasque, an early Christian bishop's seat, gives its name to the Comtat Venaissin. Jutting out on its promontory from the western edge of the Plateau de Vaucluse, Venasque commanded a strategic view for a hawk-eyed bishop, on the lookout for marauding Franks, Goths, Lombards or Saracens. The seventh-century Baptistry – simple, pure Romanesque architecture at it best, with a font in the stone floor – is one of the earliest Christian sites in France, built near pagan temples to Diana, Venus and Mercury. No mock artisanal shops clutter the lovely Grande Rue, and the purity continues the whole length of the street from church to fountain. No wonder it attracts artists – ten permanently in residence, their studios hidden away in back streets. An American girl, in businesslike shorts and boots, strode by with a sketch-pad, in a trance of creative anticipation, relishing the crisp, cloudless day.

Once a month a dinner with concert is offered by the enterprising Auberge la Fontaine, renowned for its

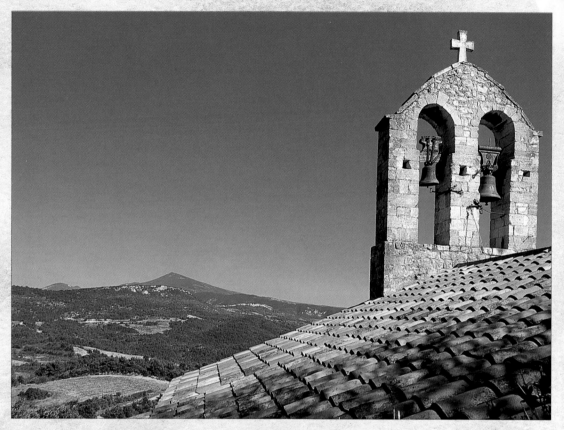

Our lone magic mountain, Mont Ventoux

A 26-mile (41km) round-trip detour by the D974 from Malaucène nearly to the summit of Mont Ventoux (6,261ft/1,908m) is a must for mountain-lovers. The road climbs through a variety of forest that has earned it UNESCO World Heritage status – pine, larch, oak and cedar. Its beech grove is a protected biosphere site. Above the tree-line, the majestic views stretch as far as the snowy caps of the Italian Alps.

Near the ski-resort of Mont Serein, where huskies attached to sleds wait to take you on snowy paths to the summit, alpine meadows and pinewoods are the summer habitat of rare birds such as wheatears and pipits. Botanists explore 1,200 plant species, ranging from Mediterranean to Arctic, for such rarities as pink saxifrage, martagon lily, and hairy poppy.

It is a holy mountain, too. Not without its witches and warlocks – goatherds have horripilant tales of goats mysteriously lost at full moon, returning with blazing red eyes and prancing on their hind legs. In the fifteenth century the Bishop of Carpentras exorcised evil spirits by building the Chapelle St-Croix, near today's mountain-top restaurant and telecommunications centre, a place of regular pilgrimage till the beginning of this century. Trekkers still make the climb, taking five hours by the GR21 from Bedoin. For the less energetic, a flat forest track leads from the D974, a 4-mile (6km) walk (round trip) to St-Sidoine Hermitage, a chapel no bigger than a shepherd's hut perched on the lower northern slopes.

Venasque – the purity
continues the whole
length of the street

produce fresh from Carpentras market, *mesclun* (mixed wild salad) and pigeon *filets* served in a cosy village ambience. Patron Christian Soehlke has opened a less pricey bistro next door, but today the weather was too good to lunch indoors. I picnicked on garlic sausage and delicious Domaine de Fondrèche Côtes du Ventoux from Mazan, below the ramparts in a meadow of wild flowers. In an hour, not a car passed.

Then a more rugged country began to emerge, of grey chalk *barres* (rock strata) slashed across wooded hillsides. The D4 climbed picturesquely with plenty of local colour. A priest in beret and carrying a thumbstick passed by, right out of an old black-and-white Pagnol movie. After patches of hilly vineyard, I plunged into a short gorge of grey, craggy cliffs. Then, up and up, zig and zag, a hundred or more hairpin bends to the top of the Col de Murs (2,056ft/627m). A sign announced Parc Naturel Régional du Lubéron. A protected habitat of wild boar, roe-buck, hare, rabbit, partridge, fox and ferret. Also, of homo sapiens in that comparatively rare species, the rich (famous and not so famous).

PARADISE NEARLY LOST

During the Great Plague of 1720, which began on a cargo ship from Syria to Marseilles and spread north like a forest fire in full flame, a wall of demarcation was built between Sisteron and Avignon. Soldiers guarded it night and day. Anyone who tried to cross it was shot. Despite prayers to St-Roch, patron saint of plagues, this particular one got the better of the soldiers, reducing a garrison of 12,000 to one hundred; infected people passed through, and all too quickly the population of Avignon was decimated.

Vestiges of the *Mur de la Peste* can still be seen on these forested heights between Venasque and Murs, a short walk from the D4. It is somehow symbolic. The countryside is sensational as you enter the Lubéron, but there's a fear that its people may be infected by a new pestilence: Lubonic Plague, a specially contagious form of one-upmanship. Hostesses tend to have a strict dress code of long skirts and ties, even in high summer, and Pétrus and Château-Yquem are served by a white-gloved servant – in the pool-house. However, a backlash could be on the way. In a refreshingly understated *mas,* a couple recently entertained *Le Tout Lubéron* to a soirée catered by the extremely picturesque Gordes pizza van, and the host bid us to come-and-get-it with a good old butcher's boy whistle. '*Très originale,*' cooed a bronzed blonde Parisienne guest.

Some 6,000 second homes, furnished with bibelots from L'Isle-sur-la-Sorgue antique market, are within easy reach of Marseilles airport and housebreakers. A £4,000 rental for a couple of weeks in August is a snip.

As I began my descent from the head of the pass, I feared the worst. Round a corner, an over-restored grey *bastide* with lavender blue shutters and obligatory landscaped pool hove into sight, as though posing for *Côté Sud,* the Lubéron's favourite lifestyle magazine. Then a hazy blue hogsback ridge came into view on the other side of the Calavon Valley. Many residents are too busy gazing at sun-blocked navels to make the trek up to the enticing hills, Petit and Grand Lubéron, which give their protected region its name. Seen from this remote back road, a paradise certainly. I decided to cross the valley by a circuitous route to see what it was like in close-up.

Round the next corner, a flock of four hundred ewes and lambs blocking the road was an encouraging start. The young shepherd told me the deserted hills on both sides of the valley were being repopulated, to a limited extent, by sheep-farmers as well as trekkers and mountain-bikers. It was a delicate ecological balance. The ancient dry-stone *bories,* mysterious beehive buildings peculiar to this area, were used as sheepfolds. Convenient for walkers caught in a storm, too.

The golden hill village of Murs, on the edge of the Vaucluse plateau, was set off by a vivid green field of winter wheat. The Crillon, more village pub than hotel, is named – like the Crillon in Paris – for Murs' local hero, the gallant knight Louis de Balbes de Berton de Crillon, known as Crillon-le-Brave. Born luckily too late in Provence's bloody sixteenth century, he did not participate in the massacre of Vaudois in the nearby cave of Barigoule. Followers of Lyonnais Protestant Pierre Valdo, hiding from persecution in several Lubéron villages, were exterminated like rats by the storm troopers of Catholic gauleiter, Baron Jean Meynier d'Oppède. Strange how Provence, ravaged by man's inhumanity to man over twenty centuries and more, manages to endow places where much blood has been spilt with a spirit of tranquil beauty. Murs was one.

The weather changed violently. At the Crillon's cosy bar at 8 a.m., a group of foresters were lacing their coffees with *marc de provence* to fortify themselves against a particularly vicious wind. 'Here we go,' said a young joker, zipping up his parka, 'off to the most beautiful job in the world.' At least there was enough forest for them never to be unemployed.

The Lubéron is a spider's web of little roads, like those from Murs to Sénanque Abbey: an unmarked right from the D15 on to the D244, then a left on to the D177 brought me down into the dramatic ravine where the Abbey catches your breath with its austere and peaceful presence. Hard to believe monks were once slaughtered here by the Vaudois in the hideous tit-for-tat that gives God a bad name. An exquisite place, even without the

lavender which so beautifully sets off the Cistercian architecture in high summer: without the high summer crowds, either.

On a weekday in spring, I had the Monks' Dormitory to myself, marvelling on such a cool day how the poor monks ever kept warm. Only one room was heated so fingers could keep reasonably agile while working on manuscripts. Books could be illustrated but the 'illuminations' had to be restrained by order of St Bernard, the Benedictines' kindly but stern guru. Their vow of silence was only excused in the superbly vaulted Capitulary where monks gathered for readings from St Benedict's rule book. As it is still in use as a monastery, the monks of Sénanque request visitors to observe the rule of silence as they themselves are still required to do. A faint hope. Like the buzzing of bees, the approach of a group suddenly grew louder in the church till it became a full-blown babble. The tour guide was in full voice, and so were his French senior citizens, battling to get their questions in about twelfth-century links of monasteries with trade routes, the financing of religious orders by local knights to do penance, and where was the nearest loo? If only we were all provided with cassette-players, silence could be as golden as a monk's.

The dramatically narrow D177 gives a fine bird-eye's view of Sénanque on the way to Gordes, where I hardly expected silence. The well-known view of 'One of the Most Beautiful Villages in France' (and the world, for that matter!) lies before you, and you can hardly raise an elbow to take your snapshot for the jostle of others taking snaps. By day, Gordes is like a star at Cannes facing a barrage of paparazzi. By night, when the coaches have gone, she becomes the Acropolis of Provence. However much artists and politicians of the *gauche-caviar* (champagne socialists) are accused of over-popularizing it, Gordes is still unmissable. One evening in the depths of winter, we visited

Sénanque Abbey's austere and peaceful presence

TH = Table d'Hôtes (guest house with dinner)
CH = Chambre d'Hôtes (bed and breakfast only)

The Lubéron may have social pretensions, but by no means all its accommodation is phoney rustic-chic or at ridiculous prices.

Le Crillon at Murs, despite garish lavender shutters, combines comfort with village pub ambience. Its Logis de France insignia is a value-for-money guarantee for budget travellers. Slightly more expensive, Le Mas de Loriot, a six-room hotel surrounded by pines, oak and lavender, has a terrace overlooking the Lubéron and tasty country cooking.

Off the Murs-Gordes road (D15), Les Hauts de Véroncle (TH) in the depths of glorious countryside is run by a couple of young nature lovers, the Corsos. La Ferme de la Huppe near Gordes (D156), an eighteenth-century dry-stone farmhouse with figs and olives in its courtyard, has a swimming pool surrounded by flowers. For

Rue du Four, Gordes, not far from the Renaissance castle

mind-numbingly sybaritic luxury, head for Les Bories (not exactly prehistoric dry-stone huts!), Gordes' answer to Eden Roc but with only 18 rooms.

Better value for money is to be had in stylish guest houses: Ma Maison (TH) at Roussillon with its abundance of green plants and frescoes; La Médecine (CH) at Goult, an ancient, sunny house getting its medical name from a Templers hospice in a former life; Le Clos de Buis (CH) at Bonnieux, a converted grocery store with hundred-year-old box trees round the swimming pool;

and Le Mas des Trois Sources (CH), with stunning view to the Marquis de Sade's ghostly château and courtyard shaded by a great mulberry tree. La Ferme du Castelas (TH) is a hikers' haven on the Big Lubéron hillside, and deep in the Aiguebrun valley Auberge de l'Aiguebrun is for silence-lovers and rock-climbers.

In South Lubéron, Lourmarin and surroundings have an abundance of good put-ups. Among the best: the seventeenth century Villa-St Louis (CH) offers bohemian comfort, and Le Moulin de Lourmarin is, quite simply, the tops.

friends in rue du Four, not far from the Renaissance castle. From chimneys less grandiose than the castle's, a sweet scent of log fires pervaded the empty street; in the crisp, crackling air, frosty stars seemed close enough to touch. Beyond the tour buses and caravans, Gordes has a simpler, secret underground life in the dark, sinuous streets of the lower town.

Outside, rigid lanes of dry-stone walls, which protect the homes of media executives, turn the approaches into a *garrigue* suburbia. Life imitates the Bories Village, Gordes' main tourist attraction, where the mysterious dry-stone huts were probably built by the Gauls, many years before Christ.

The spider's web of roads continued to perplex but never dismay. From Gordes, the D102 wound east along a hillside, passing lush meadows and fruit farms, then became the D2 before mysteriously returning to the D102. Finally, a left on to the D169 brought me to Roussillon.

With its ochre, pine-topped cliffs, Roussillon plays no second fiddle to Gordes; if Gordes is the Acropolis, Roussillon is Petra. Until you penetrate it. Just too many architects, estate agents, artists, crêperies clutter the limited space; and the ochre wash produced from its red rock, used too garishly, cheapens the effect. The Sentier des Ocres along the red cliff tops has irritatingly arcane opening dates: from the Saturday after Palm Sunday to the Sunday after All Souls. Surely they could keep such an impressive walk open for customers all year round.

I asked an elderly local if he remembered Lawrence Wylie's *A Village in Vaucluse*, a best-seller based on the very real agricultural and ochre-quarry village community of Roussillon in the fifties. 'Certainly,' he said. 'People thought Professor Wylie was doing a serious study for academic purposes. Then it became this successful book and, of course, some people thought it was an invasion of privacy. Others thought it helped the village, put us on the map. What else would we live on except tourists nowadays? Agriculture's almost finished.'

'Does anything still grow here now?' I asked.

'Car parks,' he replied.

Despite this jeremiad, the Imergue valley seemed quite flourishing. After turning right off the D105, I took the D104 to Goult. No mulberry trees fed silk worms any more; the big silkworm breeding houses (*magneraies*) had long since made second homes for millionaires. Nevertheless, vineyards, melon fields and cherry orchards were scattered about in comparative profusion.

Goult, on its hill in the middle of the valley, is a rural village, off the beaten track. Goult is quite happy about this. I had a coffee in a genuine, old-fashioned *café de la poste* with locals who looked as though their families went back more than a generation. A notice behind the bar, among the silver *boules* championship cups, warns: 'People in a state of inebriation will not be served.' A stroll up the main street led to a beautifully preserved Old Town. In rue du Château with its Renaissance bridge house, three sleepy huskies welcomed me with friendly tail-wags behind the great iron gate of a secret garden. Unusual two-storey houses with trim little gardens have been restored with love and a marked lack of chichi; on the other side, by a pinkish gold watchtower, the houses curve harmoniously with the ramparts. A most *sympa* village.

And, just below it on the D145, the pilgrims' village of Lumières celebrates the miracle cures of Our Lady of the Lights. One of the Lubéron's greatest miracles is staying alive on what used to be the Via Domitia connecting Rome with Narbonne and is now the N100. Imagine Le Mans with caravans, and you've got it. I crossed as quickly as possible to the D106 and almost immediately turned left.

Roussillon with its ochre,
pine-topped cliffs

CH. = Château
DOM.= Domaine

Côtes du Rhône, Vaucluse's largest AOC (*appellation d'orgine controllée*, a guarantee of the wine's place of origin) benefits from the Rhône valley's sunshine, pebbles, clay, chalk and sand. Perfect conditions for a strong, robust wine with plenty of fruit. 1995 and 1998 were particularly good years for red.

On my route, Dom. de Coste-Chaude is a privately owned winery, whereas St-Maurice (Drôme) and Villedieu are wine cooperatives where growers bring their grapes for vinification. Other names to look out for are: Vieux Chêne, La Courançonne, Coudelet de Beaucastel, Clos Simian, Richaud, des Grands Devers, Couturier, Rocher.

Reds are best. Drink with Drômois lamb, wild boar stew, *daube provençale*, chicken roasted with forty cloves of garlic. Flinty whites and juicy rosés are chancier but good ones (like Villedieu) go well with *aïoli* (garlic mayonaise) with salt cod and vegetables, red mullet, pistou soup, stuffed aubergine, goat's cheese.

Beautifully situated Gigondas and Vacqueyras, an easy detour from Beaumes-de-Venise (D81, D7),

are the same style as Châteauneuf-du-Pape and often better value for money. Taste Vacqueyras at Les Amouriers, Gigondas at Les Pallières. Apart from Dom. de Durban at Beaumes-de-Venise, try the Cooperative and Dom. de la Pigeade (D21). Muscat de Beaumes-de-Venise is at its lingering subtlest with melon, foie gras or Roquefort cheese.

No longer playing second fiddle to Côtes du Rhône owing to much improved vinification, Côtes du Ventoux and Côtes du Lubéron are blended from the same grape varietals: for reds, *grenache*, *syrah*, *cinsault* and *mourvèdre*; for whites, *clairette*, *bourboulenc*.

Côtes du Ventoux is a sunny, lightish wine, limpid in the glass and fresh-tasting. Names to look out for: La Vielle Ferme, Pesquié, Valcombe. For tasting en route: Fondrèche and Canteperdrix at Mazan.

Côtes du Lubéron produces good spicy reds; also, superior whites due to the slightly cooler climate. Besides Ch. la Canorgue, other impressive châteaux are Val-Joannis at Pertuis, de Mille and d'Isolette near Apt. I tasted the last with a *brandade de morue aux truffes* (salt cod with purée potatoes and truffles), proving how well the right red wine goes with fish.

Pont Julien, a Roman bridge to rival Vaison's

This took me to a lane mostly used by cyclists which follows a disused railway along the Calavon river. I reached the Gare de Bonnieux restaurant in time for lunch. Formerly a railway station bistro, it provides an admirable 65-franc lunch of crudités and charcuterie, plat du jour, cheese or dessert, and a quarter litre of wine.

Pleasurably replete, I continued on the bike lane to Pont Julien, a Roman bridge to rival Vaison's; then, right on to the D149 to visit Château La Canorgue. One of the best Côtes du Lubéron wineries, La Canorge boasts a genuine château, hidden discreetly in its park. Jean-Pierre Margan greeted me warmly in the *chaix* (wine-production and tasting premises) where I tasted his bio-dynamically produced rosé, particularly good, and a fresh young '97 red. 'Like the ancients, I work by phases of the moon,' Jean-Pierre told me. 'My pesticides are made of nettles.'

Things were getting better all the time. Just above La Canorgue, vertiginous Bonnieux is situated between the Big and Small Lubéron hills. Exhilarated by my wine-tasting, I made the eighty-six-step climb to a shady copse of cedars by the church of two saints, Gervais and Protaise. From this vantage point, I saw the south face of ubiquitous Mont Ventoux, whose north face we see from our garden. Like pampered Gordes across the valley, Bonnieux rewards penetrating – vaulted passageways, stately mansions in need of a clean, a fountain with two stone-carved swans, and the only Bread Museum in Provence, situated in a fine seventeenth-century house. From the growing of wheat and other cereals to milling and baking, the alimentary and religious aspects of Our Daily Bread are traced via the unleavened bread of Israel, medieval bread, bread of the French Revolution, and all the different varieties – six-cereal, country, rye, olive, sourdough – available in baker's shops today.

Vertiginous Bonnieux rewards penetrating

gras, monkfish roasted with garlic, potatoes puréed with olive oil, mouth-watering desserts with pears and figs). The Aiguebrun Valley has a talented Polish chef at Auberge des Seguins and the country-house ambiance of Sylvia Buzier's Auberge de l'Aiguebrun (artichokes stuffed and braised, farm chicken with crayfish, crumble with fruit in season).

Lourmarin is well endowed with Le Moulin de Lourmarin's haute-cuisine sea-bream grilled with *arquebuse,* an ancient liqueur of gentian and agrimony; and, for those with less arcane tastes and a budget, Le Recréation's delicious rabbit, wild boar, *daubes,* and fruit tarts.

An old friend, Michel Bosc, cooks Provençal at Le Bistrot à Michel, Cabrières-d'Avingon, only 4 miles (6km) from Gordes (D2); his *pieds et paquets,* an earthy Marseillais speciality, and decor of old French movie posters are worth the detour. Le Mas de Tourteron at Les Imberts (off D2), an eighteenth-century *magnaneraie* amid cherry-trees, has aroma-specialist Elisabeth Bourgeois offering hot goat's cheese with rosemary, spicy charlotte of lamb and aubergine, and peach-and-lemon verbena soup.

Cuisine lowers its prices, if not its sights, as you descend from lofty Gordes to the excellent Bistrot de Roussillon (little Provençal stuffed vegetables, rabbit with aubergine, vegetable lasagne), Café de la Poste at Goult (pasta with pistou, *aïoli,* Goult's own *andouillette* sausage, lemon tart) and the Gare de Bonnieux, already described (see p.39). In Bonnieux village, Le Fournil has a trellis-shaded terrace and dining-room built into the rocks (lentil terrine with foie

The nearer you get to the Lubéron Mountain, the less crowded are the roads. For a taste of solitude, I headed east out of Bonnieux on the D36, left on the D232 until it joins the Apt road (D943) for a few hundred yards and then continues right, signposted Saignon. This is the real Lubéron, far away from mass tourism. The straight, empty road runs parallel with the Big Lubéron, with not a building in sight, past wild country of *garrigue*, ravines and rocky cliffs. *Garrigue* is a specifically Provençal open terrain between forest and grassland; on its thin, chalky soil grow kermes and holm oaks, juniper, Aleppo pines, green and gold *baouco* grass, sumac and turpentine trees, gorse, wild thyme and rosemary; its hot, aromatic aridity is the natural habitat of warblers, crickets, lizards, praying mantises and a poisonous centipede called Scolopendra.

A memorable hike to the top of the ridge took me past sheer escarpments where the Olympic rock-climbing team trains, via a gentler route following shepherds' and hunters' tracks to the summit of the Viper's Head rock. Not a soul up there, yet I was only an eagle's short flight from the Gordes and Roussillon tour buses. Among holm-oak and Genista, I ambled peacefully along the ridge, and descended down past Castelas, a *ferme-auberge* (farm taking guests) where Sardinian Gianni provided a refreshing apple juice and couldn't stop talking about his peccorino cheeses and home-cured hams hanging in the loft. His son is a virtuoso bongo player, and concerts disturb no one, because there's no one to disturb for miles.

From the D232, at the first *garrigue* crossroads a right on the D113 begins the descent south down the Aiguebrun valley, a wooded gorge past the Priory of St-Symphorien. A good stopover for medieval travellers, its bell tower pokes comfortingly out of the forest like a lighthouse. A southerly sun shone in splendour as I joined the D943 and the Combe de Lourmarin. *Combe* means dale and this one cuts dramati-cally between Big and Small Lubéron from the Calavon Valley, up over the plateau and down to Lourmarin.

Chief town of the South Lubéron, Lourmarin on its two little hills was the home of Albert Camus and has attracted writers and artists ever since. This is a gentler, more domestic, greener landscape of sleepy villages, fruit farms and some of the best vineyards of Côtes du Lubéron. Pride of Lourmarin is its castle, reached by a shady avenue; its fine staircase and chimney-pieces rival the Renaissance features of nearby Tour d'Aigues, a château much damaged by fire which would otherwise have been one of the masterpieces of Provençal sixteenth-century architecture. All roads lead to Lourmarin, a perfect base to make short detours to other noble Châteaux of the South Lubéron. East (D27, D45 and D135) leads to Ansouis – a medieval castle atop its village with flag flying, owned by the Sabran-Pontevés family since the twelfth century, with spectacular copper pans in the Provençal kitchen. West (D27) takes you to Lauris, viewed from afar perched on its rock, where the eighteenth-century château's gardens are terraced with ponds and fountains. And finally south to Cadenet (D943), my last stop in Vaucluse, a fortress once strategically situated with bastions overlooking the town and Durance River, now in ruins, its green, flat spaces gainfully employed as an open-air theatre.

After a clamber over Cadenet's medieval trenches and a stumble down the uneven, narrow pavements of its ill-lit main street, and a queasy stomach after dinner at the so-so Restaurant Gervais, I was ready to hate Cadenet. Far from it. Cadenet is real, not rich, a working town and a bit of a mess. The Lubéron without a social pretension in sight.

The further south I got, the more the Lubéron had delivered – superb scenery, surprisingly unspoiled villages, and unblasé locals. My journey through Vaucluse ended, as the French say, *en beauté.*

St. Rémy
Arles   Aix-en-Provence

Chapter 3

LAND OF LIGHT

BOUCHES-DU-RHÔNE

This is delta country – vast expanses
of fertile flatlands producing fruit,
vegetables, wheat, rice, vines and
olives. A hallucegenic light bounces off
grey, rugged hills like the Chaîne des
Alpilles between Mouriès and Eyguières
(below right). Former Roman roads
are now long, straight avenues of
plane trees (above right), leading to
Arles, St-Rémy-de-Provence, and
Aix-en-Provence, city of a hundred
fountains and a tradition of elegant
façades (far right).

CADENET TO ST-RÉMY-DE-PROVENCE

My next *départment*, Bouches-du-Rhône, would be very different from Vaucluse. Bouches-du-Rhône is delta country – vast expanses of fertile flatlands producing fruit, vegetables, wheat, rice, vines and olives. An hallucigenic light bouncing off grey, rugged hills beyond former Roman roads, now long, straight avenues of plane trees. Nearer Aix-en-Provence there are pine woods and lush, wine-producing plateaux, the red soil of Le Tholonet and the stark Montagne-Ste-Victoire.

Aix-en-Provence was less than an hour away but to visit Cézanne country and ignore van Gogh would have been inexcusable. I decided on a three-day detour, west to the Alpilles hills and Arles which had inspired Vincent and caused him much grief.

From Cadenet, it was only a few minutes to Bouches-du-Rhône. On the D943, I crossed the wide Durance which, further upstream, I would be coming back to in depth. A hyperbole, perhaps, for such a shallow, scruffy relic of a river. Most of the water runs by the side of the river in the state-of-the-art Canal de Provence to Marseilles and the valley is primarily agro-industrial and dull.

Just after the bridge, a sharp right on to the D561 had me driving west, parallel to the canal, until a fork left on the D561A led to a glorious surprise: Silvacane Abbey. Together with its sister abbeys Sénanque at Gordes and Le Thoronet near Lorgues, Silvacane is one of the masterpieces of Cistercian architecture in Provence, that harmonious blend of Gothic and Romanesque typical of the region. It was early morning; a Polish couple from Cracow and I were the only visitors, standing among fruit trees, admiring the ascetic, perfect proportions of its church. A superb setting: near the river, in tranquil fields, with a northern backdrop of the Petit Lubéron's wooded slopes.

Years spent in construction to the greater glory of God always astonish: in the case of Silvercane it lasted from 1175 to 1300, with the church completed in 1270. Barrel-vaulting in the choir and sacristy, ribbed vaulting in the refectory and chapter house deserve special attention for their austere beauty; a stroll around the arcaded cloisters reveals a wash-place for Benedictine monks sweaty after work in the fields. St-Benedict's rules of physical labour, prayer and work on manuscripts created a unity of body, spirit and mind. As places imbued with good so often are, Silvacane was pillaged in the Wars of Religion and damaged in the French Revolution. Now it has been nobly restored.

Further along the D561A, Roque d'Anthéron's Château de Florans, now a clinic, plays host to the popular summer Piano Festival in its formal French gardens. This is another perfect setting which once belonged to Auguste de Forbin of Aix-en-Provence, a truly eighteenth-century man – painter, archeologist and Director of French Museums. Nearby, an old man was filling empty mineral water bottles from a fountain. 'Much healthier,' he said. 'Free, too.'

Immediately after Roque d'Anthéron, I rejoined the boring D561. Without wasting time in the harsh, grey rock landscape of the Durance valley running towards its confluence with the Rhône at Avignon, I broke my back-road rule and took the old N7 north via Sénas and Orgon – a nostalgic trip: it was the road Sheila and I had taken on our first encounter with Provence at St-Tropez in 1958, long before arterial routes nationales had been upstaged by France's elaborate autoroute network. The sight of such familiar landmarks as Notre-Dame-de-Beauregard perched on its cliff top were reminders of our first excitement at spotting them: we're getting nearer the sea!

This time, headed north, I was glad to turn left at Orgon on to the traffic-free D24B towards a softer, more peaceful,

Chapelle Ste-Sixte,
a gem of rural
Romanesque

TH = Table d'Hôtes (guest house with dinner)
CH = Chambre d'Hôtes (bed and breakfast only)

Big choice, prices to match. Value for money is the Auberge Provençale at Eygalières, an eighteenth-century coaching inn with log fires in winter, shady courtyard in summer. And, near the Ste-Sixte chapel at Mas Doù Pastré (CH), Madame Roumanille's old Provençal name assures spirit of place in furniture, flowers and welcome.

On a honeymoon, head for St-Rémy's Château des Alpilles, living *la vie du château* in a park of ancient cypress and cedars. Air-conditioning and saunas enhance the nineteenth-century charm. Villa Glanum, convenient for the Roman Antiquities, was painted by van Gogh, while Gounod composed his opera *Mireille* (based on Mistral's poem) at Ville Verte in the town centre. Both hotels have a variety of rooms.

Les Baux offers rustic-chic luxury and damn the expense. Le Cabro d'Or lurks discreetly in the valley, covered by virginia creeper; Auberge La Benvengudo's swimming pool is surrounded by olives and its rooms filled with Provençal antiques.

Stay in the Old Town of Arles: main sites within walking distance. Apart from the small, elegant Hotel d'Arletan (with Roman baths – remains only!), the Grand Hotel Nord-Pinus in the Place du Forum has a bullfighter's bar, wrought-iron beds and Provençal prints.

At Fontvielle, a friendly stay in an atmospheric village house can be had at Mas Richard (CH), and L'Oustalon, a modest village pub in the olive-oil village of Maussane, is a former sixteenth-century abbey. Buried in olive country near Aureille (the D24A between Mouriès and Eyguières), Le Balcon des Alpilles (TH) provides Provençal hospitality at its best but not cheapest.

Stay in the Old Town of Arles

gently rolling landscape of pine wood and vineyard, cypress and olives. Just before Eygalières, the twelfth-century Chapelle Ste-Sixte makes a pleasing few minutes' stop – a gem of rural Romanesque, perfectly proportioned and sitting well in its deep south surroundings.

On the wide, sleepy main street of Eygalières, I had a coffee at the Café du Centre. The waitress had cropped dark hair, skintight pants, long black jacket. Very chic – I was clearly nearing St-Rémy. Life's more relaxed here, though. Traffic waits, while old friends embrace in the middle of the street and dogs make love. Suitably slowed down, I climbed sinuous, cobbled streets past finely restored houses to a ghostly ruined church's stage-set façade and shining white Virgin Mary praying on a rock. My eyes, in the shimmering sunlight, turned from a plain stretching north towards Avignon to Montagne de la Caume, the rugged, romantic beginning of the Alpilles hills. A preview of van Gogh country.

Soon after Eygalières the D74A reaches a left on to the bigger, dead straight Roman Via Domitia (D99), the last stretch to St-Rémy-de-Provence. Bamboo and high cypress hedges provide shelter from the plain's relentless mistral. Approaching the town, nurseries for the gardens of the rich and famous have replaced the staple crops of yester-year. Why bother to eke out a living against Spanish competition, when you can sell your *mas* (small farmhouse) to a millionaire, your land to a nurseryman?

VINCENT'S HILLS

St-Rémy, whatever you read about it in the glossies, is much as it always was, a roundabout with a small old town in the middle and a busy, shady one-way street running around it. The Wednesday market fills the town centre with nattily clad shoppers, a high-pitched buzz of greetings and departures with laden shopping baskets to Land Cruisers and Volvo station wagons.

Princess Caroline of Monaco, whom I didn't see at the market that morning, has family connections with the Alpilles. In 1642, Louis XIII gave the town of Les Baux to her ancestor, Hercule de Grimaldi, to acknowledge Monaco's loyalty to France; it remained Monégasque till the French Revolution. The Marquis des Baux – who was a Prince of Monaco – donated the fine stained-glass windows of St-Vincent's church. The Grimaldis' legal representative, Joseph de Pistoye, built for himself the elegant eighteenth-century Hôtel d'Estrine at St-Rémy. It is now the Centre d'Art Van Gogh, where an audio-visual show illustrates the Dutch post-Impressionist's love–hate relationship with the region, and visitors can enjoy the fine plaster mouldings, wrought-iron stairway and painted ceilings.

Geographic convenience rather than chronological order guided my footsteps in search of Vincent, starting with the second, marginally less fraught period of his Provençal stay (1889–90). After turbulent months at Arles, he bitterly consented to be transferred to St-Rémy as a patient of Dr Peyron, where he painted the peaceful gardens of *L'Hôpital St-Paul in St-Rémy* and *L'Iris*. Above the clinic, the surreal, jagged crest of the 'little Alps', Aleppo-pine covered and full of pagan gods, further confused his cosmic vision. His religious mania could not cope with all those gods; he was Jesus forsaken by the Father, the doomed worker of miracles on canvas.

In spite of its grim associations, St-Paul de Mausole is far from grim to visit (signposted left-turn off the D5 at Glanum's Roman Antiquities). Still a psychiatric clinic, it revealed Vincent's irises in the garden and beds of primroses in the nearby church's delicate cloisters. There is a strong sense of the creative spirit, peace and tranquillity amid the turbulence. Bright sunshine shining through the

LES BAUX-DE-PROVENCE

Les Baux, one of the great sights of Provence, can be reached by two routes. Before visiting Arles is the more dramatic: turn left off the C138 on to the D27 to the top of the Alpilles, and you come suddenly upon a heart-stopping view almost hallucinatory at first sight. Are those houses down there or just more odd-shaped grey rocks? On the way back from Arles, turn left off the D17 on to the D78F and approach up Val d'Enfer (Hell's Valley) – not really very hellish but ghostly at full moon.

Its medieval origins are as romantic as its site, overlooking the valley and the Crau plain.

The Lords of Les Baux, 'a race of eagles, never vassals' as Mistral called them, had a strange idea of nobility. Sweet-singing troubadours, often from good families themselves, would keep the ladies happy while the Lords were off leading the Crusades, and all kinds of amorous disputes were settled in the Courts of Love. Occasionally things got out of hand. One jealous Lord killed his wife for cheating on him with a particularly lusty troubador. Then he invited the troubadour to dine and served him, among other tasty morsels, his wife's heart. Perhaps 'losing one's heart to a loved one' comes from this grisly legend.

Troubadours would serenade in the Langue d'Oc, 'the language of love', which gave its name to that region of south-west France. A version of it was spoken from Limoges round to Italy, and modern Provençal has the same sensual, musical ring.

Mar que rebumbello
  Waves of roaring ocean
Bos plen de rumour,
  Whispering woods above,
Digas à la bello
  Tell my heart's emotion
Moun langui d'amour
  To my lady love.

Today, Les Baux's magnificent Renaissance architecture keeps the grown-ups happy, while children love the fortress's siege-engines and precipitous but well-protected network of paths and steps to explore the eagle's nest ruins. At full moon, observe Les Baux's singular presence in its uneven circus of ghostly white crags and shadowed crests. You can almost hear the sounds of a lute and of a voice singing '*Mar que rebumbello ...*'

three small stained glass windows behind the altar has the attention-holding effect of a mandala.

An informative small museum off the cloisters is named for the pagan goddess Valetudo at whose Glanum spring pilgrims would come to be cured by holy water. From early Christian times to the present Maison de Santé St-Paul, the mentally disturbed were always looked after here. And now it is touching to see the paintings of contemporary patients following Vincent's therapy, on show near the room where he stayed – and another room describing the clinic's progress from cruel bedlam to humane caring.

Between Vincent's fits of madness, Dr Peyron allowed him out into the nearby countryside to work, accompanied by a minder. When Vincent departed from St-Rémy for Auvers-sur-Oise, he left a number of works in the good doctor's care; the doctor's son used them for target practice! Others survived. After visiting the museum, I walked to nearby painting sites: *The Quarry at St-Rémy* and *Olive Trees* in the grove beside the St-Paul de Mausole driveway. *Mountain at St-Rémy* and *Olive Trees, The Rock with Two Holes*, painted from near the Glanum remains, are his expressionist vision of the pierced, fretwork hills, a wild swirling vision. Of these paintings, he wrote to brother Theo: 'As far as I'm concerned, I reckon I'm less than the peasants. Finally, I'm slaving at my canvases as they do in their fields ... You get to know a country quite differently than it seemed at first sight ...'

Glanum upstages Vaison-la-Romaine's smaller, more domestic antiquities with its monumental civic remains: pompous mausoleum and triumphal arch towering over the tour buses. The Romans certainly chose their town sites well. Near a holy spring, protected by the Alpilles' bosky woodland of Scotch firs and kermes oaks, the plateau is worth visiting for the site alone. In Roman times, Glanum was strategically placed as a halfway halt on the

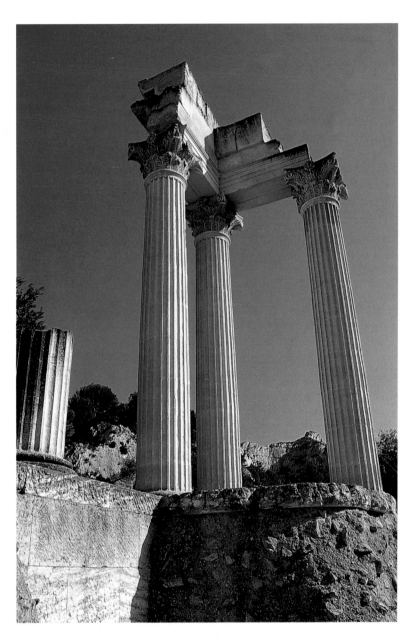

Glanum — its monumental civic remains

trade route from Spain to Italy, and linked their Provincia colonies at Narbonne and Nice – hence its civic and military importance. The principal attractions are the thermes (hot and cold baths), forum (central place), nymphaeum (Roman swimming pool), and temples (gods and goddesses of the Roman pantheon). For crowd-beating coolness, come early in the day, avoiding July, August and weekends.

Back in St-Remy, I needed a drink – at the Café des Arts, a delightfully beat-up literary establishment, where the locals on their regular bar stools don't look down noses at you if you happen to be carrying a Michelin Guide. One leisurely pastis in their convivial company set me up to continue in Vincent's footsteps.

ST-RÉMY TO ARLES

I drove along the Old Arles Road (C138), parallel with the little irrigation canal, Canal des Alpilles, which runs from the Durance river to feed secret, imposing farms on either side of the lane.

Marie Mauron, known as the Colette of Provence, evokes their market gardens in *Jardins de St-Rémy*:

The Gardens consisted of the greenest, freshest, most murmuring of waters and trees in a changing landscape. Peasants Jean-Denis Roumanille and his wife Pierrette were happy in their farmhouse there; fruit and vegetables grew in abundance as though blessing their joint efforts. Fine apple trees (so thick on the ground, so remarkable that they had given the farmhouse its name, *Les Pommiers*) adorned the orchard with pink clusters, thanks to irrigation streams whispering in the gentle breeze of spring. (*Quand La Provence nous est contée ...*)

The Bistrot d'Eygalières, a former grocery store, sets the high standard with little potatoes sprinkled with truffles, raw marinaded scallops, pigeon stuffed with foie gras and caramalized apple tart. Another bistrot in the the same enchanting village, Chez Adeline, has simpler family fare: oven-baked fish in summer, knuckle of veal in winter.

Upmarket St-Rémy does have a few reasonably priced restaurants: L'Assiette de Marie (fricassé of artichokes, fish soup, canneloni of Corsican cheese and spinach), ingredients are fresh from the market round the corner; or see and be seen with *le tout St-Rem'* at Le Bistrot des Alpilles, tucking into home-made pasta, with pistou (basil, garlic, olive oil and parmesan), smoked salmon or ceps.

Gourmets with Gold Cards head up the hill to Les Baux's temples of gastronomy. On the panoramic terrace of L'Oustaù de Baumanière, Jean-André Charial serves baby French beans picked in the kitchen garden that morning, not to mention fillets of red mullet with basil, and leg of lamb *en croûte*. In the valley, there's sumptuous *tian* of artichokes with salt cod and *aïoli* at Riboto de Taven.

Arles is more reasonably priced. Apart from the value-for-money Brasserie Nord-Pinus (artichokes with coriander, rack of lamb), Le Jardin de Manon is convenient for homely Provençal cooking when visiting the Alyscamps. For tasty snacks (Arles sausage, *tapendade*, olive bread, dessert), head for the Pâtisserie du Forum in the old town centre.

For more swanky dining under the stars at Fontvielle's Le Régalido, Jean-Pierre Michel's specialities are gratin of Bouzigues mussels with spinach, olive ravioli, green apple tart. Also on the D10: Le Bistrot du Paradou (see p.55), and Maussane's La Petite France (little pig's trotter pancakes with morel mushrooms, chocolate fondant).

The Roumanilles were parents of Joseph Roumanille, Avignon bookseller and *félibrige* poet. The movement was founded by fellow-poet Frédéric Mistral, who claimed to have heard the obscure word *félibrige*, meaning the Provençal language, at a funeral oration in his village of Maillane. In a spirit of regionalism, Mistral and others used Provençal flamboyantly to promote a return to basic rural values in an industrial age – at romanticized farms such as Marie Mauron describes.

These properties have very different inhabitants now. I stopped at Le Trévallon, a mile or so from St-Rémy.

'My father,' said winemaker Eloi Dürrbach of Alsace origin, 'bought Le Trévallon in the fifties to sculpt and garden. When I started making wine here, there were sixty market gardeners, now there are only three. A vice-president of Coca-Cola just bought a property, and Atlanta's moving in ...'

Seriously rich customers for a seriously fine wine. Le Trévallon has earned its reputation as one of the best in Provence. It's a biologically produced wine, with lucky insects discouraged from attacking the vines by a sweet-smelling insecticide made from rosemary and lavender. In an oak-barrel lined cellar, I tasted the '96 white, a tiny production of mellow nectar; the '95 red was an even higher scorer with its stylish blend of Syrah and Cabernet-Sauvignon, as different from Côtes du Rhône as the Alpilles from Mont Ventoux. In 1975 former architect Dürrbach, a true original, began blasting inhospitable rocks from the lower Alpilles slopes to make the first of his 49 acres (20 hectares) of vineyard. He also showed me a kitchen garden where the gardener was just opening the canal sluice gates to water aubergines, courgettes and tomatoes. Gentle rivulets nourish the parched plants in high summer.

The C138 joins the main St-Rémy-Arles road (D99) at St-Etienne-du-Grès, where an afternoon market – rare in Provence – sells the freshest of *primeurs* (early fruit and vegetables) and the best available all year round. From there the D32 led to the western end of Les Alpilles and an unavoidable stretch of the N570 (Avignon-Arles) to the wide Rhône flowing swiftly towards the Mediterranean. As I drove into town, a classic Camargue sunset silhouetted Arles and the sky was aflame.

VINCENT'S RIVER

Vincent's tempestuous Provençal sojourn began in the snowy winter of 1888 at Arles and lasted till 1890. It was charted by personal disaster – loneliness, heavy drinking, lack of funds, despair, self-mutilation and madness. Paradoxically, it also inspired the hallucinatory beauty of the Rhône waterfront in *The Starry Night* and the peace of a peasant's siesta in *Noon: Rest*.

Sad to report, Arles does not possess a single van Gogh; he was considered off-limits by the municipal museum curator – as, indeed, by every other art-buyer in France at the time. *Sunflowers*, also inspired by the Midi stay, fetched £24,750,000 at a 1987 Christie's auction. Touching visual tributes by fellow foreign artists can be found at the Van Gogh Foundation: themes of sunlight, madness and suicide are treated by Bacon, Lichtenstein, Rauschenberg and others. Arles is still eagerly awaiting the donation of its first van Gogh.

Sites of his paintings, however, are legion.

If you stay at the adorable little Hotel D'Arlatan, near the Arlaten Museum (founded by Mistral) with its fulsome, evocative jumble of Provençal memorabilia, you're not only central for the bullfights at the Roman

Le Pont de van Gogh, Arles

Arena but also for hanging out in the Place du Forum. Nothing is more relaxing after a heavy day's sightseeing than to dine upstairs at Vaccarès, above the little square with its statue of Mistral where Vincent painted *Café Terrace, Evening*.

Vincent's notorious ear-slashing only detained him three days at the sixteenth-century Hôtel-Dieu hospital. He paid Docteur Rey with a painting which was promptly used to block a windy hole in the wall! Now the Espace van Gogh cultural centre, it housed the 1988 Centenary Retrospective when many locals saw original van Goghs for the first time. A man near me pointed to the Pont de Langois, and exclaimed with proprietorial pride: 'That's where I fish!' The bridge can easily be visited following the sign to 'Le Pont de van Gogh' on the D35 to Port-St-Louis on the outskirts of town.

Gauguin, moving spirit behind the Atelier du Midi, a projected cooperative of Arles artists, visited Vincent later in 1888. At first they got on well together at Vincent's digs, *The Yellow House*, No. 1 Place Lamartine. They painted together, images of the Café de la Gare (now L'Alcazar) and the Roman necropolis, Les Alyscamps. Then they got on each other's nerves. Their quarrels grew fiercer. Vincent's remorse at threatening his friend with a razor led him on a rampage to a brothel in rue Bout-Arles near the Rhône. He presented his own severed ear-lobe to Rachel, his favourite girl, hardly the most endearing gift from a regular client.

Strong, sensual Midi images had literally tipped the mind of an unbalanced, puritan northerner into madness: the Greek-featured beauties of Arles, harsh sun, relentless sky, twisted olives, black cypresses, turning sunflowers.

Vincent's torment became our treasure.

Alphonse Daudet's windmill, Fontvielle

ARLES TO AIX-EN-PROVENCE

After backtracking on the N570, a right on the D17 took me to eleventh-century Montmajour Abbey, burial place of the Counts of Provence, an imposing landmark set against the Alpilles hills. Along their southern slopes, I stopped at Fontvielle for Alphonse Daudet's windmill, a much-visited literary shrine. Native of Nîmes, Daudet hated the mid-nineteenth-century grime and mud-slinging of Paris, and the renewed inspiration of Provence led to his world-famous *Letters from My Windmill*.

Daudet, like Maupassant, was a master of economy. In five crisp pages of *L'Arlésienne*, which became a Bizet opera, the wild girl from Arles drives a country boy to suicide. 'Jan never spoke again of the girl from Arles. But he still loved her; and more deeply than ever since knowing she had once been another man's mistress.' Macho tragedy and bucolic whimsy (*The Stars* and *Monsieur Séguin's Goat*) express the paradox of the real Provence, its perverse mood swings. *Le cafard du midi* (Midi blues) can blow in any time, like an ill wind. A Gipsy Kings' riot of Camargue guitars can just as quickly dispel it.

Further along the D17, I lightened up over lunch at the inestimable Bistrot du Paradou where the wise reserve and the foolish curse their imprudence. The fixed menu is classic: essential Provencal fare, wine and crisp country bread included. No choice but no complaints, either. In a region so full of tourists, it's surprising how much local atmosphere it manages to maintain without an iota of folksiness. An easy detour to Les Baux from Le Paradou can be made either before or after lunch (see page 48).

As I continued through Maussane-les-Alpilles on the D17, olive trees grew thicker as tourists grew less. Headed east, I found myself actually doing 50 mph (80 kmph) on the straight, flat road across the Crau coastal plain to the

Salon-de-Provence's eccentric moss fountain

olive-oil town of Mouriès, which claims to be the first in France and, ipso facto, the best. My neighbours in Nyons, a rival to the claim, would kill me for agreeing. A wise impartiality was the order of the day as I arrived at the Cave Cooperative (olive oil cooperative), an unpromising, scruffy-looking building so off the beaten track I thought I must be mistaken. But no, once inside the mill with its millstone, presses and *scourtins* (mats used in pressing), sniffing the familiar smell, I found an animated crowd lining up to have plastic containers filled at 95 francs a litre. It was like a party where the guests all know each other. There was no attempt at presentation, no boutique with *tapenades* (a paste of black olives, anchovies, capers, herbs and garlic), soap, honey and lavender bags. Just a homely, slightly chaotic ambience with faded photos and news clippings dangling insouciantly from the wall, showing olive-oil fraternities with producers in robes receiving honours.

After Mouriès, olives gave way to conifers, the hills grew less rugged in aspect than Vincent's, and the peaceful D24 climbed and serpented gently through a thick forest past the hamlet of Le Destet. Turning right on to the D25, I found myself on one of the most scenic hill routes so far – through the centre of the Alpilles to the eastern end of the range – weaving like a sun-struck snake between grey rock hills, *barres* and bluffs, garrigue and pines. Another right on to the D569 brought me to Eyguières, gateway to the Alpilles, a friendly, earthy little town of bull-breeders and sheep-farmers. A jolly, red-eyed man in a black Provençal cowboy hat suggested I admire the façade of the eighteenth-century town house, Hôtel Garcin. His boozy bonhommie seemed at odds with the town's forbidding motto *L'Aïgo faï veni pouli* (Sobriety is the Mother of Beauty).

The hideous, hectic approach via the D17 to Salon-de-Provence, biggest and busiest plains town, does not prepare the visitor for the charm of its city centre. Encouraged by the noble medieval city gate, Porte de l'Horloge, and the eccentric moss fountain to which years of moss-covered chalk deposit give the appearance of a dripping tree, I later visited the Musée de l'Empéri in the oldest fortress in Provence. This beautifully set-out museum, dedicated to the French army, is well-placed in territory fought-over for so many centuries and a must for anyone remotely interested in military history. Another pleasant surprise was the small, beautifully run Hotel Vendôme with its quiet, interior courtyard. A fair-skinned, blue-eyed girl called Christine – in charge of the front desk that afternoon – insisted on escorting me personally to the garage. 'No parking, not even for a minute in this little street,' she said, unusually law-abiding for these parts.

Christine, who swore she'd never go back to her native, sunless Moselle, also recommended I dine at the Salle-à-

OLIVES

The Greeks brought the olive to Provence as the fruit of civilization on the branch of peace. Now the Mediterranean's Muslim and Christian countries share the symbolism of oil as an unction of benediction; the Koran speaks of the olive tree as 'a blessed tree neither of East nor West'. All year round eternal olive groves cast a silvery grey patina over the landscape as the sun catches their leaves. An olive tree has to be pruned so the birds can fly through it. Only a shock frost can destroy it. Black olives are riper green olives. The olive year's cycle is as fixed as wine's: first blossoms in March; flowering April–June; ripening June–October; September–October green olives harvested for the table; November–December, black olives picked for oil or preserved in brine to take the bitterness out before eating; January, first pressing for oil. It takes 11–13lb (5–6kg) of olives to make 1³⁄₄pt (1 litre) of oil. Highest quality unblended oil from the first pressing has the lowest acidity and is known as Extra Virgin or Virgin, considered the best for cooking, salad dressing and medical uses. Four top categories are all chemical-free.

Black olives are used in beef and lamb stews, with chicken,

The Greeks brought the olive to Provence

and to make such Provençal specialities as *tapenade*; green olives can be stuffed with pimentos, anchovies, almonds, and also used in cooking.

Olive groves grace the sunniest, south-facing slopes. Names are like a poem: Aglandau, Grossanne, Salonenque, Picholine.

The valleys around Les Baux specialize in green olives known locally as *cachado*. Other important olive-producing areas are Nyons in Drôme Provençale and the hills behind Nice.

Manger (Dining Room). Conveniently, just next door, but I missed the entrance twice. It's run by a family in their private house, and they wouldn't sink so low as to display a menu outside. I rang the bell, my host opened the door and led me into a sumptuous, candlelit dining room with log fire blazing and exuberantly painted walls and ceilings. Francis Miège, fat and jovial like *patrons* used to be, welcomed me with a sensible two-course proposal for a reasonable 125 francs, while his wife Elyane did the cooking, and his daughter in a flowered dress with a white apron served the tables. I had a starter of haddock, garlic and potatoes in a *tarte tatin*, followed by *paquets* of rabbit with noodles, with Domaine de la Vallongue from Eygalières. 'It was once a Marseilles merchant's house,' explained Monsieur Miège. 'In summer, you can dine in our secret garden's orangery. Come back, *pourquoi pas*?'

After the rev-up of Salon's morning rush-hour on the D572 to Aix-en-Provence, I was glad to slope off to the comparative peace and quiet of the D15. It announced itself as another section of Route des Vins, which enters the Coteaux d'Aix appellation near Lambesc.

Previous visits to the town had been fully taken up with lunch at a famous restaurant which had since become a male strip club and was now defunct. So there was no excuse not to explore Lambesc. On a low hill between the Crau plain and Aix plateau, the country town takes in some half dozen turbulent centuries, including a devastating earthquake in 1909. Many of the seventeenth- and eighteenth-century stately town houses of the gentry, matching the ascendancy of nearby Aix-en-Provence, were destroyed. A few remain, like the fine example in rue Madame de Sévigné. Lambesc's arcaded wash-place is a classified *monument historique*. The monolithic façade of the parish church, Notre-Dame de l'Assomption, however, seems out of scale with the rest of the town: typical of

Medieval city gate, Porte d'Horloge, Salon-de-Provence

TH = Table d'Hôtes (guest house with dinner)
CH = Chambre d'Hôtes (bed and breakfast only)

Salon-de-Provence's tiny Vendôme (see p.56) has friendly service and much charm; those who need more formal *salons* head for Abbaye de St-Croix, a converted twelfth-century abbey 2 miles (3km) out of town on the D16. This has 'Relais et Châteaux' luxury in a wild, sunbaked landscape of *garrigue* and cliffs, with panoramic views from rooms decorated with low-key good taste.

A coolish reception in a noble, tapestry-hung hall at Hotel des Augustins, Aix-en-Provence, was redeemed by an airy, sunny room with a small terrace overlooking red-tiled roofs and church bell towers. Another favourite is Le Manoir, also in the old town – with the

The Fountain of the Four Dolphins, Aix-en-Provence

great advantage of an arcaded garden and private parking. Both of these hotels are reasonably priced by Aix's elevated standards. To be within ear-splashing distance of Aix's prettiest fountain, choose the Quatre-Dauphins – smallish, comfortable rooms with bills to match.

Two small musical hotels not too far from the city centre are Le Mozart, named for the opera festival's favourite composer, and La Renaissance, former home of Aix-born composer, Darius Milhaud. Villa Gallici is a top Aix choice when money is no object: faïence and marble bathrooms, bedroom walls

hung with fabulous fabrics, and a music room sumptuous enough to receive the Sun King himself.

On the Cézanne trail, you can stay overnight at La Pauline (CH), an eighteenth-century villa in the Pinchinats Valley, once the scene of Pauline Bonaparte's amours. At St-Marc-Jaumegarde (D10), Le Mas des Bartavelles (CH) has a studio and a family suite – perfect for a prolonged stay – with fresh-water swimming-pool and tasteful Provençal decor. Further along the road, the pleasures of Vauvenargues' simple but hospitable Moulin de Provence are described on page 70.

pompous Provençal baroque. I prefer the Jacquemard bell tower with its family of figures on top who perform their little act when the clock strikes the hour.

It was hard to get out of Lambesc on the road I wanted (D66). I kept asking, and kept getting directed to a better road to Rognes (D15). What was wrong with the D66? Should I warn the police I was taking it, as before a Sahara crossing? In fact, it was a perfectly good if narrow road via the ravishing Forêt Domaniale de Caire-Val: gently rolling vineyards of red, sandy soil; pine woods with yellow gorse and ivy; bright green fields of winter wheat.

The wine village of Rognes also suffered badly in the 1909 earthquake. Its red stone (*pierre de Rognes*) is much used for sculpture in a concentrated area of châteaux and country churches. A man shopping in the Cours St-Etienne was singing the Hallelujah Chorus at the top of his voice on this crisp, sunny morning. It put me in the best of spirits, too. I took a mountain-goat's path, clambering up to the ruins of the medieval fortress on the hill behind the village, and was rewarded by a hint of summer emanating from resiny pines, as the sun grew warmer. A spur above the village's red roofs offered a view to Montagne Ste-Victoire to the south, the Lubéron to the north, and the warm, inviting countryside of the Aixois hinterland.

On the way out of Rognes by the D543, Chapelle St-Denis (just before branching left on the D15, then right on the D14C to Aix) is a typical example of Provençal hybrid architecture of different periods: baroque façade, Romanesque apse. Its blend is a good deal more harmonious than the heavy mixture of centuries at the next stop, Château Beaulieu, whose brochure claims it as 'unquestionably the most important vineyard estate of the Coteaux d'Aix'. A boast that could well be challenged by Fonscolombe, Commanderie de la Bargemone, and my personal favourite, Vignelaure.

Through a long, cool forest, I began the descent to Aix (D14). Suburbs and lunchtime road-rage began. There is no one more tetchy on the road than a hungry Aixois (or Aixoise). Puyricard's famous *chocolatier*, whose chocolates rival Aix's famous *calissons* (sugar-coated almond candy) reminded me that I too was getting hungry and tetchy.

CITY OF A HUNDRED FOUNTAINS

Aix-en-Provence is like an oyster – difficult to open but, when you do, what a pearl lies hidden there, what a succulent taste. And as with an oyster's shell, you have to find precisely the right point of entry, or the 'opening' can lead to frayed tempers and no oyster.

For my lunch picnic, I went to where it all began: the Celto-Ligurian oppidum (fortified town) of Entremont. It was the capital of the Celtic Salyens tribe whom naturally the ethnic-cleansing Romans felt it necessary to lay waste in 123 BC. The site itself is a dramatic spur, its limestone

impregnated with springs and streams and shaded by massive pines 1,000 feet (305m) above sea level, and the Roman army had a sweaty, rocky climb up the escarpment from the camp below.

The Romans soon realized the value of their camp site. Hot and cold springs bubbling. Running water for their public baths. Proconsul Caius Sextius Calvinus founded a military post called Aquae Sextiae (later contracted to Aix). The Thermal Baths were among the empire's best, and as late as the 1920s Aix was a flourishing spa. By 1990

the spa, which hadn't received much attention since Caius Sextius Calvinus, had its seedy premises shut down by the city council. Since then, they have been handsomely refurbished and opened in the spring of 1998 to receive 10,000 *curistes*, in search of anti-stress and anti-nicotine cures. At £500 a week per immersed body, the city fathers must be rubbing their hands.

The Romans' great gift to the town is undoubtedly water. *Ville d'eau, ville d'art* (town of water and art) is its motto. Aixois say their water flows upwards. And I caught my first exhilarating sight of a fountain at La Rotonde, Aix's Piccadilly Circus, certainly the biggest in town if far from the prettiest. A typical nineteenth-century official water-works, fed from the reservoir built by Emile Zola's father, complete with guardian lions, spouting water-babies and topped by what you might think were the Three Graces. Not at all: in Victorian times a more grandiose, worthy purpose was required; the ladies represent the virtues of the city – Fine Arts, Agriculture and Justice.

Justice faces towards the cool bower of plane trees on the Cours Mirabeau. An Aixois would punch you for calling the wide, shady avenue Aix's Piccadilly, and kill you for calling it Aix's Champs Elysées. To me, it is more beautiful than both. It is the centrepiece of Louis XIV's opulent seventeenth- and eighteenth-century rebuilding of the city, and I would explore it later. At this point, in the dodgem-car chaos of the Cours' traffic, I attempted a U-turn and fell foul of Justice in the shape of a policewoman who whistled at me from the sidewalk.

Two golden rules for enjoying Aix: choose a central hotel and dump your car. Then cool off by one of the hundred fountains, each with its own evocative name: Trois Ormeaux (three elms) at the junction of three streets – Matheron, Montigny and des Epinaux – where antique dealers have their shops; or Augustins (Austin friars), conveniently close to my hotel of the same name, a former twelfth-century monastery with rich tapestries in the hall.

My exploration of the narrow, pedestrians-only streets began at Place des Prêcheurs where the present Law Courts were once the Palace of the medieval Counts of Provence. To ensure the education of competent political and judicial administrators, the university was founded in 1409. Around the original Place de l'Université are various privileged educational faculties in old buildings that few of today's 40,000 students, taught at outlying blockhouses,

get to see. French courses for foreigners, for instance, take place in the sumptuous fifteenth-century Hôtel Maynier d'Oppède. Even for them it wasn't all privilege.

'Aix is a cliquey town,' a young German student told me. 'At some cafés on the Cours, you have to be seen kissing the waiter on both cheeks – otherwise you're not in!' He preferred Le Petit Verdot wine bar and the cafés of the Place de Cardeurs where the locals hang out, heads are cooled by the modern Amado fountain, and kissing the waiter could lead to a punch-up.

It's always been a closed, cliquey town, and even Louis XIV, the Sun King himself, had a hard time opening it up. A Provençal proverb speaks of:

The three scourges of Provence,
Parlement, Mistral and Durance.

The mistral blew, the Durance flooded and members of the Aix *parlement* (high judicial court) refused to pay the King his taxes. During the Wars of Religion, they had defended Provence's independence against the central government of French Kings, and in the seventeenth century even more fiercely against the Sun King and his heavyweights, Richelieu and Mazarin. By showering them with privileges, enobling many and rebuilding their town, the Sun King tamed his rebellious Aixois bourgeoisie.

Nowadays the privilege lives on in Archbishop Mazarin's Palace with the annual summer *Festival de l'art lyrique* (opera festival), where the Espéluque fountain in Place de L'Archevêché cools opera-goers and, too hot in my glad rags, I once gratefully splashed my face.

'Elitist!' accused a leftish scion of an old Aix family. 'How can you stand all those white tuxedos and Givenchy dresses? They've spoiled the cultural fun here.' I pointed out there were now cheaper opera tickets – to no avail. 'There used to be street theatre, impromptu concerts, popular events we could afford. The council's too busy cleaning up our act for snobs, and killing the joy in the process.'

Aix has a tradition of elegant façades, whatever inelegant behaviour may go on behind their massive doors. The eighteenth-century firebrand revolutionary and skilled orator, Comte Gabriel de Mirabeau, who proposed that Louis XVI become a constitutional monarch in the English manner and thereby save his head, lost his own to women time and time again. He was one of the great lechers of Aix. The main street is named after him.

Love in a hot climate seems to permeate every inch of the Cours Mirabeau's 880 yards (804m). 'Half the distance they cover in their daily journeying is dedicated to love,' wrote the playwright Giraudoux of the modern Aixois. The best time to see the Cours is traffic-free, late night or early morning. The moss-covered Fontaine Mossue runs hot, the Fontaine Neuf Canons runs cold. The fountain by the statue of Good King René – poet, painter, composer and winemaker – does not, alas, run wine. Fifteenth-century Good King René, Duke of Anjou, Count of Provence, King of Sicily spoke Latin, Greek, Hebrew, Italian and Catalan. Happily married at twelve to Isabella of Lorraine and, after her death at forty-seven, to Jeanne de Laval, he loved his Provençals like his wives and lavished upon them festivals and jousts and endless schemes of merriment. No wonder Aix prospered under his reign.

Most important sites and events are within easy walking distance of the Cours. Just off it, on Avenue Victor-Hugo, a *santons* fair is held during December. These hand-crafted terra cotta and wood figurines represent the 'little saints', local characters like The Shepherd, The Lavender-Seller, The Tambourine-Player and The Fishwife who appear with The Wise Men in *crèches provençales* (Provençal cribs) at Christmas.

I breakfasted early at Le Mazarin on chocolate croissants and freshly squeezed orange juice, and then took a leisurely stroll up the Left Bank (the wide sidewalks are known as Banks), where the sunlight slants through the plane trees, and the sun's rays dapple the façades of magnificent mansions. 'Who would have thought,' wrote the historian de Haitze, 'that Vanity needed a house, just like people do?' The home of a newly ennobled Aixois had to knock his neighbour's eye out, going one better with fierce *mascarons* (grotesque stone-sculpted faces), sturdy *atlantes* (Graecian male figures), hand-of-Fatima door-knockers, delicate wood carving, cool courtyards with softly murmuring fountains, wrought-iron staircases and painted ceilings.

The Left Bank, now housing the city's banks and best *pâtisseries* (cake shops), is the shady side of the street. Actually, the sunny side of the street opposite, with its endless line of cafés, becomes shady too – at night, when big BMWs from Marseilles, a mere 20 miles (32km) away, disgorge blonde-streaked, teetering bimbos in skin-tight dresses and short, sharp-suited men with lethal rings, come to check out their investments. Property and the Mafia go hand in hand in Provence. A bomb has been known to go off in a Cours café.

Not that the Cours is normally more dangerous than any other city's main street. At 11.30p.m. on Saturday night it was impossible to find a café seat, and I did like the young Aixois do: sit on a bench, feet up, wait till a place becomes vacant and make a dash for it.

Saturday is also when you see well-heeled young couples carrying cakes and champagne to friends' pricey *appartements* with painted ceilings in split-up eighteenth-century mansions. Aix has become one of the high-tech centres of France, attracting young technocrats from all over the country. The new elite need lawyers to fix their housing

Salon's friendly, family-run Salle-à-Manger sets a high standard (see p.58). This standard can also be found at Francis Robin, where the chef of that name gives great value for money in classic French style: rascasse mousse, a *navarin* of lamb with green cabbage and red peppers, and a cornucopia of tempting desserts. On the D66, four miles before Rognes, Les Olivarelles occupies a modern *mas*. With traditional hospitality, Paul Dietrich serves inventive young pigeon raviolis and kidney cooked in Gigondas.

Nobody need go hungry in Aix-en-Provence, but they may regret their choice. Beware tourist traps. In the Cours Mirabeau area, restaurateur Antoine does you proud with a choice of two eateries bearing his name, Côté Cour or Trattoria. In decor and on table, a touch of neighbouring Italy in Provence – anti-pasti, artichokes with coriander-flavoured olive oil, skate with capers and hazlenut butter, fresh pasta and *tiramisu* (coffee-and-cream-cheese spongecake) –

The cool bower of plane trees on the Cours Mirabeau

unfussy food at unbeatable prices. Along the Cours, café-restaurant Deux Garçons with stunning Louis-Philippe decor boasts the terrace for seeing and being seen at festival time – with okay food at prices you could do without. Stick to drinks. Better value is the elegant and welcoming À la Cour de Rohan, calling itself a salon de thé (delicious snacks and cakes are available) but in its pretty, miniscule courtyard you can enjoy aubergine caviar, poached eggs with spinach, and cherry clafoutis. Just the lunchtime fare for sightseers.

More Provençal is the Old Town's wine bar, Le Petit Verdot, in rue Entrecasteaux, fun and cheap for quail pâté and a mixed stew of duck and beef. Best in town, of course, is still Clos de la Violette with the Banzo's superbly inventive cooking in a haven of *luxe, calme et volupté*, described on page 67.

Out of town, Cézanne country does well with the Bonfillon's Petite Auberge (see p.68) at Le Thoronet; and Relais Saint-Victoire at Beaurecueil serves poached eggs in truffle-and-cream sauce, fillet of beef fillet with *tapenade*, complex desserts made with local honey, Calisson d'Aix (almond and crystallized melon sweetmeats, which is still Aix's most famous confection), rosemary, and essence of orange flower.

Bouches-du-Rhône is rich in festivals, fêtes and fairs. In July the Roque d'Anthéron international Piano Festival's concerts in Parc de Florans or Silvercane Abbey give Chopin nocturnes, Schubert sonatas, or Bartok concertos beneath the stars.

St-Rémy is earthier with La Caretto Ramado, a colourful parade of Provençal horses-and-carts, their harnesses richly decorated. At La Grande Feria, also in August, wild guitars accompany even wilder boys snatching rosettes from young bulls let loose in the streets.

Braver, bigger bulls are fought to the kill by French and Spanish matadors in Arles' Roman Arena during Easter Week's Feria. Bodegas, castanets, swirling skirts, clicking heels – you'd think you were in Seville. To see the Roman Theatre next door at its best, go to an open-air performance during the Festival of International Photography in July.

At Les Baux-de-Provence, the *Noël des Bergers* (Shepherds' Christmas) Midnight Mass, complete with Provençal crib, is a hot ticket, only procured a year in advance. The summer Jazz Festival at Salon-de-Provence attracts top players, and Salonais fondly remember Miles Davis there in 1951. For a small country town Rognes packs them in round the year: antique fair, carnival, wine festival, harvest festival at St-Marcellin Chapel, open-air concerts and plays at Les Carrières (quarries) and a truffle fair.

Round the year, too, Aix-en-Provence jumps. There's a *santons* fair, modern dance, an artisanal fair, folk dancing and jazz. Most prestigious is the Festival d'art lyrique (opera) at the Archbishop's Palace which was converted into a theatre in 1948 with a German, Hans Rosbaud, as conductor of the first memorable *Don Giovanni*, a daring move only four years after the war. To celebrate the 50th anniversay, Peter Brook directed a modern dress production of the Don, shocking the more traditionalist Aixois audiences who exclaimed: 'Very nice but where are the wigs?'

deals and dentists their teeth. And there's no better place to have a tooth fixed than just off the Cours at Place d'Albertas, home of dentists and lawyers, where the languid splashing of its fountain bowl soothes the nerves, and the beauty of its houses confirms that you have chosen the right city in which to live. The apotheosis of fountains, however, is in another fine residential quarter, Quartier Mazarin: the Fountain of the Four Dolphins. Sculpted by Jean-Claude Rambot in 1667, its joyfully spouting dolphins dominate a crossroads, and the place seems made for them rather than they for the place.

The new Aix elite live well. Brigitte and Jean-Marc Banzo are still the best restaurateurs in town, and eating in the tranquil garden of the Clos de la Violette finished my visit in style. I relished all the flavours of the south: serious dishes with capers and basil and feather-light tagliatelle, asparagus and anchovies, sesame and savory. I was serenaded by a final fountain. Around me, bright young Aix professionals laughed and talked about money and other meals in expensive restaurants around the world. Even at my single table, I felt part of it. It seemed that I had penetrated those great doors and just a few of the secrets that lay behind. The oyster had finally opened.

CÉZANNE COUNTRY

In the nineteenth century, while nearby Marseilles became a boomtown, Aix was known as 'The Sleeping Beauty'. And no city could have been more asleep to the incipient talents of two young Aixois, writer Emile Zola and painter Paul Cézanne. They were at school together, drank on the Cours together, endlessly discussed art and literature together – and eventually fought together. The writer disappeared to Paris to make his name, the painter took years to become Cézanne. Taking umbrage at Zola for his

novel *L'Oeuvre*, wherein a failed impressionist commits suicide, which was based on Cézanne's early lack of success, the painter was only reconciled with his childhood friend at the novelist's funeral where, by then himself distinguished, he wept bitter tears. While Zola fitted in well with Paris as an outspoken journalist-novelist, Cézanne was always the rough Provençal with the funny accent. Zola used Paris frequently as a background to his novels, Aix only occasionally in *Les Rougon-Macquart*. Cézanne's work never showed Paris as it did Provence. His roots, however much he hated its bourgeois respectability, were in Aix.

Cézanne *père* had a hat shop at No. 55 Cours Mirabeau and later became a farmers' banker. Paul was born at No. 28 rue de l'Opéra, died at No. 23 rue Boulegon and went to school at the Lycée Mignet (with Zola) in rue Cardinale – all within an easy walk of each other. You might think he would soon be recognized, like Zola, as a local boy made good. Not a bit of it. The prophet, who took so long to find honour in Paris, took even longer in his own country; nowhere is this more evident than at the Granet Museum. A mere eight paintings mark the evolution of his career from *Still Life: Sugar Bowl, Pear* and *Blue Cup* (1865) via *Portrait of Madame Cézanne* (1875–76) to a drawing for *Bathers* (about 1895). The respectable Aixois hated his work at the time.

Why did Cézanne never reject the city? He certainly never painted city subjects, as the impressionists had done in Paris. Partly it was his love–hate relationship with Louis-Auguste, the autocratic father on whom he depended financially, partly because his astute eye preferred the magnificent surrounding landscape to the philistine city.

I took to my wheels again and headed along the narrow, wooded Route du Tholonet (D17). Montagne Ste-Victoire, a hazy grey monster, rose theatrically into a postcard blue sky. Cézanne captured it in a less clichéd light but not even the master could disguise something sinister about it. It derives its name from the 'holy' victory of the Roman general Marius over invading barbarian Teutons; on the instruction of a prophetess, he ordered a number of their womenfolk and children to be flung down a ravine as a thanksgiving offering to the god of war.

First stop: Château Noir, where Cézanne rented a room in 1887 to paint in the peace of its pine trees – and for the best view of Montagne Ste-Victoire. Now romantically dilapidated, the red brick house with neo-gothic windows has been in the Tessier family since 1825. Pousy Tessier, the present owner, will receive Cézanne enthusiasts but dislikes art buffs. 'Kenneth Clark floated in grandly with a photographer,' he said laughing, and showed me the rare pistachio tree that was the subject of a watercolour in 1900.

Tessier, a dedicated Green, also dislikes smokers. 'Anyone can start a forest fire,' he said. 'The last big one was begun by a stupid accident, someone filling a chain-saw motor with petrol. And bang went another lot of Cézanne landscape!' We looked at the charred trees, like black pencil marks on the grey cliffs of the mountain. Happily, greenery sprouts fast in this climate. And at least the familiar red-soiled vineyards and pine woods around Le Tholonet had been spared.

I lunched at the Bonfillon family's La Petite Auberge where they have been since 1530 – *escalope de loup avec beurre d'oursin* and a half bottle of white Château Simone from the tiny Pallette appellation near Aix.

Continuing by the D17 on the Cézanne Country circuit proved easier said than done. Slowed down by lunch and the complexity of roads around Greater Aix, I had a hard time. After Le Tholonet's fine château, right on the D46 via Beaureceuil to the now industrial town of Gardanne where the master rented an apartment for his wife and child, and the father of cubism painted 'this still-life of roofs and cubes of houses'; east on the D6 to La Barque with vantage points to his mountain, subject of more than sixty canvases; across the Arc River after a left on to the N96 which joins the N7 to the Pont des Trois-Sautets. Then I got hopelessly lost trying to find the Pont de L'Arc at the junction of the N8 and D9, so I gave up and returned to my hotel for a siesta. Which is what I should have done in the first place.

For minimum hassle, take the Cézanne bus tour organized by the Office de Tourisme. That way, you see it all comparatively painlessly – including a lot of unlovely peripheral Aix. The trouble is so much has changed since Cézanne painted it; the artist would have detested the antiseptic satellite town taking its name from Jas de Bouffan, his parents' country house. He loved to depict its golden façade, grey shutters and red roof, its pond, trees, pots of flowers and park at different times of year. It is now owned by a doctor and cannot be visited inside. The best stop, which can easily be made in your own car, was Cézanne's studio, perched high above the city on Avenue Paul-Cézanne (via the D14 – my entry road). Ablaze with geraniums, the little house with pink shutters was specially constructed with a huge northern window. Its decor is suitably atmospheric: a canvas of *Bathers* on an easel, skulls and apples waiting to be painted, an ulster and parasols ready for the vagaries of Provençal weather, sheaves of corn and dried herbs, a fig tree at the door. The studio exudes a warm, sunny fragrance. It is a happy place, a place of final achievement after years of struggle without recognition.

CH. = Château
DOM.= Domaine

Pebbly clay at the base of chalky cliffs makes ideal sun-baked soil for Les Baux de Provence, the latest, most southerly AOC to excite wine buffs. Rare frost and comparatively high rainfall help, too. Seven communes grouped around Les Alpilles make reds of *grenache*, *syrah*, *mouvèdre* and sometimes *cabernet-sauvignon*, the grape of Bordeaux. Only reds and rosés are AOC, but whites can also be well-structured, subtle and fine.

Besides Le Trévallon (see p.52), wineries could be easily visited on my route: Dom. des Terres Blanches, near Eygalières, with *garrigue* aromas in its white wine, perfumes of Provence in its red; Dom. Hauvette, near Glanum, biologically produced red and white vinified in barrels; Mas de Gourgonnier, in a niche of Les Alpilles at Le Destet, which produced a terrific '97 rosé.

Les Baux's sister AOC, Coteaux d'Aix, is much larger, stretching from the Durance to the Arc Valley near Aix. Dom des Béates, near Lambesc, was my first tasting – and very good, too. Its light rosés are the perfect summer accompaniment to *aïoli*, grilled sardines, stuffed vegetables, pistou soup, salade niçoise. Tasty, supple reds for drinking young (two or three years) go with calf's liver, roast duck with braised turnips, and barbecued meat. A small production of fresh, dry white goes well with bouillabaisse. A tiny, separate AOC of La Palette near Aix produces a superb, pricey white at elegant Château Simone, well worth a visit.

From the rustic Co-op of Rognes to the super sophistication of La Source de Vignelaure, wine-tasting in Coteaux d'Aix is a particular joy for the beauty of the domaines, often containing houses with a history. Proprietors of eighteenth-century Ch. de Fonscolombes in the Durance Valley also own Dom. de Crémade on the sight of two Roman villas, their remains still visible. All make excellent wines.

AIX-EN-PROVENCE TO VAUVENARGUES

Pick the right time of day – mid-morning or mid-afternoon – and avoid Aix's traffic snarl-ups. Heading east on the D10, I was soon in leafy suburbs and crossing little streams like the Torse tumbling off the Egremont plateau.

Provence's terrain is like continuous variations on a theme. Not fifteen minutes from Aix, I thought myself in the wilds of Canada. Lac Bimont may not be a natural lake, merely a larger replacement for the reservoir built by Zola's father, but its deep green water surrounded by forest and a backdrop of Montagne Ste-Victoire create the grandest of illusions. I walked out to the middle of the dam to take in the deep gorge on one side and the lake on the other. Topped up by the Durance valley's Canal de Provence, it provides irrigation for 19,767 acres (8,000 hectares), water for twenty-two communes, the industrial zone of the Arc valley, and the electricity plant at Gardanne. It is also a nice place for stressed-out Aixois to come to cool off and breathe fresh air at the end of the day.

'Welcome To The Valley of Vauvenargues', said the sign. 'No Campers or Caravans'. Conservation, on the north side of the mountain, is strict. The natives like it wild and want to keep it that way – with none of the charred patches left by forest-fires that deface the south side. An understated sign on the right of the road at Les Cabassols points to the priory of Ste-Victoire – *site historique*, from which you'd imagine the priory to be a short walk from the parking place. In fact, it's an hour's hike – the classic path to the summit refuge (3,001ft/915m) former Benedictine hermitage with chapel and terraced garden. On top is La Croix de Provence, a 30-foot- (9m-) high cross with appropriate inscriptions: south, in Greek for Marseilles; east, in Latin for Rome; west, in Provençal for Aix; and north, in French for Paris.

The northern, more gently inclined slopes are easier to climb than the steep, rugged south cliff. Sheepfolds of the transhumance are dotted about. The view from the crest extends from the Rhône valley to the Esterel hills over rich alluvial plains and expanses of wooded wilderness with wave-like folds of chalky hillocks and rural valleys. Serious walkers continue along the crest, having read their marching orders, posted at the car park: be fit, don't light fires, keep to marked paths, no walking on Sundays or holidays because hunters might mistake you for a wild boar, nor between 1 July and the second Saturday of September because you might start a fire, nor on days of high wind.

Further along the D10 Vauvenargues village is unspoiled, despite the presence of the famous château occupied by the Counts of Provence in the fourteenth century, and by Picasso in the twentieth. A flamboyant man in an artist's scarf, smoking a cheroot, greeted me as I took a snap.

'How d'you like it here?' he asked.

I gave the right answer, for he turned out to be Gérard Yemenidjian, owner of the only hotel, Au Moulin de Provence. I was invited to eat my own picnic on his terrace, offered a glass of wine on the house and not unnaturally ended up staying the night. Good salesmanship. An off-duty chef even helped with my luggage.

Yemenidjian was yet another of the many inhabitants of non-French descent – Russian, North African, Italian, Spanish – encountered on my journey. After the Turkish massacre of Armenians in 1915, refugees benefited from the traditional open-door policy of Provence and many settled there in the twenties.

That afternoon, I walked on the wild northern slopes of the mountain, two hours on foresters' tracks without seeing a soul except one girl on horseback. It worked up an appetite. After dinner, the Yemenidjians showed me their copious scrapbooks on the Picasso connection. Gérard and Magdeleine, as they quickly became, were amateur archivists. Picasso was, after all, a fellow immigrant to Provence – via Andalucia, Catalonia and Paris.

When he announced to a friend in 1958: 'I've just bought the Montagne Ste-Victoire', the friend imagined he meant a Cézanne painting – 1,976 acres (800 hectares) sounded a little large for a painting. Not too large for Picasso, though, happily at work far from the eyes of the world. He filled his turreted bastion of privacy with his own collection of nineteenth- and twentieth-century art from Courbet to Matisse. And, of course, Cézanne. He

Not too large for Picasso, the Château de Vauvenargues

owned *Five Bathers*. As a prophet of cubism, Cézanne had written: 'Treat nature as cylinder, sphere and cone.' Picasso felt at home here, walking the paths of his master.

For a sun-loving Spaniard, winters can be gloomy in a castle at the bottom of a valley, and the peripatetic Picasso was never content in one place for long. After marriage to Jacqueline Roque in 1961, he spent more and more time in Mougins, near Cannes. When he died in 1973, aged 91, Jaqueline followed his wishes to be buried at Vauvenargues, and came every six months to the grave. A familiar fresco in the bathroom and a large photograph in the hall only added to her grief. Twenty-five at the time of their marriage, she had much leftover life to live. In 1986,

unable to bear the loneliness, Jacqueline Picasso took her own life. She is buried beside the artist in front of the house, beneath the shade of a tree he loved.

What would become of the Château de Vauvenargues in the shenanigans of the Picasso inheritance? There was talk of its becoming a Picasso Museum. Former Culture Minister Jack Lang was all for it. The village was divided. Trades people rubbed their hands, while conservationists dreaded the arrival of eyesores like Pizzeria Pablo and La Galerie Minotaur selling Picasso *santons* and tee shirts. 'Better than selling to an Emir or a sect,' said some. 'If they'd proposed a nuclear power station, it couldn't be worse,' said others. The mayor had the last word: in respect for the 'final union', as the graves of Pablo and Jaqueline were known, there would be no museum. The castle is still not visitable.

Catherine Hutin-Blaye, Jacqueline's daughter by a former marriage, was the inheritor. According to the Yemenidjians, Catherine's Argentine journalist husband, Milton, dislikes the castle's spooky ambience; they prefer the house at Mougins. It is called Notre-Dame-de-Vie, Our Lady of Life, and from the very name, who can blame them?

When I went out on my balcony next morning, an eerie mist hung around the château. Despite the beauty of its setting, there was something infinitely melancholy about it. I was happy to be on my way.

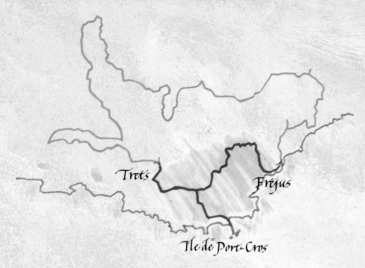

Trets

Fréjus

Ile de Port-Cros

Chapter 4

GREEN HILLS, BLUE BAYS

VAR

Among the bays, creeks and sandy beaches of the Côte d'Azur, so called because of the brilliant clear blue of its water, Cap du Dramont (below right, far right) is a protected area within the Forêt Domaniale de l'Esterel. The Corniche de l'Esterel is a priceless gem among the costume jewellery of the Côte d'Azur's built-up roads. Along the more peaceful hill roads of the hinterland are villages like Fayence (above right), popular but unspoiled.

VAUVENARGUES TO LA STE-BAUME

Var has the longest coastline of the *départments* – 270 miles (435km) of bays, creeks and sandy beaches – known as the Côte d'Azur from the brilliant clear blue of its water. That's the poster image, of course, an image too often tarnished by high rises looming above and trash floating upon those pristine waters. The Concrete Coast more accurately describes it. Thanks, however, to stalwart Greens like *Conservatoire du Littoral* (Coastline Protection) enclaves of beauty have escaped the heavy hand of property developers and gangsters traditionally associated with this part of France. And there was no need to pack a pistol driving up into hill villages of the Basses-Alpes (Low Alps), where the only danger is tumbling down a slope of endless green. Between sea and hills, I found a gently rolling landscape of vineyards and parasol pines sprinkled with sacred sites.

Soon after leaving Vauvenargues, the D10 along the Infernet valley develops into a mini-pass, Col des Portes (2,069ft/630m), with gradients steep enough to warrant chain warnings. It may not snow for long but nasty black ice patches and frozen slush can be hazardous.

I crossed the border into Var where the D10 becomes the D223. Parasol pines, the *départment's* most characteristic vegetation, began in earnest as I turned south on the D23 at the eastern end of Montagne Ste-Victoire and meandered through the Bois de Pourrières into the wide valley of the Arc.

Pourrières – from the French word *pourri* (rotten) – is cruelly named for the decaying bodies left there after the Roman general Marius's victory over the Teutons. The village is prouder to be the birthplace of Cézanne's grandparents, wig makers, and an itinerant mystic poet, Germain Nouveau, admired by Verlaine and Rimbaud. The D23

became the D6E as I returned to Bouches-du-Rhône for a short stretch. The dullness of the valley here reminded me how scenic my route had been so far; then, to make matters better, bridges took me under highway N7 and over the Aix–Nice autoroute, towards enticing, traffic-free coastal ranges south of the Arc valley. Beyond was the sea.

Trets, on the northern slopes, is one of those towns you think you'll pass up but, instead, where you spend a happy hour or so. Unhurried explorers are rewarded. A medieval fortified precinct, unencumbered by the obligatory boutiques, lurks behind hefty ramparts. Way off the tourist beat, the Porte St-Jean gateway leads to twelfth-century Notre-Dame-de-Nazareth Church on a fourth-century Paleo-Christian site. And you soon sense the nearby presence of Marseilles with its plethora of pretty girls, North Africans and exaggeration. 'Oh, it'll take you well over an hour!' said the butcher who provided my deliciously herby *pâté de campagne*, when I asked him how far to the Grotto of Ste-Baume. Well over an hour for 22 miles (35km) Typical Marseillais exaggeration, I thought, but I was wrong.

First, the streets of Trets were undergoing a face-lift. Deviations galore. Moroccan road workers shouted merrily: 'Not that way, the other road!' After two blind alleys and somebody's back yard, I finally ended up on the D12, the right 'other' road to St-Zacharie.

Up and up I climbed into the Regagnas, one of the mountain chains that lay between me and the sea. Over the Pas de Couelle pass (1640ft/500m), past St-Jean-du-Puy's oratory (pilgrim's place of prayer), and back into Var. The D12 became the D85 heading down and down to St-Zacharie at the bottom of the Huveaune valley. Up-hill, down-dale Provence calls for plenty of time. Time for photo opportunities, an occasional few minutes' walk to a hill top oratory, and surprises like St-Zacharie, a village of

OVERNIGHT IN VAR

TH = Table d'Hôtes (guest house with dinner)
CH = Chambre d'Hôtes (bed and breakfast only)

Near Pourrières, Mas des Graviers (TH), run by patron of the arts Andrea McGarvie-Munn, has a gallery to exhibit artists who stay and work there. With its own vineyard, ancient mulberry trees and swimming pool, it has an unpretentious, friendly ambience.

Nothing but the spartan Hôtellerie de la Ste-Baume (see p.77) offers itself until the tastefully decorated Mas de Fontbelle (TH), in the depths of the country near La Roquebrussane. The Belgian owners, former restaurateurs, also give cookery lessons.

On the coast near Bormes-les-Mimosa, Les Palmiers at Cabasson is a small, comfortable hotel tucked away in the woods with its own footpath to an unspoiled beach five minutes away. For the Relais and Châteaux set, there's Les Roches at Aiguebelle, spectacularly terraced into the rocks with cacti and swimming pool overlooking the sea. It's essential to reserve at Le Manoir, the only hotel on the island of Port-Cros. This old, white, colonial-style manor-house, shaded by eucalyptus near an enchanting blue bay, is a Var must.

Back in the hinterland, La Grillade au Feu de Bois (The Wood-Fire Grill) at Flassans-sur-Issole is as appetizing as its name. Hostess Madame Babb is an antique dealer. It shows in the decor. And the winemaking of Brigitte Grivet at Domaine St-Jean-Baptiste (CH), Lorgues, can be sampled after her delicious breakfast with homemade bread and jams (see p.89). The more luxurious Hostellerie Les Gorges de Pennafort south of Bargemon (D25) has rock-pools in the gorge when you need a change from the hotel pool. Nearer village life is the Hôtel de France, Seillans, a comfortable pub complete with fountain and shady plane trees in the square nearby.

Back on the coast at Fréjus, your best bet is L'Aréna in town, while along the Corniche de l'Esterel two notable havens of charm stand out among overpriced overnighting. At Boulouris, La Potinière is a peaceful villa-hotel in a garden of eucalyptus and parasol pines; and Sol e Mar at Dramont is the kind of easy-going, quiet seaside hotel that would make Monsieur Hulot come back for his holiday year after year.

La Ste-Baume's enchanted forest

curving up a ravine, it had barriers to prevent you even attempting it in icy weather, while the Ruisseau de Péroy's waters tumbled noisily beside it from the plateau above. Clumps of parasol pines rise nobly above humble holm-oaks where they colonized spaces left empty by peasants' exodus to Marseilles in the Industrial Revolution. Finally, I reached the Plan d'Aups plateau, lushly wooded and fertile amid arid surroundings, with all the majesty of the rocky ridge of Ste-Baume in front of me. A left on to the D95 at a T-junction led quickly to the Dominican monastery near the Holy Cave.

I looked at my watch. Allowing for my stop at St-Zacharie, those 22 mountainous miles (35km) from Trets had taken one hour and twenty minutes. The butcher had not exaggerated.

HOLY CAVE

Baume is Provençal for cave. The Ste-Baume Massif's 7½ mile (12km) length and 3,280 feet (999m) height (Mont Pilon) is named for one small but very important cave in a sacred wood.

The legend is one of the most treasured in Provence. After leaving her boat from the Holy Land at Les Stes-Maries, Mary Magdalene followed her vow to do penance

potters and fountains. There's even a potters' fair in June at the Maison du Peuple, a fine art deco building. At the Château du Moulin, just out of town on the Marseilles road (N560), naturalist Gaston de Saporta's arboretum of rare trees and English-style garden are graced by the stillness of a lily-pond whose open spaces reflect willows and surrounding mountains. I had a coffee at Le Cercle du 21-Septembre, a café where the *patron* explained: 'A *cercle* used to be very special to us Varois. You had to be a member of the circle to buy drinks, even. Like a club. Royalists wouldn't be allowed in, because we've always been super Republican here.'

An elusive, unsignposted left-turn at the optician's shop in St-Zacharie took me once again upwards – on to my wildest road yet (D480). One-vehicle width, constantly

for being a prostitute by preaching the word of God in different lands. After converting the pagan Prince of Marseilles to Christianity, she made many other conversions in Provence before retiring to her hermitage – the Holy Cave. In 1279, her remains were found at St-Maximin in the valley below where a tomb and massive Gothic basilica still honour her today.

She could hardly have chosen a wilder spot for her hermitage. Nor one more pleasant for a pilgrimage; Christian pilgrims in their thousands – on foot, horse and donkey, by carriage, car and bus – have been coming here since the eleventh century. The shrine had once been pagan: engaged couples would make little piles of stones as votive offerings to fertility gods. Then the Church integrated the enchanted forest into Christianity where it has stayed firmly ever since. In 1319, King Robert the Good gave it royal protection, and ensuing French monarchs, much as they loved hunting, forbade the killing of its animals and the chopping of its beech trees.

Over the years, it gained a magic reputation. 'Enchanted forest' New Agers, freaks of today, come in for gentle mockery from Brother Eugène Colin of the Dominican community. 'In twelve years living here,' he laughed, 'not an elf or sprite has crossed my path, alas! And frankly, I much prefer our friendly wild boars and badgers, and there's a little tom-tit that wakes me up for morning prayer with its song.'

The Dominican hostel, Hôtellerie de la Ste-Baume, is a large, rambling, workaday complex of buildings on the road from Plan d'Aups to Mazaugues (D95). When I arrived, a group of Italian pilgrims, excited as school children on an outing, were being issued sheets and pillow cases from a pristine pile. Girls with sun-glasses pushed up on their foreheads and stylishly sporty men looked more dressed for a Milanese disco than a Provençal shrine,

and the supervisor went along with the high spirits. Friendliness is next to godliness here, and makes up for the run-down shabbiness of the hostel. In the last year alone 13,000 pilgrims lodged and 9,000 ate here. By the delicious smells wafting from the refectory, there would be no complaints. The inevitable souvenir shop, too, had a spartan seriousness about it, refreshingly free from weeping plastic madonnas and model grottos with winking lights.

The real grotto is a forty-minute walk from the hostel. The path known as The Way of the Cross leads between sturdy, unharassed beech trees. The alternative Chemin des Rois (Kingsway), built for Louis XIV, is stepped to make an easy, gradual climb towards the sheer limestone cliff towering 300 feet (90m) above – an alpinist's practice paradise. In front of the cave's entrance, a terrace provides a fine view over forest and plateau. The cave itself, complete with impressive marble altar and statue of the saint, is theatrically lit. St Cassien, founder of St-Victor's abbey in Marseilles, hallowed it as a votive grotto around AD 415. Nowadays, at Christmas Midnight Mass the whole cliff is floodlit, and the cave takes on the aspect of a life-size stable and manger.

On the way down, a distant bell echoed through the beech trees. I passed the Miette oratory where the Dominican Fathers lead pilgrims in prayers of thanksgiving. With its power to instill interior calm and harmony, La Ste-Baume is an all too rare place of spirit, worth a visit whatever your beliefs.

LA STE-BAUME TO FORCALQUEIRET

From the hostel, the D95 continues along the plateau through woodland of oak, yew, holly, lime, and maple, parallel with the massive grey mountain on my right. Glacial and north-facing, with no balmy breezes from the

Mediterranean to warm its chilly wastes, Ste-Baume is usefully the source of four rivers – Argens, Caramy, Gapeau and Huveaune. Along its ridge, trekkers can take GR28 footpath with views south to the sea, north to Montagne Ste-Victoire. Descending from the plateau, I came out of the woods to a wild panorama of Var, not a building in sight, just forested hills in hazy light, wilderness as far as the eye could see. In the Forêt Domaniale de Mazaugues, the feeling of space was even more pronounced than in the Lubéron hills, the village of Mazaugues itself too small and isolated to warrant a service station. It's wise to check your petrol gauge before embarking on the Massif de Ste-Baume. Mine was wavering around the empty mark.

After another nail-biting mini-pass, another tense mini-valley, the serpentine D64 delivered me safely to La Roquebrussanne: petrol and Café de la Loube's much-needed refreshment. La Roquebrussane has the sweetness of Var villages away from the Concrete Coast – plane trees to shade a boules game, a stream to feed a fountain and at least one local boy made good. In this case, the chef J-B Reboul, author of the cookbook *La Cuisinière Provençale* (The Provençal Cook), my bible of local recipes now in its twenty-third edition.

After La Roquebrussane, vineyards return. The problem is finding your winery in the maze of new roads. Continuing on the D64 from La Roquebrussane to Garéoult, I searched for the D554 to Forcalqueiret. In a state of surreal disorientation where every farm building, road, vineyard looked the same, I came – God knows how – to the D43, the Brignolles-Hyères road, and a momentous decision. It was time to head for the sea. I turned south with relief.

Large seaside Côtes de Provence wine properties

And thanks to the greenhouses instituted in the sixties - plastic eyesores we've learned to forgive - so are irises and lilies.

On my route, 120 varieties of mimosa are cultivated at Pepinières Gérard Cavatore at Bormes. At Hyères, Serge and Brigitte de Montgolfier sell 2,000 different flowers. The Jardin Aquatique at Bagnols-en-Fôret has a display of waterlilies Monet would have loved and painted, while fifteen gardeners attend to their floral tributes beyond sweet-scented magnolias around the pond of the Villa Marie at Fréjus. In the same town, the Hong Hien Buddhist temple has a garden around its pagoda with statues of sacred animals. And, in the Parc de la Villa Aurélienne, the Roman aqueduct's remains are romantically set in a woodland of parasol pines, eucalyptus, cypress and oaks.

Where would the *Corso Fleuri* (Battle of the Flowers) at Bormes-les-Mimosa be without flowers? Or the Clos St-Bernard at Hyères? In that fabulous cubist garden of state-of-the-art-deco Villa Noailles, the Comte de Noailles showed what Var, *département* with the most sun in France (2,650 hours a year), could do for simple bouquet flowers as well as exotic tropical plants.

While azalea, oleander, hibiscus, mimosa, bougainvillaea, lemon and orange trees in pots grow naturally outdoors, Var is the biggest producer of flowers to bring their colours and scents indoors when the weather isn't so bright. And to whisk fresh flowers to the northern capitals of Europe in their darkest hours.

Var delivers three-quarters of France's anenomes and tulips, nearly a half of her roses. Dahlias are destined for French wreaths, carnations for wedding buttonholes, and gladioli for the vases of yachts moored in St-Tropez harbour. Snapdragons are cultivated all year round.

A Coastal Detour

The 80-mile (130-km) round trip was worth every mile. I discovered a coast I had thought long dead. The D43 became the D14, then the D12 skirting the western end of the wild Massif des Maures. That mysterious, romantic chain of hills, covered with chestnuts and cork oaks, separates the Var central valley from its coast almost from Toulon to Fréjus. I stopped for a pot of Collobrières chestnut jam, a delicious remembrance of things past.

The D12 joins the unavoidable, traffic-heavy N98 coast road. After less than 4 miles (6km), however, I turned right on to the D42bis to Port-de-Miramar. Though modern and makeshift, Port-de-Miramar's bit of coast is still pleasantly uncluttered and its little marina was my first chance to stop and breathe sea air, to scan the misty panorama of the Hyères islands: Porquerolles, Port-Cros and Ile du Levant. A ferry was leaving for the 30-minute crossing to Porquerolles where Georges Simenon had Inspector Maigret observe:

As I approached on a silky sea, the contours of the island grew clearer, with its capes, bays, ancient forts amid greenery and right in the middle, a little cluster of bright houses, a white bell tower emerging from a kid's building blocks.' (*Mon Ami Maigret*)

Hopefully, he put his pipe out to breathe the heady maritime mix of ozone and eucalyptus.

An unnumbered but easy-to-find lane (often closed in the high season) penetrates a coastal paradise between Port-de-Miramar and Cabasson. Driving east, I was in a Virgilian landscape, just a field away from the sea. Vineyards stretched down to the pine- and palm-fringed coast, set against a backdrop of the Maures hills. The land

Cork oaks near Fort de Bregançon

partially owes its freedom from building to two large seaside Côtes de Provence wine properties, Châteaux de Brégançon and de Léoube. Walkers will be as astonished as I was to find a coastal footpath from Cap de Léoube to Cap Bénat with nothing but a beach shack restaurant or two on the clean, white sandy beach near the village of Cabasson. So peaceful you could almost hear – or at least imagine – the cries of jungle parrots and toucans at the nearby Parc des Oiseaux (bird sanctuary); on this warm March day, it seemed like some faraway beach in the tropics. Or, at least, the Côte d'Azur of long ago.

A cynic might find a political reason for this: at the eastern end of the beach, on a rocky island linked to the

mainland by a dike, stands the rugged Fort de Brégançon, the French President's official residence for entertaining foreign VIPs. The last thing he wants for Tony Blair or Gerhard Schroeder is a Concrete Coast vista. The image of *La Belle France* prevails.

The benevolence spreads inland to Bormes-les-Mimosa, perched on a ravishing coastal hillside, just 4 miles (6km) of country lane from Cabasson. It sits like an amphitheatre facing the sea with a permanent show of islands, ferries, yachts, fishing boats, sunrises, sunsets, different moons and twinkling lights at night – a Mediterranean festival that need only cost the price of a car-park ticket. Top tourist attractions, yes; eyesores, no. The medieval town, like the nearby coast, has been perfectly preserved for walkers, though a certain fitness is required for its steep flights of steps and alleys burrowing beneath houses in a warren of tunnels. 'Can't you just *smell* the mimosa?' panted a backpacker from Oz, adding proudly, 'It comes from Australia, you know!' I sniffed and sure enough the fragrance had wafted into town from nearby trees. The yellow flower, which can blossom up to four times a year, is at its most spectacular from January to March. The Mardi Gras carnival has mimosa-covered chariots rumbling through the town, and all year round its prize-winning flowers dazzle the eye and titillate the nose.

Even Le Lavandou, the town's port, bears traces of once being a fishing village amid the characterless buildings along the waterfront. It has nothing to do with lavender, as you might think; the name comes from its *lavoir* (wash-place), and the fragrance here is more pizza than mimosa. As coastal towns go, however, it does contain vestiges of opulence in nearby Aiguebelle's villas 'with their feet in the

A coastal paradise between Port-de-Miramar and Cabasson

The Brignolles-Hyères road skirting the wild Massif des Maures

water', as the French say. I dined memorably at Les Roches, an old-style Côte d'Azur hotel with its terrace above the rocks; my fish was so fresh it might have jumped from the water on to my plate. At the next table, slick-suited Italian 'business-men' were being entertained by their equally sharp French hosts, they were clearly men of influence on the coast. The rough-and-tumble of property development began early in Bormes-les-Mimosa's history: its medieval lords were tough extortionists, in 1416 kidnapping the prior of the Chartreuse de la Verne in the Maures hills and holding him to ransom in exchange for a few church possessions.

From Le Lavandou, I took the ferry to Port-Cros, the apotheosis of my coastal detour. Salt spray splashed my face and the ferry rolled gently in a cross-wind, an exhilarating, unscary fifty-minute crossing. We stopped at Ile du Levant, where you either wear uniform at its military base or nothing at its nudist colony. Port-Cros is a smaller, friendlier island, its sheltered port a handful of ochre and pink houses and a couple of shops grouped around a jetty. I was struck at once by the absence of cars. Even bicycles are rare. Feet are favourite on Port-Cros.

All around the bay rise thickly-wooded hills. Owned privately until 1963 by Marceline and Marcel Henry, their 1,463-acre (592-hectare) island was presented to the State on condition it became a nature reserve; it is the smallest Parc Naturel National in France. Also, it receives a 'pearl

Besse-sur-Issole, a village with seven fountains

of the Mediterranean' accolade as one of the sea's least polluted spots . A lyrical path, well-shaded by Aleppo pines, took me to the Fort de L'Estissac, a bastion ordered by Richelieu for Louis XIV's extensive defence plan against pirates, British, Spaniards and other Mediterranean marauders. Its rooftop offers a spectacular view north across the Rade (roads) d'Hyères's white-flecked waters to the hazy coast and Massif des Maures. From there, the Sentier Botanique (botanical pathway) is dotted with sharp-scented bilberries, whose liqueur is used with rosé wine to make a *myro,* Provence's *kir*; white and pink cystus, Jupiter's beard and Cineraria; and a rare form of spurge, the reddish bush which sheds its leaves in summer to protect itself from the dry heat.

On the Plage de la Palud below, I encountered a group of schoolchild-ren struggling out of wet-suits, excited and out of breath, teeth chattering. They had just been on a different nature ramble – the Sentier Sous-Marin (underwater pathway) – where markers guide you through an oasis of tropical rarities, said to have appeared in the Mediterranean due to global warming. Among swaying green, brown and red seaweed, red grouper and peacock-fish glide. *'C'est super!'* the schoolchildren assured me. *'Allez-y!'*

I didn't have a wet suit and, anyway, had to hurry up a coastal path to catch the last ferry back to Le Lavandou. It is a place to dawdle – particularly in June or September when the waters are really warm and the crowds less. Now it was time to get back on course – via the N98 in the Hyères direction, branching right on to the D12 towards Brignolles. It was the way I had come, but very few Provençal roads look the same going back. I could have done without the truck traffic. Never mind: with the salty tang still on my lips and face tingling from the sun, I did not have any complaints.

FORCALQUEIRET TO LE THORONET

I caught up with my route where I'd left it at the Forcalqueiret crossroads, now turning right off the busy D43. Heading east on the D15, I was suddenly slowed down by a big flock of sheep – in a green valley with the Issole river running clear and peaceful. Besse-sur-Issole had seven fountains with fantastical gargoyles, a little lake nearby, a couple of medieval gateways and fine seventeenth-century church. It was the birthplace of eighteenth-century Gérard de Bresse, swashbuckling brigand and terror of Esterel hill travellers.

Next stop north on the D13, Flassans-sur-Issole, in the heart of Côtes de Provence wine country, is a village split in two by its river, with an old bridge leading to an eighteenth-century mill once owned by the aristocratic Bourbon-Condé family.

At Cabasse I took a riverside stroll, a typically Varois thing to do in this land of abundant streams where fisher-

Ablutions for medieval monks

men contemplate and occasionally catch. The pathway was an ancient transhumance route when flocks were moved from the Var valley's winter quarters to the summer grazing and sheepfolds of the Verdon highlands. They still are, but mostly by truck. Some customs go back even further: dolmens and menhirs (pre-historic stone sepulchres and monuments) were nearby. Situated by a classified seventeenth-century well, the Hotel de Cabasse was having its doorway remodelled by a girl making cement while her male assistant lounged about, smoking. Back to work, he flicked his cigarette butt into the well.

Shortly after Cabasse I left the Issole valley, turning right off the D13. Through blissful woods, the D79 brought me to the most harmonious ensemble of all Varois buildings, Le Thoronet abbey.

SACRED AND PROFANE

Le Thoronet is surrounded by perfect Var countryside – terraced vineyards in russet soil, sugar-loaf hillocks, little valleys with limpid streams, winding lanes and tucked-away country houses with aromatic gardens. Only a disused bauxite mine's scraggy red cliffs or a village's over-spill of mock-Provençal villas spoils the picture.

In harmony with nature in their work and with each other in their Gregorian chants, the routine of Cistercian monks was well-balanced. A harmony reflected in the

The ascetic beauty of Romanesque architecture at Le Thoronet

CH. = Château
DOM. = Domaine

My itinerary through Var took me close to more wineries than any other *départment*. The AOC Côtes de Provence is vast, dating from Greek and Roman times, and is associated with the frosted bottle of cool pink wine waiting for you invitingly with grilled sardines and salad after a swim. Eighty per cent of production is rosé but a greatly improved fifteen per cent red and five per cent white are grabbing the attention of connoisseurs.

At Pourrières, besides Mas des Graviers (see pp.74-5) which exports to three continents, Dom. Pinchinat produces a velvety red by ecological methods. Hidden away on the bucolic hillside of Mont Olympe near Trets, Dom. de Gran' Boise (Bouches-du-Rhône) is an enchanting place to visit as well as taste.

The lesser known, smaller AOC Coteaux Varois has an enclave at the eastern end of the Massif de Ste-Baume. The best wineries near my route were: Dom. La Rose des Vents at La Roquebrussane, Ch. Trians at Néoules (D468 from La Roquebrussane), Dom. des Chaberts at Garéoult, and Dom. de Déoux at Forcalqueiret. As at Bandol, the

Côtes de Provence's Route des Vins

finest coastal AOC (drink the wine!), Bormes-les-Mimosa benefits from microclimatic conditions (no frosts) and sea air to keep the vines healthy and pest-free. Londe-les-Maures (N98) has no less than four top wineries, including Ch. de Jasson run by a former restaurateur who knows what he's doing with his red Cuvée Eléonore. Nearer the sea, Ch. de Brégançon matches its stunning position overlooking the Hyères bay with its deliciously fresh Reserve du Château rosé.

The Issole valley scores high with one of the region's all-round best, La Commanderie de Peyrassol at Flassans, and Ch. Réquier at Cabasse for its white exuding tropical fruit and lilac.

The Lorgues area has an embarrassment of riches: besides Dom. de St-Jean-Baptiste, Dom. Rabiega offers classically made rosé, red and white for drinking young, while Ch. Les Crostes is known for its aromatic white and full-bodied red. Not to mention Ch. de Berne, Dom. de la Rose Tremière and Dom. Ott.

Rosés are best drunk with *pistou* soup, Mediterrean seafood (red mullet, sea urchins, bouillabaisse) and goat's cheese; lighter reds with crudités and roast meat, heavier with game *civets* and beef *daubes*; *blanc des blancs* (white wine from exclusively white grapes) with lamb *daube*, piquant cheeses and Bouzigues oysters.

ascetic beauty of Romanesque architecture contemporary with the Gothic elaborateness of Notre Dame in Paris: the purity of the Cistercian Brotherhood compared with the complex dogma, rituals and machinations of the main body of the Church.

Inside the austere but lovely abbey where a Music Festival of singing is held in summer, I was greeted by the sound of a mystical chant, not Gregorian, more contemporary. Relishing its well-balanced acoustics, three musicians were rehearsing under the eagle eye of Madame l'Impressario. One played a strong, almost strident wood-wind instrument while two bearded singers weaved around his melody, almost like improvised Corsican *paghella,* the soul music of the Mediterranean. It followed me, at various levels, through the buildings. Each area was connected for continuous prayer: from the church to the vast dormitory; from the dormitory, down a double stone stairway to the cloisters where a communal *lavabo* dripped water for chilly ritual ablutions in the early morning, before and *after* meals (medieval monks ate with their hands); from the cloisters to the cellar with its wine and olive presses; from the cellar to the chapter house where a chapter of St-Benedict's rules was read daily to remind the monks of their vows of humility, obedience and poverty.

Spiritually refreshed, I continued to Lorgues on a section of Côtes de Provence's Route des Vins linking vineyards. A left off the D79 on to the D84 brought me to the pretty hamlet of Pont d'Argens, a narrow bridge over the Argens river, and a right on to the D562 into Lorgues.

Despite Le Thoronet's harmonious vibrations, this is a tough part of Provence, not the region's most law-abiding. In solidarity with other drivers against the police, Provençals flash headlights to warn you of a checkpoint. I had been flashed. Sure enough, at a roundabout on the outskirts of Lorgues, a fierce squad of *moto-flics* were checking papers, gorilla-like and menacing, as the hurtling aggression of rush-hour slowed down to the pace of a Sunday afternoon granny-trip.

I slunk slowly by and took refuge at Domaine de St-Jean Baptiste, wine property of Madame Brigitte Grivet. Set back from the busy Vidauban road (D10), it was a small *mas* conveniently near to its *chaix*. 'Well, I was just closing,' said Madame Grivet with a smile. 'But please – *dégustez!*' Madame Grivet methodically prepared her wines for me to taste. Her winery was all the better for its feminine touch, products well displayed for sale and tasting: three shades of wine, and vinegars – rosemary, balsamic ('very hard to make, that!') and mint. 'The British around here love it for their lamb,' she said.

Côtes de Provence is another greatly improved Midi wine with new methods of production, including such ecological practices as night harvesting when the dew is on the grape and bottling by moon phase. Brigitte Grivet's Special Cuvée Harmonie was clearly going to be a wholesome wine, though too tannic yet, needing time to age. Having trained at Châteauneuf-du-Pape, she started production in 1994 on only 22½ acres (10 hectares). 'With just one man,' she said. 'And occasional visits from my parents to give encouragement.'

Touring Provence involves networking, and Madame Grivet recommended me a cheap-and-cheerful restaurant in Lorgues, Chez Pierrot. Despite being also the local butcher, Pierrot served a good *filet de rascasse,* garlicky salad and chunky lime sorbet – and here I was, back in the land of *le petit rosé de Provence,* the classic pink summer wine of holidays.

At the next table, a 12-year-old boy was obsessed with swivelling his baseball cap to all angles, till his mother made him take it off. Sulks. The man with them was not, I reckoned, the boy's father. They never spoke. In a manner most unlike a husband, he slithered his arm surreptitiously round the woman between courses. With jet-black hair, aquiline nose, she wore a clinging red polo neck sweater and black leather waistcoat. A louche trio. After dinner, another mother – younger and prettier – flounced along Cours de la République in hot pants and black tights, with a toddler in each hand. A café I passed might have been in North Africa; no women, men with black moustaches, drinking Orangina and mint tea, one orator in a woolly hat holding his audience with an impassioned monologue.

The comparative closeness of Tunisia, Morocco and Algeria (formerly French-governed countries known collectively as the Mahgreb) accounts for the heavy concentration of Mahgrébin Arabs in Provence. It explains, even if it does not excuse, why Toulon, Vitrolles and Orange have all had National Front mayors. Racism is aggravated by the more bigoted *pieds noirs*, former Mahgrébin citizens of French origin, who settled in Provence as farmers and in business after their own sun finally set. Others, of course, make the best of it, working and living amicably with Provençal Arabs whose language they often speak and manners they understand.

All is not sweetness and light in Var. There is a certain irony that Le Thoronet is where it is – bang in the middle of a political set-up comparable to the medieval Church's often violent power game which the Benedictines campaigned so hard against. Scratch my back and I'll shoot yours ...

Not far from this very spot, on 25 February 1994, occurred the assasination of Yann Piat, parliamentary representative for Hyères and known for her *milieu* (French underworld) connections. Suspects behind the hit included two mayors (Marseilles and Fréjus), whose motives were imputed to be that Piat must be got rid of because she knew too much about their alleged own deal-ings with the *milieu*. Political assassination or underworld settling of accounts? The politicians were not surprisingly cleared and the hitmen took the rap.

I do not want to give the impression that Lorgues, just because it is a little louche at night and close to the scene of Yann Piat's murder, is anything but a blameless, hard-working Var town. Brigitte Grivet is typical of its energy and friendliness. For its visitors, it has plenty of action: a good, well-signposted walk around the medieval town; Collégiale St-Martin with many fine baroque features; and an ancient Palais de Justice (law courts) which is only slightly crumbling.

LORGUES TO FRÉJUS

The back roads of Upper Var took me through some of the most beautifully situated villages in Provence – in pre-Alps too high to be called hills, not high enough to be called mountains.

From Lorgues to Flayosc, on an unnumbered lane to the left off the Draguignan road (D562), I ascended gently, past a waterfall, across a ford and through a sleepy hamlet called Sauve-Clare. I arrived on top of Flayosc, above red-tiled roofs, a typical Varois curve of tall houses making a defensive wall along its ramparts. Below the village, a bucolic slope of vines, meadows and orchards. The Place de la République's fountain serenades an awninged general store displaying a profusion of flowers.

Flayosc was once famous for its shoes. An artisanal tradition began when the Villeneuve family's château needed the protection of a garrison, which in turn needed servicing by armourers, saddlers and cobblers. After the castle was destroyed in the French Revolution, only the cobblers remained. Nowadays the village depends on outsiders for its prosperity.

BOULES

trespasses on someone else's game. A small wooden ball known as the *cochonnet* (piglet) is chucked between 20–30 feet (6–9m). Throwing one of his or her three balls in turn, a player either gets as near to the 'piglet' as possible, or thwacks a rival's ball away from it, or preferably both. All players carry a tape measure and minutely check out apparent equidistances. Arguments are loud and Pagnolesque but punch-ups are rare. A fraction of an inch/centimetre can make all the difference between winning or losing in the contest of 13 points.

Although *pétanque* is not played professionally, villages and towns have teams which regularly compete. It is as good an excuse for a party as any, and silver cups are proudly displayed in local cafés where the players meet, drink pastis, and tear each others' game to pieces.

Boules is played all over France, but the specifically Provençal version, *pétanque*, was invented by a Varois in Le Ciotat in 1910. Unable to move his legs – legless from too much pastis? – he threw his ball in a knees-bent and stationary position (*pieds tanqués*) instead of taking the three paces which had been a rule of the game since its eighteenth-century invention. From then on, Provençals were delighted to save their energy for the friendly fiendishness of the sport.

The rougher the ground, the tougher the contest. Ideally, it should be between 50–70 feet (15–21m) long. Any reasonable number, women included in these marginally less macho times, can play – in teams of one upwards. Several teams may be competing in the same area, and God help the player who inadvertently

Châteaudouble, 'the village in the sky'

pub. 'I may go to prison, but I acted in good faith...' a man was saying at the bar when I arrived. I never discovered what he might go to prison for; it was a clam-up on a stranger's entry.

Surprisingly for so small a village, Ampus has a Michelin one-star restaurant, La Fontaine. I had been warned to reserve a table. Madame Haye welcomed me into the tiny, country dining-room seating only fifteen, and regaled me with roast guinea fowl and polenta, crème brulée flavoured with pumpkin and vanilla. Ampus is also famous for its honey. A sign above a door in one of its circular streets reads Lentier, Beekeeper, Father & Son. I followed further signs to The Tomb of Christ: modern naif mosaïcs by a British artist simply called Geoff showed The Stations of the Cross, leading to a collage in a hilltop grotto. It had been presented to the village in 1985 by Abbé Volpato, *curé* of Ampus, who was responsible for restoring some twenty chapels. A few miles detour on the D49, there is the twelfth-century chapel N-D de Spéluque (cave) which in fact has no cave but does have a singular statue of the Virgin Mary. Beware if she starts wobbling on her plinth – it's a portent of climatic catastrophe!

From Flayosc on the D557 down into the valley, then left on to the D57 to climb again, I passed through one of those suburbias that suddenly spring up in the midst of idyllic Var countryside. After another left on the D49 to Ampus, not an eyesore in sight. Industrial Draguignan, distantly glimpsed, was a hazy conglomeration framed in a V at the end of the deep Nartuby d'Ampus valley. You could hear the silence. Only one car passed; mountain-bikers sweated upwards and onwards.

Ampus, first seen after a bend in the road, was a lone clump of houses packed together on a hillock. More austere than villages lower down, its harsh brick reminiscent of Corsica. Over a *myro* in the Auberge des Braconniers (poachers), I was among hill people, reserved, polite but a little wary – as they would be in the poachers'

As I climbed higher, grateful for the cloudless blue, taller mountain pines began. Descended upon via the D51, Châteaudouble seems about to tumble into the Gorges de Nartuby which it overhangs like someone leaning dangerously out of a window. Not for nothing is it known as 'the village in the sky'. A 430-feet (130-m) sheer drop begins where the village ends. Luckily, I could squeeze through

Bargemon's familiar roofs

La Fontaine at Ampus

Lorgues, Chez Pierrot

Le Clos Gourmand at Trets (Bouches-du-Rhône) is off the tourist beat but near enough to Marseilles for good fish. Locals flock for the *daurade* (sea bream) roasted with fennel.

On the coast, even French holidaymakers make do with salads, sardines and *le big mac*. Bormes-les-Mimosa gets out of the rut Chez Silvia, an original pizzeria serving brochettes flavoured with mint and bay leaf, spaghetti with baby octopus and aubergine, fig tart and herb-teas with herbs fresh from the garden. More serious is La Cassole's terrace with its gambas salad, garlic soup with red mullet, sweetbreads in flakey pastry with almonds and morel mushrooms. By the water, Les Tamaris at Plage de St-Clair, Le Lavandou, has a pleasant terrace to watch kamikaze jet-skiers while digging into untranslatable but deliciously fresh fish from the gulf - *pageot*, *pagre*, *chapon* - or straightforward bouillabaisse (to order). Perfect after a swim.

Apart from the basic and good Chez Pierrot at Lorgues (see p.89), Chez Bruno in a nearby country house has a classier, very reasonably priced single menu. Bruno's extrovert welcome gets you off to a good start for little green vegetable ravioli with truffle sauce, alpine pigeon with foie gras and truffles in flakey pastry, *clafoutis* with cherries from his garden. L'Oustau, Flayosc, serves honest-to-Provence daube, and La Fontaine at Ampus (see p.92) is village gastronomy at its best.

At L'Hostellerie Les Gorges de Pennafort, beneath the lime trees of its luxuriant terrace, former Parisian chef Philippe de Silva regales you with fillet of sea-bass with preserved tomatoes, fillet of roast lamb with aubergines and a touch of tarragon, and sherry sorbet. Less costly, La France in Fayence scores with rascasse fillets and pears in red wine, served impeccably in a welcoming dining-room with big bar.

L'Aréna at Fréjus lives up to its reputation. In an unusually friendly hotel dining-room, I was offered baked *daurade* with feather-light tomato tart, *filet mignon* of porc with buttery polenta, and banana tart with caramel sauce. Meanwhile, St-Raphael next door has the inestimable Pastorel, a genuine local bistrot, with market-fresh sardines marinaded with basil, aubergine caviar, and *bourride* (fish soup) with *aîoli*. Both are good alternatives to the coast's tourist traps.

the narrow streets and *placettes* in my diminutive Panda, taking care not to damage flowers in pots and sleepy cats, or go over the cliff. Eglise N-D de l'Annonciation, a fine example of Provençal baroque, has a seventeenth-century gilt-and-wood altar table with painting by Draguignan artist, François Mimault.

The corniche of the D51 brought me down to the Nartuby river at the bottom of the green, towering gorge and a left on the D955 up again on to an open *garrigue* plateau. Soon after a right on to the D19, the isolated Favas Romanesque chapel had been turned into a sheep-fold. Lucky sheep. As I stopped to take a snap, I thought I heard thunder. Where? The sky was blue with wispy clouds, and the Virgin had not budged on her plinth. I looked at the map. I was all too near the desolate Canjuers military zone's short-range missile practice.

A few minutes later, the village of Bargemon rose to greet me. As I drove slowly downhill, familiar roofs and church came into view, the hallucinatory panorama of southern hills with the draw of the sea beyond. We had spent time there as a family, thirty years ago, in the house of a close friend. The distant rocket-fire was replaced with the tolling of a medieval church bell.

From 1350, Bargemon was a fiefdom of the ubiquitous Villeneuves who owned the Château de Reclos among the olives and vines below. Rather more modestly, we drank pastis beneath a fig tree on the terrace of our friend's little house in the ramparts. 'You'll find a lot changed,' said Monique Santini whose 10-year old daughter, Colette, had taken our daughters on a mass village outing to pick yellow Genista flowers for the perfume factories of Grasse. I turned a blind eye to changes, and even found the *boulangerie* where we used to take our Sunday joint, spiked with garlic and with wild thyme tucked under the string, to be cooked in the baker's oven. You could still swim in the cooling rock pools of the nearby Gorges de Pennafort. Place Moreri seemed much the same, too. Shaded by a huge *micocoulier*, Provence's nettle-tree, its graceful buildings are celebrated by the words *L'art embellit la vie* (art embellishes life) carved on a stonemason's house; on either side of the door, two stone carvings show the stonemason with hammer and chisel, his wife at work in the kitchen.

More corniche greeted me along the Rieu de Méaux valley, a mass of streams cascading under the twisty D19. Then open country again: a misty, translucent view to the Maures coastal range as the road ran along the southern slopes of Mont d'Auzières. Seillans was *en fête*. With as much panache as Nice for its Carnival, the town was putting on a smaller version. An old trouper in a clown's hat, all the more comic for his utter seriousness, spoke pidgin French when my own slipped and I said *carnival* instead of *carnaval*. Clearly, he had an idiot foreigner to put wise. 'Afternoon is children *carnaval*. Night, big ball for adults. *Compris*? You stay for ball?' I went but would have liked to 'stay for ball'. The village felt Italian with its palms and cypresses; little boys dressed as red devils, apes, wizards and little girls on frisky ponies gave it a Fellini look. Of former residents, surrealist Max Ernst would probably not have painted the scene, but composer Charles Gounod might have worked it into a romantic opera.

On the way out of town, the chapel of N-D de l'Ormeau is where Seillans began. A Roman tomb with pagan votive inscriptions marks the site of the ninth-century village, centre of a vast agricultural property belonging to the monks of St-Victor abbey, Marseilles. A viscount of Marseilles, who helped get rid of Saracen invaders from North Africa, started building a château on the hillside where the village now stands. Successive monks and viscounts were constantly fighting over who owned what

The Missiri Mosque, Fréjus

Emperor Napoleon III. From here, an up-and-down exploration of the old town includes a Saracen gate, double-vaulted tunnels, little gardens round every turn, miniscule pedestrian alleys. An intriguing town, popular but unspoiled, like Bormes-les-Mimosa.

The D563 (which becomes the D4) leads south through Lower Var valleys and pinewoods towards Fréjus. Shortly after Bagnols-en-Forêt's paleolithic caves, I sight misty sea beyond the flat Argens delta. Industrial zones, round-abouts, and heavier traffic began. On my right, a strange desert blockhouse in red ochre, more suitable to Mali than Provence, turns out to be the Missiri Mosque, built for former Senegalese sharpshooters in the French colonial army. There is also the Buddhist pagoda Hong Hien built in 1919 by Indo-Chinese soldiers, in memory of comrades lost in the First World War. Fréjus, a recruitment centre for all colours and creeds of soldier and sailor, is still typically Provençal polyglot.

until, after the Revolution, seigneurial rights passed to the villagers. The chapel's sixteenth-century altar table makes up for a hideous porch stuck on to the chapel's exquisite Romanesque structure.

Further along the D19 is Fayence, star of Var hill villages. Another Fellini image appeared in a field on the outskirts: a camel and a lama that have seen better days chomp grass as the circus big-top goes up for tonight's performance. The lama spits at me, so I take the hint and wind my way up into town. Bearings are best got from the 360-degree panorama on the clock tower's terrace near La Farigoulette hotel. You can see the village spread out below, a glider coming in to land at the gliding-school on the plain and the Esterel coastal range in the distance.

Just off Place de la République, the eccentric Town Hall is a gate-house built over the main street on the orders of

FORUM IULII

Suddenly I was back on the N7, turning left after the mosque for a short, sharp stretch of insane traffic into Fréjus. At first sight, it's the kind of Concrete Coast town I had been avoiding on this trip. It had also once been Forum Iulii (Julius's marketplace), a Roman town on the Via Aurelia, founded by Julius Caesar in 49 BC. However, it does deserve more than a cursory glance, and greatly rewards penetrating.

From 600 BC to 49 BC, the most important port in southern Gaul had been Massilia (Marseilles). With Pompey's defeat by Caesar in a Roman civil war, Massilia fell and Forum Iulii took over as the naval base at the Empire's most glorious hour. A colony of veterans, who were former foreign legionaries of the Roman army, given their freedom and land to farm, was settled there. In historian Pliny the Elder's words 'settled in peace and by the fleet'. This fleet later soundly beat the lumbering great ships of Anthony and Cleopatra at the Battle of Actium (31 BC), thanks to light, high-speed galleys developed by Octavius at Forum Iulii. When Octavius became Emperor Augustus, the lantern-turret to mark the entrance of the harbour was named Lanterne d'Auguste after him. A portion of the defensive wall along the quayside still exists, with a plaque to denote the site.

Sleuthing Fréjus's elusive Roman remains, like a treasure hunt in a maze of modern town, can be a lot more fun than visiting Fréjus-Plage or Port-Fréjus, sad and soulless monuments to today's property-empire builders. A canal 1,650 yards (1,508m) long led the victorious galleys of Actium into a sheltered haven. After the cramped quarters on board and the exertions of battle, officers would head for the Thermes of the port, the entrance to a vaulted hall still visible at the Porte d'Orée gateway. Filthy bodies sweated off dirt in steam baths, aching limbs were massaged before a peacock strut through the Forum with tales of victory. It is now Place P. Vernet where walls of the Roman naval arsenal can still be seen.

Water was brought for the Baths and grand, red-roofed villas of Roman VIPS (governor, prefect, shipbuilder) by an aqueduct. A few pillars and ruined arches are still visible near vestiges of the Roman theatre. From its Siagne spring, 26 miles (42km) away, water descended from 1,712 feet (520m) nearly to the sea – quite an engineering feat in those days. In the Reyran valley, where orchards, meadows and bamboo once flourished, there is a more substantial section of aqueduct at the Arches du Gargalon, named for the onomatopoeic Provençal word *gargoulon* (spring). Nearby are man-made ruins which are much more recent: the terrible collapse through negligence of the Malpasset dam in 1959, which killed 430 people and devastated peach orchards, farms and whole villages in the Fréjus area.

To the casual visitor, no sign of this tragedy remains. From the Roman villa-style Hôtel L'Aréna, it was a short stroll to the Roman arena, not exactly up to Arles standard but still good enough for bullfights; a plaque commemorates a matador killed there. Today was Sunday. In the Old Town centre, people were carrying cakes in neatly tied cardboard boxes to family lunches. A long-bearded old salt in a captain's cap sat in his usual café place, while *motards* prepared their fat-tyred racers for a roar-up along the Corniche de l'Esterel.

Fréjus's present is lively but its past continued to fascinate. The next great phase, after Saracens destroyed Forum Iulii, was the restoration by tenth-century Bishop Riculphe. The massive medieval episcopal quarter reveals a magnificent reddish-brown stone church with double-tiered cloisters and fifth-century baptistery as old as Venasque's. There was hardly an empty seat at Mass.

The port, a run-down breeding ground of disease, was closed in 1774, but the Church's power continued despite wars and rumour of wars. A bishop's elegant town house in rue Fleury and other fine eighteenth- and nineteenth-century buildings bear witness to prosperity. From then on, preoccupations were commercial rather than cultural, and a chapel decorated (but unfinished) by Jean Cocteau at the end of his life is a rare, recent addition to the town's considerable heritage.

FRÉJUS TO LA NAPOULE

How Fréjus ever lost ground to its neighbour, St-Raphael, I can't imagine. St-Raphael nowadays has little to recommend it except a TGV station. On the D98c to N98, I escaped as quickly as umpteen traffic signals allowed, remembering with astonishment that Scott Fitzgerald had written *Tender Is the Night* there. St-Raphael also claims to have invented bouillabaisse, which is enough to attract a guerrilla force of Marseillais in a gunboat.

Things got better. Between St-Raphael and La Napoule, the Corniche de l'Esterel (N98) is still a romantic Mediterranean road, with sea like Scott and Zelda's, 'as mysteriously coloured as the agates and cornelians of childhood, green as green milk, blue as laundry water, wine dark' (*Tender Is the Night)*. If the water had been warm enough, Boulouris – a cove right by the road – would have been perfect for a swim. At Tikki Plage, a handful of bodies were prone on a clean, golden beach in a red-rock bay.

From there, I walked for an idyllic hour round Cap du Dramont near the pebble beach where 20,000 GIs disembarked on 15 August 1944 for the liberation of southern France from Nazi occupation. Today was quieter. A staggering 79,000 acres (31,971 hectares) of Mediterranean forest burn each year, but Cap du Dramont is a protected area of the Forêt Domaniale de l'Esterel. There's not a building to be seen except the lighthouse and foresters' cabin. Behind me, azure Agay Bay was backed by bare, red, shredded pinnacles and spires of the Esterel hills. I was glad of good boots on the rocky smuggler's track along the coast, which I had all to myself, with paths descending to cerulean bays where secret caves once hid contraband from mean-spirited *douaniers* (customs officers). It was so

quiet I mistook the flapping of a jib, raised by a yachtsman a little way off the coast, for nearby seagulls's wings. Sweet-throated goldfinches swooped around the *maquis* (heath) where cystus, dwarf iris, myrtle, heather, thyme and bay flourished with no shadow of a bulldozer. And, in autumn, arbutus fruit would be gathered for jelly. The path creates the illusion of a time-warp, back to when Virgil or Ovid were writing of such paradises. A primeval wilderness reigns where, just off the north coast of the cape, the Ile d'Or's tiny sea-bound hillock sprouts a mock-medieval Genoese tower, built at the beginning of the last century by a charming eccentric who proclaimed himself Monarch of the Wave-Battered Rocks.

I drove on east towards Agay's hill, where explorers of the Esterel turn inland on the D100. The Corniche de l'Esterel is a priceless gem among the costume jewellery of the Côte d'Azur's built-up roads. Rocky creeks of purple porphyry and violet sea greet you all the way. There are stark views of the Pic d'Ours (Bear Peak) and Cap Roux (Cape Russet). From Agay's ancient harbour with vestiges of Ligurians, Greeks and Romans, to Le Trayas's seventeenth-century tunny-fishing centre, it's hard to keep one's eyes on the road. After Anthéor, the hills' steep slopes hug the sea, and there's hardly room for road and railway to slip between.

At Miramar, I crossed into the *département* of Alpes-Maritimes. Traffic, nearer to La Napoule, built up. Crowds filled the little *calanques,* power boats skudded about, fishermen cast their lines, and white-skinned hedonists in thongs lay strewn upon the rocks. Although swimsuits would have been bigger and speedboats smaller, I was time-warped back to the Côte d'Azur of Scott and Zelda, Cole Porter songs and Elsa Maxwell parties. Just for a brief, nostalgic moment.

HIKES AND BIKES IN THE ESTEREL

The Esterel is a piece of Africa dropped into France. Behind the hectic coast, there's a wild, volcanic cauldron of red lava and green vegetation against a blue sky, a spatial paradise for hikers, mountain-bikers, and snails-pace drivers. In summer, cars may be prohibited on the forestry roads because of fire hazard. The costly infernos that traditionally transform green forest into smouldering grey ash and skeletal black sculpture are actually beneficial – according to ecologists – to the natural regeneration of plants and bushes.

A right turn, well signposted, takes you off the Agay-Valescure D100 to the Grenouillet farm where bikes can be rented. Detailed maps show forestry roads and walks. When cars are permitted, it's easy driving but limited – more fun to hike or bike. Choose spring for the wild flowers and heady aromas. High summer is too hot. Autumn smells of wild fruit and mushrooms. Winter sea views show the Mediterranean emerald, violet or cobalt.

A four-and-a-half hour walk starts at Gratadis forestry hut. From a grove of eucalyptus trees, it leads to the Mal Infernet ravine, once the hideaway of notorious brigand Gaspard de Besse; along Lac d'Ecureuil, where frogs croak, green lizards

Idyllic Cap du Dramont, a protected area

bask in the sun, and deer sip the water; climbing up to the Balcony of the Côte d'Azur where views extend to Cap d'Antibes and yachts like paper-boats on a silvery Bay of Cannes; from Col de Notre Dame pass, on a resin-scented track round the jagged peak, Pic de L'Ours (1,627ft/496m), to the sweet-sounding Col des Lentisques (Cashew Nut Tree Pass); and back down through cork oaks and Aleppo pines to the Gratadis forestry hut.

A shorter, three-and-a-half hour circuit begins three miles from the forestry hut, up the Pic de l'Ours road; via Grotte de Ste-Baume holy cave, fifth-century refuge of St-Honorat who founded the famous monastery on the Lérins islands, along rough, volcanic tracks to the Pic du Cap Roux (1,435ft/437m), with views to St-Tropez; back down to the holy cave, passing Mont Pilon's spectacular cliff with rocks like pink and ocre teeth sprouting everywhere.

Myrtle and oleander bloom in the Vallon de Perthuis, north-west of the Gratadis forestry hut. Nature-lovers will enjoy an easy stroll of an hour or so through the valley's biological reserve to catch rarities like exotic forms of bracken, American agave, and *lavatère d'Hyères* with luscious pink flowers. It also affords views of the Esterel's highest point (2,033ft/619m), Mont Vinaigre (Mount Vinegar).

Valberg

Nice

La Napoule

Chapter 5

HIGH SPOTS

ALPES-MARITIMES

High Alps, inhabited sparsely by sheep and trekkers in summer are invaded by winter sporters; Riviera beaches, over-crowded in summer, can seem deserted in winter. Nice, however, is a city for all seasons. The Negresco (below right) is one of the great privately owned hotels of the world. While isolated villages of Upper Provence contain more rugged buildings like the ruined castle at Guillaumes (above right) and Roure's church (far right) with its unusual triple-bay bell tower.

LA NAPOULE TO GRASSE

Of all the *départements* in Provence, Alpes-Maritimes has the most varied terrain and shifting population of visitors. High Alps, inhabited sparsely by sheep and trekkers in summer, are invaded by winter sporters; Riviera beach resorts, overcrowded in summer, can seem deserted in winter. Nice, however, is a city for all seasons. Italianate Nice, with its cosmopolitan people and special gastronomy, was to make a perfect halfway halt before beginning the return journey by an upland route. Lonely alpine passes and isolated villages of Upper Provence would put my tiny but infinitely reliable Fiat Panda to the test in rally conditions.

The Riviera has traditionally attracted eccentric Americans, a sadly endangered species in these times of corporate conformity. On arriving at La Napoule from the Corniche de l'Esterel (N98), I headed straight for a curious Château-Museum, once the home of American millionaire-sculptor, Henry Clews, built with his second wife, Marie-Elsie. It epitomizes the Jazz Age when Clews, though nearly fifty, was lavish host to the bright young things. Completely reconstructed between two fourteenth-century towers, it is a mish-mash of styles from Romanesque abbey to Beverly Hills baronial. Personal credos, literally writ in stone, are carved on the façade: 'Myth, Mystery, Mirth' – 'Political Altruists' – 'Once Upon a Time'.

Clews identified with Don Quixote whose statue he placed in front of the house. Son of a mega-rich Victorian banker, scorned by critics as a rich dilettante at an exhibition of his work at New York's Metropolitan Museum of Art, Clews came to Paris to study sculpture with Rodin. His tilting at windmills is evident in the studio, filled with sculpture that Marie-Elsie hid in cellars from the occupying German soldiers. Though a romantic, he portrayed people with savage realism; his animals have a certain emblematic charm.

You can't helping liking the Clews. They were generous to La Napoule, frequently inviting the villagers – as they were before La Napoule's expansion from fishing-village to resort – to the intimate Italian and classical French gardens, and judging by the eulogies in their Gothic sepulchre, the village clearly adored them. The terrace of the château is spectacularly placed, below the northern end of the Corniche de l'Esterel, in a sheltered inlet of the Gulf of La Napoule. Here the fishermen's children would play with Mancha Clews, Henry's son. Mancha, now over eighty, still visits from the States.

A Frenchman with our group asked suspiciously: 'Is this a *monument historique?*' When the guide told him 'No', he looked miserable at the waste of his time. For the French, a *monument* that is not classified *historique* is like a wine bottle without a label. Definitely not to be taken seriously.

A branch left (D92) near the château lead me to the N7 for a short bout of pestilential traffic in La Napoule's twin town, Mandelieu, mainly important for its airport and golf club. Only owners of private jets and golfers need bother with it. After a minor hassle finding the hidden turn left (D92 again) to the Massif du Tanneron (by the Agence de Thermes blue shop front), quite suddenly I was winding up a bucolic lane high above the Siagne valley. Bird's-eye views of the ocean and smoggy Cannes appeared before entering an 11-mile (18-km) stretch of mimosa forest, much of it still in bloom after the high season of January and February. Related to the Australian eucalyptus and first brought to Cannes in 1880, mimosa is now exported all over the world. One of the pleasures of winter is a fresh bunch scenting our living-room and, even when it all too quickly fades, the fragrance lingers. Growing wild, mixed with cork-oak, the yellow-and-green expanse of the

The cornucopia of Nice restaurants

Riviera *haute-cuisine* begins at La Napoule with Stéphane Raimbaut's Le Oasis. Asian flavours and Mediterranean ingredients on the tropical patio under a great palm-tree might include lobster with Thai herbs. You could be in Phuket. And if the price puts you off, there's the Oasis Patisserie next door where an éclair and a packet of macaroons won't exactly throw you off budget. Better value could be the flower-bedecked Le Coelanthe, convenient for *tian* of rascasse when visiting the Clews château.

The Auberge de Nossi-Bé at Auribeau-sur-Siagne (see p.104) would be hard to beat in the Grasse area, though the place to be seen and spend is La Bastide St-Antoine. Lounging beneath a parasol, one feeds sumptuously on ravioli with truffles, beef with aromatic juices (far from synthetic!), mandarin ice cream. Another haven in a gastronomic desert is tiny Pierre Baltus for salmon terrine with asparagus, panfried prawns with aniseed butter, and veal sweetbreads with morels. Three miles (5km) from Grasse, Magagnosc's friendly La Roque Blanche has addicts returning gratefully for sweetly spiced duck breasts in honey and roast *lotte* with poppy seeds.

At the Gorges du Loup, Gourdon has the value-for-money Au Vieux Four, if you can't get into the Auberge de Gourdon (see p.108). Vence has plenty of choice, working upwards from cheap and cheerful Le P'tit Provençal's old town terrace for such local specialities as Niçois little stuffed vegetables. Middle-range good value are Provençal *taboulé* with lobster, courgette flowers stuffed with *mousseline* of rascasse, and roast duckling with preserved cherries at Le Vieux Couvent. Treat-time is La Commanderie's sea-view bay windows and tapestries, while feasting on delectable Provençal inventions like grilled red mullet fillets with Niçois broccoli and an *aoïli* sauce.

Besides the cornucopia of Nice restaurants mentioned on pages 115–16, others to try in the international mix are Le Barachois (Réunion Island), Poco Loco (Mexican), L'Auberge de Théo (Tuscan), Fjord (Scandanavian) and Zucca Magica (Vegetarian).

Local wines, rare in Alpes-Maritimes, are the Nice hills' trendy Bellet (Ch'x. de Bellet and Crémat, Dom. Augier) and earthier St-Jeannet (La Bastide du Collet de Mourre).

Tanneron hills is even more exotic. I passed an Equestrian Centre, and couldn't think of a more pleasant way to travel than on horseback through sweet-smelling hills as unexpectedly unspoiled as these. No building allowed – and no picking the mimosa, either.

Continuing on lanes D138 and D509, I came to Auribeau-sur-Siagne, a protected twelfth-century village which, after being abandoned during the Plague of the fourteenth century, was reconstructed within its medieval ramparts in the sixteenth century. It has one pretentiously fancy hotel, and one friendly auberge (the Nossi-Bé) which had a treadle sewing-machine and harmonium on the landing outside my room. I also ate extremely well there. In an oak-beamed, tiny dining-room I was regaled with two *tapenades* (made with green and black olives), duck breast with preserved turnips, and an exotic iced pecan-and-raisin pudding perfumed with *marc de Provence,* served with a honey sauce. The price was as reasonable as the welcome was friendly – a mere 8 miles (13km) from Cannes where I have been sullenly served an overpriced *steak frites* at Film Festival time.

Seen from my room window, the lights of Grasse cover a distant hillside, and stars compete for brightness above the flat ridge of pre-Alps behind; at dawn, lights and stars expire as the rising sun spreads over a peaceful, romantic landscape of valleys and hills. A golden eagle planes overhead, distracting me from inspection of a municipal garden display of the soil-and-plant difference between here and Grasse: at Auribeau, on gneiss and sandstone grow pistachio-trees, arbutus, heather and bracken; the more chalky soil around Grasse favours Aleppo pines, green oaks and *garrigue* plants. In the Siagne valley's micro-climate, a variety of trees and plants flourish – white poplar, hazelnut, willow and wild orchid.

The perfumes of Grasse, imagined as I breathed the sweet air at Auribeau, soon changed to carbon-monoxide as the D509 and D9 brought me nearer to the town itself.

GRASSE ROOTS

When you first get closer to Grasse from the south, it reveals urbanization run riot, flyovers under construction, even its celebrated hillside seems a visual mess. A Grassois friend warned me: 'When I was a child, I remember waking up in summer to the smell of jasmine wafting through my bedroom window. Not any more.' Summer houses in the quieter, cooler purlieus of Grasse were at one time a way to escape the mad, hot whirl of the Riviera. 'Nowadays my mother's is surrounded by service stations, roundabouts, and hypermarkets,' he said with a resigned smile.

Not a whiff of jasmine greeted me as I parked at the modern Fragonard factory in similar surroundings. In summer, perhaps, the scent of prolific flowers and plants, near a vast, squiggly-shaped bronze alembic for distilling them, may well triumph over the carbon-monoxide. The flower-beds make an inviting shop-window. The perfume-makers of today, however, are very different from the sixteenth-century's artisans when Grasse's flourishing glove trade demanded scents for the increasing fashion of perfumed gloves. Today's production is mainly the creation of essences, often synthetic, that perfume-makers throughout the world can blend for themselves, or aromas for the flavouring of food.

Some essences do actually come from local tuberose, jasmine, mimosa, lavender, genista and particularly orange-flowers from the Gorges du Loup. Others are claimed to be Australian eucalyptus, Ivory Coast bergamot, Sri Lankan cinnamon, Taiwan citronella, Russian coriander and sage, and Brazilian cardamon. Lab assistants hover

over their test-tube babies, and assist at the birth of long sausages of soap emerging from a machine, cutting them into the shapes we know and love. In a boutique that would not have disgraced a shopping-mall, a visiting group of school children sniffed their wrists which smiling salesgirls squirted indulgently. Gift-wrapped soaps and cosmetics and even a perfume called 'A Year in Provence' were doing a brisk trade. The sweet smell of success.

Still brisker trade was going on at the Fragonard Perfume Museum, reached by the Route Napoléon (N85) zigzagging up into town. While visiting a Good-Old-Days display of labour-intensive processes, including the costumes and tools of the trade, visitors could sniff for themselves the different elements which made up different perfumes, and see how they were blended. A bit like a wine-tasting – without the tasting.

Grasse – the sweet smell of success

There's an irony about Grasse museums: the commercial enterprise of Fragonard (established 1926) has no entrance fee and is open 9a.m.–6p.m. every day of the year; the municipality-run Fragonard Villa, celebrating the artist who gave the perfumery its name, has an entrance fee and variable opening hours throughout the year. It's wise to check. Commissioned and then peevishly turned down by Madame du Barry, works by Jean-Honoré Fragonard, eighteenth-century Grassois painter of ladies on swings in idyllic countryside, were brought to his cousin's elegant country villa when he was recuperating from an illness. The originals are in the Frick Collection, New York.

My visit to Grasse got better as it went along. The Belle Epoque esplanade, complete with bandstand and white Casino, was once *the* place for a *grande dame* to parade in a long white dress, twirling her parasol as she swotted up on her system for infallible gain at the tables. On a long, losing streak, Napoleon Bonaparte stayed the first night in Grasse after escape from exile in Elba, having been snubbed in Cannes; his nephew Napoleon III's Empress Eugénie led the rich to winter here.

Its roots go back a lot further than the nineteenth century, of course. I penetrated the Old Town's labyrinth of alleys and steps, and found an inscription on the tower of the Town Hall, commemorating the sixteenth-century

For those who love twentieth-century art enough to put up with a bit of traffic, the detour starts pleasantly from Grasse to Antibes via surprisingly unspoiled, sixteenth-century Valbonne (D2085, D3237, D3, D13, D35 – by no means as complicated as it looks). At Château Grimaldi (the Picasso Museum), works express the master's happiness at time spent there: 1946, just post-war, a 60-year-old artist in love with a beautiful 20-year-old artist, Françoise Gilot. The mood is reflected in *Joie de Vivre or Antipolis:* Antipolis, meaning 'opposite the city' was the ancient name of Antibes which faces Nice across the bay. In return for the loan of the castle, Picasso donated his entire collection to the municipality, including Mediterranean pagan themes: *Satyr, Faun and Centaur with Trident, Woman with Sea Urchins, Ulysses and the Sirens.*

Next stop, the Fernand Léger Museum just before Biot (N7, left on the D4). A sporting theme in monumental mosaic and ceramic startles the eye on arrival; vivid primary colours and water play enchanting light tricks. Sun, optimism and vitality are everywhere. In 1926, Riviera socialites Gerald and Sara Murphy were Léger's American connection; he later taught art at Yale, and was a considerable influence on the American Pop Art movement.

His populist vision depicts ordinary people at work and play – footballers, cyclists, construction workers, musicians, picnickers, divers.

For Renoir's last home, return to the N7 and head east to Cagnes-sur-Mer. His farmhouse and villa in an olive grove high above the town make an idyllic spot for a picnic. Renoir bought *The Farm of Les Collettes* for its much-needed sunshine in 1908 when crippling arthritis began to deform his hands and waste his body. His studio has its own melancholy resonance: the bronze bust of his beloved Aline; the costume of Coco the Clown in which Renoir painted his son, Claude; a photo of Renoir painfully thin, hands gnarled; his cloak, wheelchair, daybed and open wood fire.

A climb on the D7 brings you to the Maeght Fondation, just before St-Paul-de-Vence. Art dealers Aimé and Marguerite Maeght's visionary concept for a country museum was a 'family' show, with contributions and technical advice from sculptors and artists: Braque, Chagall, Giacometti and Miró. Green lawns and tall pines

are a cool decor for a Calder stabile and Pol-Bury's kinetic fountain of stainless steel tubes. Beyond the main gallery (Chagall's *Life* and Bonnard's *Summer*), the Giacometti Courtyard opens on to the valley, towards Virgilian olive-groves, vineyards and the distant Var hills.

By the D2 from St-Paul-de-Vence, the 34-mile (54-km) detour joins up with the main route at Vence and the Matisse Chapel (see pp.108–9). For the Matisse Museum in Nice, Allée Dizzy Gillespie is an appropriate approach to the red Genoese mansion which houses Matisse's *Jazz: Improvisations in Colour and Rhythm. Odalisque with a Turkish Chair, Veiled Woman* and *The Hindu Rose* were the Matisse girls, posing languidly for him in his hotel room. Decor and costumes, too, were exotic: from harem pants to white fox furs, Moorish screens to richly draped chaise-longues. Those rooms with a view seem like an invitation to love in the afternoon – and a Diaghilev ballet in the evening.

Another Riviera Russian, Chagall, was more spiritual, though no less colourful. A few minutes down Boulevard de Cimiez from the Matisse, the smaller Chagall Museum has made a holy place of the artist's life-enhancing religious symbolism. A series called *Biblical Message* is dedicated to 'To Vava, my wife, my joy and lightness of spirit!'

Rabelaisian poet, Bellaud de Bellaudière. Constantly in and out of jail, this well-bred Grassois soldier of fortune wenched, wined and warred all over France, and did much for the ribaldry of the Provençal language.

> Oh blood-red God, God of all the bottles,
> God of every goblet, jar, and beaker,
> God without whose juice ham's worth nothing,
> Nor sausage either,
> I beg you, winey God,
> Just for me, your good friend,
> To kindly release me from this dingy prison
> Which holds me with untold grief in its trap.

I was anxious to find out what the inscription in Provençal meant, and a helpful official at the Hôtel de Ville kindly left his desk to translate for me. On the way, he let me into the secret of little crosses engraved in the stones of a medieval gateway; certain citizens – including poets – were denied Christian burial in the town cemetery, and families would bury them here at dead of night. Recent bulldozing had revealed skulls and bones. He translated the inscription in tribute to the poet as 'He who can speak well, speak. He who wishes to do good, do.' Though probably better in the original, it sounded far too sanctimonious for balladeer Bellaud.

Place aux Aires, immortalized by painter Raoul Dufy, is the place to lunch. Its cool arcades, terrace cafés and restaurants are where anyone who's anyone in Grasse relaxes, chats, drinks and does deals. Real-estate heavies, one dapper with crinkly grey hair and maroon blazer with crested buttons, the other with a paunch from all that pasta with the Mob, were looking at plans over lunch and pointing towards the wrought iron-balconies of the Hôtel Isnard, maybe copying the style for their next block of

luxury *appartements* 'Résidence Fragonard-Golf'? The Place aux Aires is a fine style to copy, tall Italianate houses with arcades surrounding an airy square; its elegant fountain with three basins one on top of the other tinkled away, accompanying the cool jazz of a woman sax player entertaining lunchers.

And if a faint smell of drains mingled with the smell of cooking, at least it was an earthy, very real perfume. Nothing synthetic about the Place aux Aires. Grasse had definitely won me over.

GRASSE TO NICE

Heading out of Grasse on the D2085, a choice now faces the intrepid traveller: art or landscape. Whether to brave the back-ups on a coastal detour to see some of the finest twentieth-century art museums in France – Antibes (Picasso), Biot (Léger), Cagnes (Renoir), St-Paul-de-Vence (The Maeght Foundation); or to enjoy the more outdoor pleasures of the Gorges du Loup. The art detour (described in Light Motifs opposite) meets up with the main route again at Vence.

I knew the museums already but had never done the Gorges du Loup. A 17-mile (27km) loop begins with a left-turn at Châteauneuf-de-Grasse off the D2085 on to the D3, the high road along the top of the gorge as far as the junction near Bramatan; then, back down the low road along the bottom (D6).

The high road takes you through Gourdon, an eagle's nest village with Saracen castle, hair-raisingly perched on the edge of the valley's stygian depths. Gasp-making views extend over 30 miles (48km) of coast from Cap Roux to the mouth of the Var river, the Loup serpenting at the bottom of the gorge, and snow-covered alpine peaks in the distance. From the château, Italian hanging gardens plunge into the gorge; lime trees shade the Court of Honour which leads to neatly clipped box hedges of the formal French garden, allegedly laid out by the royal landscape gardener André Le Nôtre. I could see ancient orange groves at the mouth of the gorge. Apparently, though not more than 20 per cent of Grasse essences are made from natural products (the rest are synthetic), local orange flowers are still used. Oranges, lemons, grapefruits, clementines, mandarines, limes and kumquats all flourish in the Riviera's micro-climate and rich soil.

Touristy in high summer and school holidays, Gourdon's best bet for lunch is the Auberge de Gourdon, a *café-tabac* where the *patronne*'s warm welcome is by no means the Riviera rule, nor her genuine Provençal cooking with plenty of *aïoli*: lamb stew with aubergines, *faux-filet* steak with cream of olives, and crispy Swiss chard at prices by no means as vertiginous as the spot.

The ancients used to say that the Gorges du Loup linked the lowlands of the olive with the highlands of snow. On the return journey down the low road, alpine waterfalls spumed from on high; the Cascade de Courmes had a particularly spectacular tumble. And the reverse angle on Gourdon, now way, way above me, gave it the appearance of an alpine village. Crossing the river at Pont-du-Loup took me a mile off route on the D2210 to Le Bar-sur-Loup, where there's an orange wine festival in April, and worth the detour at any time for St-Jacques-le-Majeur church's exquisite fifteenth-century wood painting entitled *Dance Macabre*.

Backtracking on the D2210 to Vence, you have to concentrate hard on the bends of the hill road, not to be distracted by views to the sea – or the appearance of Tourettes-sur-Loup jutting out on its bluff. My wife Sheila and I once nearly bought the Old Jail to convert into a cosy cottage but were put off by sinister hooks and chains,

said to be of historical note. In fact, Tourettes was made of gentler stuff – the cultivation of violets whose fragrance wafted down its sinuous, vaulted streets. A crop of titivated artisanal boutiques stuck out like a tortured thumb.

At first, Vence seems tarred by the same brush. Its equally pretentious contemporary art galleries, aimed at the rich and dumb, may well fade into the background when the town is enlivened by such events as the Nuits du Sud World Music Festival with bands and singers from Cuba, Argentina, Portugal, Mexico and Mali. Vence loves to whoop it up in summertime, and I'd be unfair to misjudge it in the more sober month of March. No doubt its serious resident artists – Chagall, Matisse, Soutine, Dufy, Modigliani, Dubuffet and, more recently, Arman – preferred it in the quiet months. Chagall did a mosaic of *Moses Rescued from the Waters* for the baptistery of Nativité-de-la-Vierge cathedral, symbolic of a child's purification by baptism. It was presented in 1970, the year he left for Nice to begin his Biblical series. Outside, Latin inscriptions from Gallo-Roman times are inlaid into a superb baroque façade. Vence is a town for all centuries dating from the Ligurians; a Roman stronghold on a strategic plateau; a circular medieval warren of red-roofed old houses in cool, coiling alleys. A fine 1822 fountain graces Place Peyra, while an ash-tree to commemorate a visit by François I shades Place du Frêne.

The star turn of Vence, however, lies just outside it – on the continuation of the D2210 to St-Jeannet. Tucked away on the right amid suburban houses but recognizable by its tall wrought-iron cross, Matisse's Chapel of the Rosary is only open on Tuesday and Wednesday, or by special appointment made 48 hours in advance. It has a strange history. Matisse had once been ill in Nice, and the nun who nursed him proposed the idea of the chapel to a Dominican father, who proposed it to Matisse, at that time a neighbour in Vence. The theme of *Stations of the Cross* was agreed on, a design executed in a couple of hours. The actual work of 'architectural painting' took him from 1947 to 1951. The austere, contemporary chapel has an almost Cistercian purity.

'Simple colours act upon inner feeling, with all the more power for their simplicity,' declared the artist. And the primary blue, green and yellow of the stained glass windows, expressing The Tree of Life, play light games upon the pure white floor, walls and ceiling. The altar is constructed of warm reddish Rognes stone from the Bouches-du-Rhône village already visited. Inside and outside, ceramics depict Mother and Infant, and the life of St-Dominick. The Stations of the Cross, with all their suffering, had a particular resonance for Matisse who suffered severely in later life, yet managed to bring an exquisite lightness to his work.

St-Jeannet, to the left off the D2210, has one of the best positions in the region – high above the valley of the Var, nestling in the protection of Baou de St-Jeannet's craggy cliffs. Witches and faith-healers have always flourished beneath the magic hill, and villagers would take to its benificent caves in time of siege or plague. Rather more recently, Hitchcock shot scenes of *To Catch A Thief* there, Chagall painted it, and chic middle-aged women from Nice in purposeful hiking gear scale it (the round trip takes two hours). From Place Sur Le Four, I caught the panorama from a shady, arcaded terrace: below me sun-drenched vineyards, orange and olive groves sloping down towards distant St-Laurent-du-Var and the Mediterranean. Near the Mairie, a plaque publicly thanks 1905's mayor Clary-Louis who paid for the village's electricity supply out of his own pocket. Apart from a scattering of villas-and-pools with all mod cons, it can't have changed much.

In the Gorges du Loup, alpine waterfalls spumed from on high

TH = Table d'Hôtes (guest house with dinner)

CH = Chambre d'Hôtes (bed and breakfast only)

The character and convenience of the Negresco and Beau-Rivage

Just across the Var-Alpes-Maritimes border, Théoule-sur-Mer has the posh Miramar Beach in a red-rock crique on the Esterel Corniche. Sea-water therapy is available here. More modest is Mas Provençal with its own swimming pool. At La Napoule, nostalgic Riviera pampering is available at Ermitage du Riou, an inviting yellow *bastide* where your room has delicious sea views of the gulf and Lérins Islands.

Besides the classic village pub Auberge de Nossi-Bé at Auribeau (see p.104), the Grasse region offers modest, comfortable rooms at the charming Petite Auberge at Magagnosc. A minimum of two nights' stay is required at Le Coteau de Malbosc (CH) in Grasse itself, where the Malbrels welcome non-smokers to their hillside villa overlooking a pretty garden. Less rules apply chez Ringenbach (CH) near Valbonne, another recently built villa de luxe in its own park. To make certain I didn't get lost finding it, Monsieur Ringenbach kindly met me at the service station in his Mercedes. He also cooked my breakfast, while Madame Ringenbach left for work in her Mercedes.

For the independently minded at Vence, an evocative Victorian private house La Villa René (CH)

is a romantic stopover in a tiny valley, while La Roseraie near the Matisse Chapel is a charming family hotel with Provençal-style furniture and bunches of lavender in the bathroom. At St-Jeannet, Le Ste-Barbe is a village pub with stunning views from its room balconies and untouristy prices.

Not all Nice hotels have the character and convenience of the Negresco (p.118), Petit Palais (p.111), and Beau-Rivage (p.112). Château des Ollières, pink-and-white Belle Epoque oppulence, is

a small palace-hotel in an exotic garden (see p.115), where guests dine on a candlelit verandah like Russian princesses or English milords. The central and very friendly Windsor has an artistic ambience, plus hammam baths and sauna and plants as exotic as the guests round the pool. Also central and reasonably priced are Madame Vimont-Beuve's charming Les Camélias and La Fontaine which serves breakfast round a fountain, only a few steps from the Promenade des Anglais.

As I returned to the D2210 and serpented down into the Var valley, the not-so-sweet smell of smog met me – the first since Aix-en-Provence. Agro-industries thrive here, their plastic 'tunnel' green-houses shimmering in the hazy sun. Quickly over the river at Carros by a busy iron bridge, a mile or so hurtle south on the double-track N202, and I was escaping left on to the tiny D514 and D414 to Colomars, tucked away in the uncrowded hills on the eastern side of the Var. Just after Colomars, I turned right on the D914 into an unspoiled, undulating Nice hinterland of little valleys and hilltop villages. If I was a breadwinner in the city, I'd prefer the comparative quietness and safety of this leafy dormitory area to a Promenade des Anglais highrise – even if it meant driving a thousand hairpin-bends a day. Suddenly, at St-Pancrace, still on the traffic-free D914, I had the whole city of Nice below me, the Bay of Angels' curving away towards Italy, familiar landmarks like Cimiez hill, the Acropolis and the Hôtel Negresco as clear as on an aerial photograph.

And, equally suddenly, I descended from no traffic to traffic jam. It was mid-afternoon. A *lycée* was disgorging students, and the street was blocked with the Peugeots and Renaults of parents picking them up. It gave me a chance to look at my map of Nice. I decided to check out the best route to the Carabacel quarter with an efficient-looking *maman*. '*Oh, zut!*' she said pityingly, as though I'd asked her the way to Timbuctou. 'Take the Boulevard Gambetta to the Interior Autoroute and come off at the exit for Cimiez. *Bon courage!*' Then she had a better idea. 'Follow me.' And, having picked up three children laden with homework, she led me to where I could get my bearings.

Arriving at my first and only seriously big city was quite a culture shock. As Niçois kindness was my first experience, it augured well.

SALADE NIÇOISE

Nice is a truly international city; its culture mix has as many ingredients as a *salade niçoise*. Communities have their distinctive churches, synagogues, mosques and temples. But nowhere is its variety more impressive than in its places to eat, drink and stay.

Take the Hôtel Petit Palais, an old friend. Once the home of actor-playwright Sacha Guitry, it is Belle Epoque to perfection, a little palace among other palaces in Nice's once fashionable Carabacel quarter of quiet, winding streets. Exotic gardens, which mid-nineteenth-century English winterers on the Riviera did so much to develop, proliferate with palm trees, barbary fig cacti, agave, hibiscus, jasmine and bougainvillaea. English-sounding names like Ranelagh are everywhere. Nowadays it is a pleasant, unflashy place to stay, with a touch of faded elegance, a place to contemplate the lights coming up and the sun going down on the city below – from the perennial Promenade des Anglais (built so the English wouldn't have to walk on the pebbly beach) to the modern California-style Palais des Arts, du Tourisme et des Congrès Acropolis. The hotel is also convenient for the nearby Chagall and Matisse museums.

The Matisse museum is at Cimiez, about a mile's climb up the Boulevard Cimiez from Carabacel. The artist passed the last years of his life in an *appartement* at the nearby Excelsior Regina Palace, another extraordinary Nice hotel of yesteryear. Looming surrealistically like an ocean liner washed up on top of a hill by a replay of The Flood (Chagall would have approved), it is still one of Nice's biggest residential buildings. The late Victorian concept of a Nice banker and Grasse perfumer to cope with the tourist boom, it had four hundred rooms. Arriving with her own furniture, Queen Victoria stayed there three times, descending to watch the Prince of Wales cavort with carnival queens on a float at the Battle of Flowers. She *was* amused – or so the Niçois claim.

Matisse loved Nice for its cosmopolitanism. Memories went back to the first winter (1917) he spent at the Hôtel Beau-Rivage, which is still flourishing at the corner of rue St-François-de-Paule and Boulevard Jean-Jaurés. A north-

Nice's cuisine, the most distinctive of Provence's cities

erner already seduced by southern sensuality at Collioure and Tangier, he loved its light even in foul weather. *Storm at Nice* endows the Promenade des Anglais with a grey limpidity, even when buffeted by waves, its palm trees like shaken feather dusters, and one brave couple (*Anglais*?) venturing forth beneath a huge black umbrella.

And the sun shone through his hotel window, on to the intimate indoor Mediterranean scene he made his own. The Mediterranean was a closed sea, intimate as his hotel

room, with North Africa just across it, Spain, Italy, Corsica, Sardinia intermingling their histories, and boats arriving from French Indo-China, black Africa and the Antilles with beautiful, exotic models for Matisse to paint and make love to.

Architecturally, however, Nice is firmly an Italianate city. Place Masséna – all pinky ochre tranquillity in midtown, with fountains, a statue of its Napoleonic general, and baroque Chapel of the Holy Sepulchre. Nearby, another noble square is named after another heroic son of Nice, Garibaldi, who helped mastermind the nineteenth-century unification of Italy. Until 1860, Nice belonged – on and off – to the House of Savoy, so some of its population are descended from Piedmontese and Sardinians whose King once ruled them. It is still fiercely independent, with Nissat its own language, and a cuisine which combines the best of French and Italian, yet manages to remain its own.

Nice's cuisine is the most distinctive of Provence's cities. Not *haute-cuisine* but popular, of the streets, of the sea, the best of local products in the best of hands. Although disgraced ex-mayor Jacques Médecin could hardly be called 'the best of hands', jailbird Jacquot (as he's still affectionately known in the Cours Aleya market), cooker of books, also wrote a cookery book, *La Cuisine du Comté de Nice.* Until his death, this best seller provided him with a living in Uruguay and us a chance to make *pissaladiera,* flaky pastry and onion, liberally flavoured with purée of anchovies and black olives. *Boeuf à la niçoise* is a rich beef pot-roast with onions, tomatoes, black and green olives. The olives, ideally, should be the small ones from the Nice area. Sardines are stuffed with Swiss chard or tomatoes.

Then there's *socca,* a wickedly fattening pancake made of chick-pea flour, tastiest when hot off the griddle in the market with pigeons pecking up your crumbs; *ratatouilla,* a stew of aubergines, courgettes, peppers and tomatoes

Nice is firmly an Italianate city

Music lovers of all persuasions should make the trip in high summer – and to hell with the crowds! Besides the Nuits de Sud World Music Festival at Vence, jazz-lovers begin early in July with concerts beneath the stars at the Roman Arena of Nice, then move on till late July for concerts beneath the pine trees of Juan-les-Pins.

Soprano Barbara Hendricks, baritone Ruggiero Raimondi and the Philharmonic Orchestra of Monte-Carlo are the quality acts expected at the Menton Music Festival in August, while July's festival at Cannes concentrates more on chamber recitals and solo virtuosi. Music chosen is popular classical rather than avant-garde.

All through the year, Nice is a ball. After February's Contemporary Music Festival in the Chagall Museum comes the perennial Mardi Gras Carnival and Battle of Flowers with parades and fireworks on the Promenade des Anglais. March sees flower shows and cycle races. In April, there's chamber music, symphony concerts and veteran car rallies. The May Festival celebrates Nice folklore, while champion surfboarders compete in the Bay of Angels. The Fishermen's Festival, more cycling and sacred music take up June. In July there's jazz, athletics, fireworks and another Battle of Flowers. August celebrates the Liberation with a ball, and there's yet another Battle of Flowers, more classical concerts and yacht races. 'Holiday on Ice' cools everyone down in September for the Wine Festival, after which autumn events taper away in interest till the December Luna Park Fair for parents and children and the traditional mass bathing on the first Sunday after Christmas. Then it starts all over again...

flavoured with herbs and garlic; *porquetta,* milk-fattened piglet; *tourta de bléa,* Swiss chard tart; and *salade niçoise,* that good old stand-by for lazy lunches in the sun, which properly made is a mixture of peppers, tomatoes, hard-boiled egg, black Nice olives, red onions, artichokes and baby broad beans. A visit to the market, usually known as The Flower Market, on Cours Aleya is always a pleasure. Here you see, as well as flowers, the freshest of

Mediterranean fish that you'll be eating round the corner at Les Dents de Mer. Don't be put off by the corny galleon decor of this famous fish restaurant: its basil-flavoured fish cannelloni, salt cod with sweet peppers, and bouillabaisse with little stuffed vegetables are all classic Niçois combinations from market fresh products.

Over the years, I've been lucky enough to savour some of the best Niçois cooking to be had on home ground: pasta with *pistou* at La Mérenda, an eccentric hole-in-the-wall with no telephone (worth a walk to reserve); *fleurs de courgette,* beignets of courgette flowers, on the sunny terrace of La Cambuse in the Flower Market; and *stocaficada,* dried cod stew with tomatoes, olives and herbs, at Lou Balico, a family restaurant of great vitality and fun near the Museum of Modern Art.

So much for the Niçois of French, Savoyard or Sardinian origin. I was eager to find out where Niçois from other lands now congregated and what they consumed to remind them of home. The British, for instance, were once a strong community. Gale Potphar, elegant in her black tailored suit, is British manageress of Château des Ollières, an intimate small luxury hotel converted from a White Russian prince's love nest. I asked her: 'Where do you Brits get together these days?'

'Marks & Spencer's on Avenue Jean-Médecin,' Gale replied, rather to my surprise. 'Not just Brits. Canadians, Australians, Irish. You always bump into someone you know. When I get homesick, especially at Christmas, I pop in for my Christmas pud and brandy butter. And Marks & Sparks do a lovely Carol Service, with the choir of the Anglican Church.'

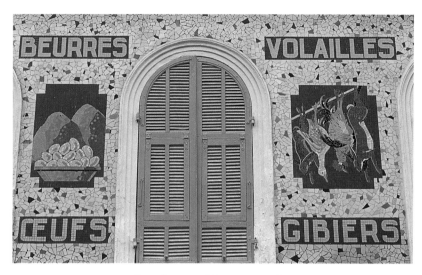

The Cours Aleya market

Melbourne-born Father Ken Letts, the present vicar, memorably described his own Australian city as 'theatre, art, and the second bottle of wine at lunch'. That's why he loves Nice, 'a city with a soul'. Theatre, art, and ... for the 50,000 English-speaking readers of the *Riviera Reporter*, more likely beer than wine, drunk at one of many locals. Pub Oxford, Scarlett O'Hara's Irish Pub, Church Street Inn, Big Ben, The Hole in the Wall are just a few of some thirty listed in central Nice alone.

Americans, nostalgic for a taste of home, will find McDonalds typically installed on the city's best corner – between Avenue de Verdun and the Promenade des Anglais. It is conveniently near to the Ruhl, now a Las Vegas-style casino where American punters feel at home combining a flutter at the tables and *les show-girls* on the floor. As I crowd-watch on the corner, a young American in tight black jeans and yellow shirt emerges blinking from the Casino, yelling curses into his mobile, clearly having

Russian Orthodox St Nicholas cathedral

'Russians come here and do a lot of laughing and crying,' said Madame Ghislaine from Beauvais, co-owner of the Transsibérien in rue Botero, where I consumed delicious aubergine caviar, salmon's eggs with thick cream, six different herrings, spicy meat balls, blinis and dill with everything, iced vodka and a glass of the Cahors wine made specially for the Tsar – in a decor of the Trans-Siberian Express, complete with train sounds and soulful Russian songs.

Like the synagogue, the nearby Russian Orthodox St Nicholas cathedral is very much the centre of its community. It is also one of the most impressively original buildings in Nice. I imagined myself in Moscow or Yaroslavl, as I stood dazzled by its six onion domes catching the sunlight. 'Of course I'm Russian!' smiled the freckled, red-haired Niçoise at the entrance

suffered a losing streak. He nearly bumps into a pretty Niçois mother with pram, deep in conversation on *her* mobile. The American cheers up visibly, pockets his mobile and gives chase.

In the eclectic variety of Nice cuisines, Chagall as a Russian Jew would have found something to please both appetites. There is kosher take-away cous-cous at Epicerie Fine Chez Mimile in rue Pertinax, opposite the Algerian Kabyle Restaurant Djurjura; and not far from rue Gustave-Deloye's synagogue, bottles of Passover wine were displayed at a popular fish restaurant, Le Leviathan. 'But our food is French,' said *la patronne* emphatically.

desk, almost indignant that I might have doubted it. 'But our bishop is English.' An English Russian Orthodox bishop? How could that be? Monseigneur Paul, as he was affectionately known, had been happily married to a Russian who died young. He became a monk, and after studying in Paris, was appointed Bishop of Nice.

The cathedral was inaugurated in 1912 by Tsar Nicholas II, ironically only five years before the Revolution, for the large Nice population of Russian royalty and aristocrats. Hence the opulence of its icons and wood carving. Nowadays Russian tourists in increasing numbers visit it with some astonishment.

If you enjoy ferreting about in search of a particular subject, here are a few Nice themes.

'Baroque in Old Nice' takes in superb polychrome frescoes, stucco and marble altar pieces decorated with Rococo art at churches like St-François-de-Paule and chapels like Miséricorde. Concerts are frequently held in them, too. Palais Lascaris shows the Italian Baroque influence of Genoa.

'Belle Epoque Nice' leads one to the stylish villas of Mont Boron overlooking the sea. There's Château Valrose with its 25 acre (10 hectare) botanical gardens and the Beaux Arts Museum (both once palaces of Russian aristocracy), the English *milord* hotels and gardens in Carabacel and Cimiez, and Les Musiciens quarter full of gaily decorated bourgeois house façades. Ending up, of course, with afternoon tea at the Negresco.

'Markets of Nice' are legendary. The Flower Market (also fruit and veg) on Cours Saleya is only closed on Monday

Place Masséna, all pinky ochre tranquility

when antiques take over. The Fish Market takes place every morning on Place St-François. There's also a Flea Market at Place Robilante near the Opera House daily except Monday, an Antique Market daily except Sunday, near the Old Port, and Books and Magazines in the Place du Palais de Justice every Saturday.

'Henri Matisse' - visit Hôtel Beau Rivage, his house on Cours Saleya, Promenade des Anglais, the Regina, and Cimiez museum.

'Lesser Known Artists of Nice' - view the work of: the superb Ludovic Bréa whose sixteenth-century religious paintings can be seen at the Franciscan Monastery in Cimiez, also in Antibes, Biot and Monaco; nineteenth-century water-colourist Alfred Mossa and his weird symbolist son, Gustave-Adolfe at the gallery on Quai des Etats-Unis; thirties poster-artist Paul Chéret, inventor of fey, floating models known as *chérettes* at the Beaux-Arts Museum; and modernist, Yves Klein, at the superb Contemporary Arts Museum. All five were born in Nice.

Contes' old village on its rocky spur

'How do you like the New Russians?' I asked Sebastian, barman at the Negresco, the palace to end all palaces, and one of the great privately owned (by the Augier family) hotels of the world. Half litres of vodka had, I knew, replaced miniatures in the mini-bars, and at least got the New Russian guests through breakfast.

'*Eh bien,*' said Sebastian guardedly. 'Let's say we have had, uh, better guests. The first free market *aparatchiks* – they looked just out of school, some of them – threw their dollars around, hiring Lamborghinis to show off to the sexiest girls they could find. Now we have quieter Russian big spenders with their families.'

I mingled with a few Russian big spenders at the Negresco's Chantecleer, arguably the best restaurant in Nice. A value-for-money 280-franc lunch menu finished my Nice stay in style. And to add another gastronomic nationality to my list, the chef Alain Llorca was of Catalan origin. While New Russians tucked into their 550-franc Tapas menu, I was delighted with my more modest gaspacho and stuffed squid, accompanied by fine Bellet red wine from the Nice hills. In this very room, Mayor Jacques Médecin and his glamorous Californian wife (long since ex) would entertain VIPS lavishly at the taxpayer's expense, surrounded by a posse of gorillas in dark glasses. At the end of the meal, the ambassador or CEO or opera star being entertained would invariably receive a beautifully wrapped gift: a copy of Monsieur le Maire's cookery book.

The *salade niçoise* may not be quite as exotic a mixture as it was in Matisse's day, but it still has a surprise or two in the bowl.

NICE TO ST-MARTIN-VÉSUBIE

Leaving Nice was simpler than my arrival. From the Petit Palais, up the Boulevard de Cimiez, past the Regina's noble pile and chic clinics in the good, clean air near the Roman remains, I joined the D14 which took me speedily into the Nice hinterland. In a matter of minutes, I was facing north towards an up-country landscape of little dormitory villages perched on hills or nestling in valleys.

The nearest of these villages, on a hill reached by the D214 off the D14, is Falicon (pop. 1,070), only 8 miles (13km) from Nice (pop. 520,000). The village name plaque shows four suns in different moods: happy, very happy, not so sure, miserable. Welcoming me in 'very happy' mood, its tiny baroque church was actually open, sadly a rarity in these light-fingered times. Painted friezes on the houses, cobble-stone streets and the charming little Hôtel Bellevue's panoramic terrace already predict the Alps. It was quite a shock to face south and see an urban perspective of the monolithic Regina's back view, Promenade des Anglais, autoroute to Italy, and industrial valley of St Pons.

The D214 continued past a dramatic quarry, a sheer cliff with strata seams clearly demarcated, as though for a geology lesson. Turning left on to the D19, a sign indicated that I was entering 'Levens – the Canton of a Thousand Smiles' with terraced orchards and pastureland. Along the bucolic Gabre valley, the occasional gorgelet penetrated pre-Alpine Mont Chauve (2,568ft/783m) on my left and Mont Macaron (2,650ft/808m) on my right – Bald and Macaroon. The next village, Tourettes-Levens, was truly Niçois in its nineteenth-century architecture with richly painted *trompe l'oeil* façades. The turreted, castellated, reddish-grey château was presented to the village by the Chabot family whose dynasty began with the Consul of Nice in 1210, and who were grand enough to give themselves numbers like royalty: Jacques I, Philippe-Emmanuel II, Honoré IV. Very feudal, the Nice aristocracy. The castle museum was not officially open, but an eager young man, cataloguing the collection, was only too glad to let me in. It housed a superbly presented collection of butterflies, beetles, caterpillars, spiders and giant crickets.

Tortuous climbs and descents began, as soon as I turned right off the D19 on to the narrow D815 to Contes. Before a hairpin bend, a man signalled me to slow down for three cars concertina-ed. The front one had stopped too close to the bend, and the others, coming round blind, had piled into it. No one was hurt. Even these lowish sugar-loaf hills can be dangerous; the eye is so often distracted. Coming down from the Col de Châteauneuf (2,059ft/628m), I nearly came off the road myself when I caught sight of an enticing village below, framed in apple blossom, and the first snow-patch on a distant, hazy mountain. The village was Châteauneuf-de-Contes where the 'new castle' was built on higher ground to protect the inhabitants of Contes in the Paillon valley when medieval barons rampaged down valleys laying waste anything and anyone in sight.

By the time I joined the D15 at Contes I'd been travelling two hours, yet Nice was still only 10 miles (16km) away. Contes' old village on its rocky spur is surprisingly well preserved in the industrial Paillon valley. Once a Ligurian oppidum and Roman castrum, it proved to have a bustling modern town, useful for a coffee and picnic shopping. It was near enough to Nice for much ribald Niçois humour as *flics* pulled a double-parked van driver out of the café. 'What's the matter with you boys? Haven't you got a mayor to arrest?' laughed the van-driver. Soon after Contes, continuing north on the D15, more jokes. When I stopped to take a photograph, a man working in his garden called, 'Sorry, no photographs today!' I told him it was the blaze of mimosa forest behind his house I was taking, not him. 'What's the matter with *me*, then? Am I so ugly?'

In the micro-climate around Coaraze, sheltered by the Alps from northerly and easterly blasts, lupins, hollyhocks and delphiniums grow in profusion in little gardens that could be in Berkshire. The village is at the head of a valley with no hills to keep the sun off it. Abstract, gaily coloured sundials by Cocteau, Douking and Valentin decorate the façade of the Town Hall while others in Place Felix-Giordan are the work of artists Goetz and Ponce de Leon. In the long, circuitous tunelled streets and little squares signs are in melodious Nissat: *lou jardin, plaça dau Pontel Savel, carriera plana*. A local legend, told me by a near-blind old Abraham with long white beard and guide-dog, surrounds the name Coaraze (*cou rasa* – cut-off tail). 'The villagers trapped the Devil by his tail,' said the old man in all seriousness, 'and he could only escape back to Hell by cutting it off.'

The Col St-Roch (3247ft/990m), further along the D15, proved to be my most isolated drive of the whole trip: not another vehicle encountered in over two hours. It was an alpine terrain, occasionally vertiginous, with

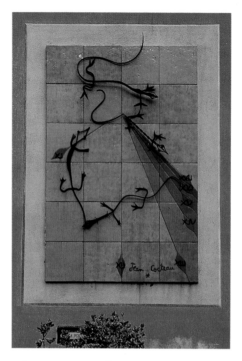

Abstract, gaily coloured sundials at Coaraze

lonely, austere hamlets sprinkled about fire-charred hills. A rugged Provence, this, though not even the rusty wreck of a car on the roadside can make it sinister. It's adventure country, sufficiently near the Riviera for bright, southerly light, yet far enough away to be utterly peaceful. Contemplative between bites of my lunchtime *pissaladière*, I listened to the silence. Turning right on to the D2566 to Peira-Cava, scenery became more spectacular at every twist and turn. Mediterranean trees were changing to mountain chestnut, Norway pine, fir, maple and beech. Chalets began, as the narrow road climbed upwards and

onwards. The air was crisper, cooler. I put on a sweater. Then, round a bend appeared the snow-covered Alpes-Maritimes peaks in all their glory. Peira-Cava (5,412ft/1,650m), my first ski-resort, had no one about; hotels and ski-lifts were out of action. It was unfair to judge it between seasons: a bit grim and grey, despite its alpine balcony position. The vividly scrawled graffiti VIVE LES LOUPS! (Long live Wolves!), agit-prop from wolf-lovers, made me eager to discover more about the wolf's controversial return to the Mercantour National Park.

Botanists and enthomologists can enjoy an 11-mile (18-km) circuit into Mercantour's Massif d'Authion, by taking the D68 at the Col de Turini (5,270ft/1,606m) junction. At this altitude, it's surprising to find rhododendrons in larch woods, meadows with rare species of lily, wild orchids and carnations, attended by a multitude of butterflies. Leave butterfly nets and clippers at home, however, or risk arrest by park wardens.

People come from Nice and Menton to these sweet forests and nature reserves to cool down in high summer. From Col de Turini, where there's a pleasant chalet-auberge, L'Aiga Blanca, I descended by the D70 – a well-made pass road with a tunnel, a gorge, a forest with belvederes to admire the views – to La Bollène-Vésubie. Just behind the church, a millwheel was turning. An exhausted woman, carrying shopping in a laundry basket,

La Bollène-Vésubie – steep paths and cobbled streets

was not getting much help from three children larking about. If you don't have a car, still a luxury in poorer Provence, every item has to be humped up and down steep paths and cobbled streets. Some houses are only reachable by steps. Harsher, mountain customs were evident, buildings a little shabbier. The Town Hall displayed a colourful mural on its façade, evidence of a pushed village putting on a brave face.

Further down the D70, the junction at the bottom of the Vésubie valley called for a right-turn on to the D2565 to St-Martin-Vésubie. A sign to the right (D65) indicated *ski du fond* up the Gordalasque valley. Hard to imagine *any* kind of skiing at this time of year; or the stunning autumnal tints for which the valley is famous – reds, russets, browns and greens – which bring visitors flocking from Nice. At Roquebillière-Vieux, palm trees began again in the soft, sheltered climate. Lovely old stone houses with wooden balconies, a semi-ruined bell tower with polychrome onion dome were all badly in need of restoration. St-Michel-du-Gast, a St John's hospitaller church later rebuilt in typically Provençal Romanesque-Gothic style originally served worshippers fallen sick on their way to or from the Crusades. That, too, was in a state of romantic dilapidation. Only this comparatively short distance from the wealthy Riviera, you sense the pinch.

VIVE LES LOUPS!

St-Martin-Vésubie, centre for Mercantour National Park, does not feel the pinch quite so badly. It is known as the capital of the Niçois Switzerland. Two valleys, Boréon and Madone de Fenestre, lead to the Park from the lively eighteenth-century town built on a rocky spur at the confluence of two rivers. Seen from my balcony at La Bonne Auberge, a spotlight of morning sun hit the snow-

capped Pic de Colmiane; by the time I'd finished shaving, its arc had spread down the forest and illuminated a long log truck winding its way along a precipitous road.

At breakfast in the cosy dining-room, full of copper pots and potted plants and a wild-boar's head on the wall, Monsieur Roberi's daughter arrived with arms full of fresh bread. 'There's bakers and bakers,' she said. 'If you prefer brown bread to white, our baker's is famous!'

Fuelled on warm *pain de siègle* (rye bread) I went to explore the town. A gully of water, known locally as a *gargouille* (gargoyle or water spout), ran down the middle of the cobblestone rue de Docteur Cagnoli, making the main street easy to clean. The Chapelle des Pénitents Blancs (penitents from rich families) with its ornate baroque interior, glistening gilt altar table and crystal chandeliers, was at odds with the rather austere houses. 'The onion-domed bell towers,' explained Monsieur Stramaccioni, a distinguished, town-proud gentleman who greeted me like a long lost friend in the street, 'naturally remind you of Austria, because St-Martin was once occupied by Austrians, who were allies of the House of Savoy. Later, Napoleon – then an artillery general – helped kick them out and Nice became French for a few years. After that, back we went to the House of Savoy! Ping-pong, it was – with us as the ball.' Monsieur Strammacioni was pro-British because of the Scottish and Irish mercenaries who fought for Nice; you could find McMahons in the Nice telephone directory even today, he said. He called Duke, his spaniel, to heel and said, 'Good day, sir!' in English, shaking my hand.

The Chapelle des Pénitents Noirs (penitents from poor families), filled with pre-Easter foxgloves, carnations and roses, was a small gem, as was the Gothic house with solid arcade of the Counts of Gubernatis. At the Tourist Office, a helpful (or so I imagined) woman told me where I could

A PARADISE FOR WALKERS AND ECOLOGISTS

Nowhere in France has a greater variety of species than the Mercantour National Park's fragile ecology. Near the Mediterranean, a walk may take you from olive trees to rhodedendrons, giving way to rich alps lush as lawns; higher up, in the Vallée des Merveilles and Cirque de Montanalbe, forests and lakes, glacial valleys and mountain slopes are the natural habitat of free-ranging fauna. And on my route, from the Col de Turini to Guillaumes, in the park or just outside it, these are some of the animals to be seen.

Curved-Horn Ibex (long, curving horns): About 100 in Upper Vésubie valley, 40 in Gordalasque valley; after annually crossing crests from winters in Italian Alps, visible from mid-May to mid-September.

Wild Sheep (short, curly horns): They migrate in flocks from safe, snowy slopes occupied in winter to valleys in early spring in search of food, returning to the heights in May; 400 in Upper Vésubie, 200 in Upper Tinée.

Chamois (short horns with little curl on top): Most frequently spotted, with 3,000 in all the Mercantour valleys; in the summer coolness of morning and evening, they make their moves, and can also be seen in autumn during the rutting season.

Marmoset (short, furry with bushy tail): They live in warrens, can be seen after hibernation in April all over Mercantour playing and fighting from May to July, at cool times of day.

Ermine (long, furry stoat): Its fur (now non-pc to wear) turns white in winter, making it difficult to spot. While trekking in mountains, watch for him or her lurking behind a rock for your picnic remains.

Royal Eagle (brown with yellowish neck and head): Makes furtive appearances everywhere in summer, planing over combes and alps, swooping on marmosets.

Ptarmigan (dove-like bird, white in winter, brown in summer): Visible in June during the mating season around Mont Mounier.

Blackcock (black grouse with lyre-shaped tail): A discrete forest-lover known for its autumn and spring song in the Upper Vésubie and Tinée.

Chocard (black daw with yellow beak and red feet): Living in mountain rocks, their acrobatic antics are particularly evident in autumn and they are post-picnic foragers.

Circaete jean-le-blanc (brown-and-white bird of prey like an eagle and buzzard): They plane and swoop on snakes and lizards, migrating to Africa and returning to Mont Mounier, Upper Var and Tinée valleys between mid-March and end of September.

Animal Rights activists, please note: foxes and hares are also protected. So are the wolves!

Long live wolves!

and could not walk in Mercantour in spring, mostly 'not' with still so much unmelted snow on the higher ground. For lengthier treks in summer, it is wise to check on conditions and leave your proposed itinerary with the Gendarmerie. They are responsible for looking for you, if you get on the wrong side of a wolf.

Mercantour National Park is one of the wonders of Provence. Its 154,000 acres (62,323 hectares), running north-west along the Franco-Italian border, stretch approximately from Sospel, 8 miles (13km) north of Menton, to Barcelonette, 105 miles (170km) north of Cannes. Its protected plateaux, lakes and mountains include Alpine peaks: Mt. Bego (God of Thunderbolts, 9,423ft/2,872m), Mt Pelat (10,007ft/3,050m) and Cime de Gelas (10,309ft/3,142m).

Now its fragile ecology is threatened by a beast worshipped by Greens and detested by sheep farmers: the wolf. A comparatively rare visitor, it must be admitted. In all that space, numbers officially counted and marked vary between fifteen and thirty. At a wintry 'wolf moon', a full-lunged howl of defiance, celebrating a return from the dead after seventy years of absence, works its horror-film effect. For the past four years, the neatly stripped carcasses of wild sheep and chamois have been found in the valley. Also, in summer when transhumance brings flocks back to alpine pastures, the prey is reared sheep – to the fury of their farmers. Controversy rages, for the wolf is a species protected by the Berne Convention.

A French Alpine mayor, Philippe Langenieux-Villard recently authorized sheepfarmers to shoot wolves which crossed the Alps from Italy to France and have so far massacred 160 sheep in his Allevard Commune. He has been accused of flagrant deliction of the Berne Convention, and risks prosecution.

So, in these parts, you go dancing with wolves at your peril, both from the wolf and sheep farmers – as I was to find out later. Right now, having turned off the D2565 on to the D89 to Lake Boréon on the edge of the Park, all was perfect peace. Mirror-still water flowed to a tumbling cascade. The peace, however, was short-lived. The track to Les Vacheries de Boréon, where the woman at the Tourist Office said I could park, was covered with slippery, rutted snow. The Panda jolted and bucked in protest. So I left it at the lake and added another hour to my three-hour walk, by walking through the larch forest to the cow houses. No complaints. I was totally alone, except for one snow-plough clearing the road for Easter visitors. My well-booted feet crunched contentedly, my eyes feasted on the sunlit, snowy peaks marking the Franco-Italian border only a couple of miles (3km) away.

Near the grey-stone cow houses with solar-heating plaques, I reached the official entrance of the Park. A board informed me that this was a place of contemplation, discovery, encounter, knowledge and protection, with two thousand species of flora and fauna. Full of hope for a wolf cry higher up, I started the normally easy climb to the Refuge de Cougourde (6,855ft/2,089m), exactly as the woman at the Tourist Office said I could. Only I couldn't. Not without snow-shoes. The enticing track through the forest was deceptive; my boots kept sinking into the melting frozen snow. Twice I fell down. A careless fracture, apart from providing wolf fodder, can be a thorough bore for rescuers. There are enough idiots risking their lives and others' in the Alps without my adding one more.

Turning back, I borrowed a plastic chair from the stack on the terrace of the shuttered Alpages du Haut-Boréon café, relaxing with an apple and chocolate. Soft adventure, perhaps, but I considered myself the luckiest soft adventurer on earth. A superb alpine view to myself, tanning sunshine, snow all around, and one noisy woodpecker representing the two thousand species of flora and fauna. I resolved to return at a better time of year (May-September), and sample some of the fifty well-signposted walks on offer.

The Panda backtracked on the D89 and, after a few mountainous miles, the D2565 changed direction from north to west, pointing me in the direction of home for the first time since Nice. Skirting the southern edge of Mercantour, I passed the hideous modern high-rise ski-resort hotels and shopping centres flung up on the Plateau de Colmiane with no respect for nature, drab blocks of brown amid the green, white and blue landscape.

The upside of Colmiane is the sensational Baous de las Frema *via ferrata,* mountaineering made easy on a totally safe five-and-a-half-hour route with ladders up cliff faces, protected passages between jagged rocks, and aerial bridges across depths. Vertigo-sufferers abstain! Other summer sports – trekking, mountain-biking and grass-skiing (dangerous, that one) – have proved more lucrative than growing wheat at Val de Blore, a wide-open plateau

of alpine pastures surrounded by gentle slopes. St-Dalmas, a seventeenth-century farming village amid ski-resort anonymity, has an air of solidity with its fine brick houses, strong wooden balconies, and an arcaded building dated 1655. Jean Alcoy, an affable *prof* sporting a tweed cape, showed me the Romanesque village church which revealed one of the best architectural treats of the trip: a small, intimate, vaulted crypt which had only been unearthed and restored in 1978. It was ten centuries old.

I took a short detour from the D2565 by the D66 to Rimplas, a village perched high above the Tinée valley. Its scruffy, neglected fortress, a relic of the southern section of the Maginot Line which successfully defended the French from the Italians in 1940's brief campaign, offered a 360-degree birds-eye perspective: east to Val de Blore, south along the valley towards Nice, north up the valley towards the popular ski-resort of Isola 2000, and west to an equally perilous village clamped on to the mountainside opposite. Roure – my destination for the night.

After serpenting down the D2565, I turned right on the D2205 at the bottom of the gorge-like valley. A short tunnel through maroon-mauve rocks led to St-Sauveur-sur-Tinée, a good place to stay for trekkers to the ghost village of Valabres, uninhabited but preserved just as it had been when peasant polyculture still thrived in the valley. I crossed the Tinée river on a fragile-looking bridge, serpented up again on the D30 to the turn-off to a scary, one-track cliff road (D130) with tell-tale dents in its crash-barriers. My eyes firmly diverted from the 1,000 foot (305m) precipice, my prayers for no oncoming vehicle rewarded, I arrived at Roure aloft on a sheer cliff high above the Vionène, a tributary of the Tinée.

Ramshackle and dour at first appearance, with brown corrugated iron roofs steep-sloped for snow, Roure was shrouded in a light, grey mist. Unloading the car, I was greeted warmly by an old woman with mauve head shawl, grey stockings, button boots, apron and a St Bernard dog. 'Don't take pictures of our village today,' she said with civic pride. 'Tomorrow the weather will be beautiful.' A European Community flag flew over the seventeenth-century Saint-Laurent church with its unusual triple-bay bell tower undergoing restoration and tiny graveyard packed with building materials. A builder was full of praise for the mayor. 'He's trying to pump some life back into the village,' he said. 'We're not a ski-resort so we depend on summer visitors to the Mercantour Park.' Here, it was an even more delicate balance between visitors and locals than I had encountered in the more prosperous Var.

Auberge Le Robur doesn't need a balcony, because the whole village is one. Twilight at Roure, as the mist rose, was a fine free show: features of forests and valleys fading till just the mountain crests were silhouetted, and the lights of Rimplas on the other side of the Tinée a lone cluster, occasional headlights piercing the gloom of the valley below. I told *la patronne,* Madame Brassard, I found Roure a particularly friendly village. 'We're more open than most mountain people,' she said, 'because we're basically Niçois up here.' As if to prove it, her chef husband Gérard had made a cold-weather *pistou,* the famous Nice vegetable-and-bean soup, normally served in summer with a relish of basil, garlic, olive oil and parmesan. This was like a warming minestrone for a chilly, mountain night.

Next morning I was up early to visit Bernard and Brigitte Masson, sheep farmers, whom the Roure mayor encouraged to bring pastoral life back to his Mercantour commune. On a hair-raising mountain track high above the Tinée valley, I drove to their sheep-fold. Three loudly barking border collies had to be secured before I was allowed out of the car. 'Their bark is worse than their bite,' Masson told me. 'I've got a couple of much more aggres-sive Pyrenean mountain dogs.' 'Frankly, on a dark night, I'd rather meet a wolf,' I said. 'You're right,' he replied. 'A wolf doesn't attack humans unless threatened, only sheep. These dogs will guard my flocks against wolves when I take them to the Longon plateau this summer.'

In the sheepfold, it was the lambing season : 400 vocifer-ous ewes and as many bah-bahing lambs. What were the pros and cons of pastoral life in Mercantour? 'The Park management have made big improvements,' Masson conceded, 'bringing water where there was none, provid-ing enclosures for shearing. We have a good relationship with the management. On the other hand ...' He paused, smiled, and shrugged. 'As President of the Sheepfarmers Association, I'm not saying who brought *canis lupus* back into the Park. Some of my farmers are furious, though.' I had read that they and hunters were threatening to take action – with guns – for the 'liquidation' of the wolves. Was that true?

Again, Masson was guarded. 'Look, a pack of wolves even got down into the village. One of my sheep was killed, four others just disappeared. Last summer, three of us did all-night relays up on the plateau, keeping watch every night. I've seen five wolves in a pack at full moon. By the time we got there, they'd already slaughtered four lambs.' Masson felt sheep farmers were true ecologists, helping keep the Park in trim – on the spot. 'The city folk have nothing to contribute except reports,' he continued, his tone mocking. 'They sit on their backsides in offices, come here for a weekend once a year, sniff the air, and say how lovely and green everything is! We work here.'

In more ways than one, the balance of visitors and locals was delicate. Especially when the visitor is a wolf. The battle rages. Liquidate wolves or sheep farmers? In a bid to find practical cohabitation, a former Minister of the Environment, Corinne Lepage ordered a Commission

Roure aloft on a high cliff

which proposed Mountain Zoning for the wolves: 'There will be places where the wolf is welcome and others not.' Try telling that to a wolf, Madame le Ministre.

VIVE LES LOUPS!?

ROURE TO THE GORGES DE DALUIS

Backtracking on the D130, I rejoined the D30 for a westerly climb up the Vionène valley, between larch-covered slopes, via four short tunnels through purple rock bluffs jutting out over a gorge, to Roubion. There's a one-upmanship about these villages: which is the *most* perched, the *most* clamped on to its mountainside? Now I was looking down on Roure from an even greater height. A white ribbon of road trailed up one side of the valley. The view was like a scale model of mountain reliefs.

In the peace and quiet of Roubion, I was serenaded by fountains; particularly impressive, Fontaine du Mouton's diabolic-looking ram spouted water as though in defiance of a wolf. A lizard was enjoying the sun, while I explored gently stepped alleys and houses with murals of eagles, an eighteenth-century church with two bells at different levels of its castellated tower and, inside, impressive painted plaster of Paris ceilings.

At the top of the Col de la Couillolle (5,503ft/1,677m), a couple of chamois leapt across the road. Further on, the little town of Beuil, guarding the mouth of the Gorges de Cians, was known for its bloody-mindedness. In the eighteenth century, its fiercely independent Grimaldi barons stood up to the House of Savoy, and Hannibal Grimaldi was executed for his pains in 1621. Nowadays, beneath sturdy larch-log roofs with overhangs to protect *souleiaires* (balconies for drying cereals and fruit), the people of Beuil make goat's cheese, not war. Somehow goat's cheese tastes best within sight of the goats, particularly with appetite

In the peace and quiet of Roubion

sharpened on a wide open, sunny plateau with wisps of cloud settling on and rising from Mont Mounier (9,239ft/2,816m), summer home of sheep after the transhumance. Beuil is a centre for all seasons and all sports: flat or mountain skiing, para-gliding, horseback riding, climbing, archery. Not without cultural attributes, either: Chapelle des Penitents Blancs with finely painted *trompe l'oeil* façade, baroque church with painting of the Veronese School.

Winding along the flattish D28 to Valberg, it struck me how few people or cars I had seen since Nice. The difference of population intensity between coast and back country had never been more vividly evident; nor the back country's dependence on tourism. Brave are the Communes that are trying to balance their ecologies with local activities, keeping the land and villages alive with goat's cheese-making and sheep-rearing. Will the young respond, though?

Valberg was once a handful of sturdy chalets to house shepherds during the transhumance. In fifty years, it has proliferated into a sunny winter sports resort, which also attracts summer visitors to the western end of Mercantour. Shortly after Valberg, a *table d'orientation* details the peaks of the Alpes du Sud, first sighted in all their glory on the descent into the Var valley. The 180-degree expanse of snow-covered mountains and forests would be hard to beat, even in the Himalayas or Andes. As it would be my last big mountain view, I feasted on it as an accompaniment to my Beuil goat's cheese.

The D28 joins the D2202 at the bottom of the valley near Guillaumes, a medieval garrison town; later, the town shuttled between the Counts of Provence, the kings of France, and the House of Savoy to the chagrin of its inhabitants, obliged to change loyalties with each occupation. They are resigned to foreign influence. Nowadays, Ingo

On the descent into the Var valley

and Beate Langenbach at the Ferme-Auberge du Traouc follow Austrian philosopher Rudolf Steiner's theories of biodynamic agriculture, strictly observing the ascendent and descendent phases of the moon. The proof is in the Langenbachs' wholewheat bread, baked with *épeautre* (spelt – a Provençal mountain cereal particularly good in soup) and served to their guests with dishes all made from organically produced ingredients. Healthily restored, you can set out from here to explore the western end of Mercantour.

The Var river, once the natural border between Provence and Savoy, is wide, pebbly and fast-running. Tough kayakers were preparing for a rough-and-tumble through the Gorges de Daluis, a narrow defile of oddly coloured and surrealistically shaped rock formations 260 million years old. Arthur Rackam country, this, Gothic but not sinister. Descending traffic on the D2202 goes through a series of one-way tunnels; upward-bound, you get the view, as the road splits and goes round the outside of each tunnelled bluff. Whether upward or downward bound, there are plenty of stopping places for photo opportunities. A British film crew were making a television documentary called *Bridges*; they'd certainly picked a good one in Pont des Roberts, a single metal arc straddling the Var at the upstream entrance of the gorge. 'Nice work,' we all agreed. We could hardly complain about the traffic, either, directed when necessary by a couple of *flics* for the film crew's benefit: only one bus and a mail van passed during my twenty-minute stop.

A few miles after the Gorges de Daluis, I crossed the border into the *départment* of Alpes de Haute-Provence. Already, the mountains were getting smaller. My alps had already been crossed. Like Hannibal's elephants, I would never forget it.

OVERNIGHT AND EATING OUT IN THE ALPS

TH = Table d'Hôtes (guest house with dinner)
CH = Chambre d'Hôtes (bed and breakfast only)

North of Nice, food and hotels tend to be simple, more for feeding hungry skiiers and trekkers than gastronomes. Places of character and charm are few and far between.

Le Bellevue at Falicon, apart from its stunning panorama of the Nice hills, has particularly good Provençal starters like sardines stuffed with Swiss chard and pinenuts and a warm *bavaroise* of vegetables and scampi, followed by classic French main courses. At Coaraze, Auberge du Soleil, a real village inn with panoramic terrace, reminded me: for reasonably priced overnighting with local atmosphere, look for the Logis de France sign.

At the Col de Turini, L'Aiga Blanca is a reliable head-of-the-pass chalet hotel, whereas the Grand Hotel du Parc has a certain period charm and a garden at La Bollène-Vésubie.

In need of sustenance or a bed on reaching the junction of the D70 and D2565, take a detour left for a mile or so to Lantosque where L'Ancienne Gendarmerie is the best hotel for miles, though it's by no means grand, being an old police station with a restaurant overlooking the Vésubie valley (salt cod raviolis, home-smoked salmon, quails with foie gras). Cheaper is the cosy Auberge du Bon Puits. Both are convenient for the Mercantour National Park, as is La Bonne Auberge at St-Martin-Vésubie (see p.122) where most friendly service provides terrine of grouper, trout *meunière*, duckling with olives or quail casserole.

Simple but comfortable alpine stopovers with food, in interesting places, are the nine-room Auberge des Murès at St-Dalmas, convenient for winter and summer sports; St-Saveur's hotel-restaurant Le Relais d'Auron, at the bottom of the Tinée valley; and the precipitously placed Auberge de Robur at Roure (see p.126).

The biggest ski-resort on my route is Valberg. Hôtel Le Chastellan, on the main square, is a seven-room family hotel,

La Bonne Auberge at St-Martin-Vésubie

open winter and summer; more unusually for a Provençal ski-resort where food tends to be Savoyard (*raclette* and *fondus*), there's a gourmet restaurant, Côté Jardin, serving *croustillant* of scallops, oysters and mushrooms, and duck breast with spiced orange.

The more adventurous will head for a night or two at Ferme-Auberge du Traouc (TH), near Guillaumes, where Ingo Langenbach farms the biodynamic raw materials for his wife Beate's delicious Swiss chard lasagne, *beignets*, and baked vegetables. Everything you eat - charcuterie, meat, cheese, vegetables, fruit and jam - is home-produced.

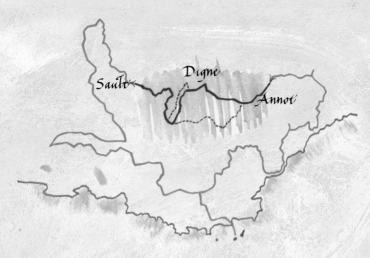

Chapter 6

PANORAMAS WITHOUT PEOPLE

ALPES DE HAUTE-PROVENCE

As writer Jean Giono, native of Manosque, said: 'The production must have cost God an arm and a leg.' Dramatic scenery of high plateaux, snow-covered mountains, deep gorges, seen on back roads such as the D20 from Norante to Digne-les-Bains (far right). Napoleon took this route on his return from Elba and stayed overnight at Malijai château (above right). An unusual feature of the 'production' is Les Pénitents rock formation (below right), with its erotic legend.

GORGES DE DALUIS TO DIGNE

Where did all the people go? This is the first impression of Alpes de Haute-Provence, one of the least populated *départments* in France. Although not exactly as empty as Australia, it does have equally dramatic scenery of high plateaux, distant snow-covered mountains, deep green gorges and wide open spaces bisected by the wild, once untameable Durance river. Views extend forever over lavender fields, forests rich in mushrooms and sleepy villages where television creates an anxiety among its ageing inhabitants that life has passed them by. Then, another slow look at their terrain and a breath of their scintillating, clean air, compared to soulless, polluted city life seen on the box, and they take heart: nowhere in France is more majestically unspoiled. As Jean Giono, native of Manosque, said: 'The production must have cost God an arm and a leg.'

Just south of the Gorges de Daluis where the Var and Couloump valleys meet, I turned right from the D2202 on to the N202, the old Roman road which cut through the mountain valleys of Provincia linking oppidums at Cimiez (Nice) and Dinia (Digne-les-Bains). A rail track runs beside the road. No ordinary rail track, either. It carries the *train des pignes* (fir-cone train), an affectionate name still used because the old steam train from Nice to Digne went so slowly you could pick up fir cones for your home fire or feed the engine. I followed the rail track as it wound between mountains hardly high enough to be called Alps, and reached Annot by a short branch right (D908) from the N202.

Often, places I hadn't expected much from revealed intriguing secrets. Annot was one. The station is like a nineteenth-century doll's house with not a soul to be seen, nor a distant whistle to be heard. A snow-plough was taking a lunch-break, so was the booking office. With only four trains a day, it's the quietest place in a quiet town. The wide, straight main street – betting shop, pizzeria, souvenirs and an old coaching inn, Hôtel de l'Avenue – does not prepare you for the medieval Gran' Rue which twists and turns, ups and downs through an untouristy Old Town. Annot is part Provençal, part Piedmontese. Piedmont consists of the foothills on the Italian side of the Alps, and many of its builders emigrated to Provence to find work. Annot's earliest houses, in rue Notre-Dame, have the name of the builder carved in stone in Gothic type, together with the date, '1484' or '1533'. The town has an alpine feel, yet the elegance of its sculptured wood doors and a seventeenth-century arcaded house would pass muster in Aix-en-Provence.

The parish church, under the protection of Niçois St-Pons, has typical Provençal twin belfries. At the door there is a request for a donation towards the *minuterie* (timed lighting), if you want to see its pitch dark interior. The lighting, however, was too feeble, the timing too fast for me to find the collecting box, and each time I restarted the *minuterie* to look for it, the lights would go out leaving me stumbling about in darkness. I gave up, only to be confronted with another hazard: a sudden tidal wave swept down the Gran' Rue towards me, and I sprang into a doorway. 'They do this twice a week,' explained a man who had taken refuge with me. 'They open a sluice-gate to clean the street. We're used to wet feet.'

On the edge of town, a welcome dry path led between orchards sprinkled with primroses and violets, crossed the railway line and reached the Chapel of Notre Dame de Vers-la-Ville. Our Lady Facing-the-Town does so from a circus of dramatic sculpted rock formations, known to geologists as *grès d'Annot* (Annot sandstone); one resembled an eagle's beak. From this vantage point, the town

THE FIR-CONE TRAIN

Train buffs will park their cars for a day or so for an unforgettable experience. Though the affectionate name has stayed, the regular service of the *train des pignes* is no longer steam-powered – either by coal or fir-cone. Four times a day between Nice and Digne, the Fir-Cone Train takes just over three hours to do 90 narrow-gauge miles (144km) in smart, blue-and-white diesel rail-cars, sometimes with dining facilities.

Its motto is musical: *andante ma non troppo*. Moving but not too fast. On its scenic journey, it negotiates 27 tunnels, 16 viaducts, and 15 bridges. After chuntering through the streets of Nice, it zigzags from one side of the Var river to the other, heads up towards snow-covered summits and snakes across fragrant plains, plunges into darkness then out into sunlight, seduces the eye with one splendid vista after another – without having to keep the other eye on the road.

The Chemins de Fer de la Provence offer 60 'works of art' to be viewed on the way, so you can stop off for a look at, among others, an altar table decorated by Ludovic Bréa at Villars-sur-Var's church; a Maillol statue of a naked woman in chains at Puget-Théniers; Vauban's fortifications at Entrevaux; or, in the mushroom seasons, get permission to go looking for *ceps* or *chanterelles*

At Annot station, a snow-plough was taking a lunch break

from the Mayors of Saint-Benoit or Annot.

From May to October, holiday-makers flock to the old steam Fir-Cone Train. Its 1909 locomotive (classed *monument historique*!) and clattering wooden coaches run – or, more accurately, waddle – between Annot and Puget-Théniers (12 miles [19km] in just over an hour); and special excursions wheeze and creak as far as St-André-les-Alpes and Digne. It's well worth the occasional smut in the eye, as you lean out of the window to take snaps of the Alpes du Sud.

For the gourmet-and-gorge alternative route from the Lac de Castillon to Manosque, turn left on to the D955 just before St-Julien-du-Verdon. Surrounded by mountains, Castellane has excellent value-for-money at the slightly kitschy Commerce which is renowned for its sauces (also Sisteron lamb and chocolate cream); and at the Auberge du Point Sublime (D952, turn right on to the D317), well-named for its perched terrace with a superb view of the Gorges du Verdon while eating your morel omelette or local river trout.

Continuing high above the grand canyon on the D952, then by the D23 loop, you catch glimpses in summer of enviable bathers and pedalo-peddling couples enjoying the calm, emerald green water between the Verdon's spectacularly plunging cliffs. At the western end of the gorge (back on the D952), Lac de Ste-Croix reservoir appears on your left before arriving at Moustiers-Ste-Marie, star turn of this route. Never mind the well-known faïence and limpet-like hillside position spanning an ocre crevasse with rushing torrent, Moustiers' trump card is without doubt La Bastide de Moustiers. I had to book three months ahead for an October reservation. Alain Ducasse, chef of Monte Carlo's Le Louis XV, masterminded its luxury farmhouse ambience and strictly non-chichi service which he has now entrusted to colleague Benoit Witz. Terraced pool, olive grove, and only twelve individually styled rooms. Their high price is balanced by a single 280 franc menu, changing frequently according to the market and kitchen garden: for instance, salad with marinaded anchovies, farm rabbit with baked vegetables, cheeses from the plateau de Valensole, crispy strawberry sticks with vanilla ice cream. *Ça vaut le détour.*

On the D952 at Roumoules, a cheaper alternative is seventeenth-century Le Vieux Castel (TH) where the Comettis wine and dine you royally. A mile or so further on, Riez is the oldest town in Alpes de Haute-Provence, with a fifth-century Christian baptistery from Gallo-Roman times. Original, simple food is to be had at Auberge des Abeilles (tomato polenta with country sausage and egg). After crossing the lavender and wheatfields of the Plateau of Valensole by the D6 – with a stop at Valensole for its fountains and seventeenth-century houses – you meet up with the D907 that takes you to Manosque.

church's fine Renaissance tower with four Evangelist statues makes a film-decor centrepiece for a French historical drama, with houses clustered round it like limpets.

Backtracking on the D908, I continued on the N202 towards Digne. A few miles further on, alpine features returned: Norway pines in the Forêt Domaniale de Chamatte, a forested pass Col de Toutes Aures (3,686ft/1,124m), La Sommet de la Bernarde still covered with snow (6,366ft/1,940m), and a romantic Romanesque chapel (Notre-Dame-de-Valvert), solitary in a meadow just before Vergons. Then, round a bend appeared the vivid emerald green waters of Lac de Castillon in the Verdon valley. Just another of many man-made water-works – dams, canals, lakes – in the postwar development of industry and tourism. Unfortunately, it feels artificial. St-Julien-du-Verdon, enticing as it appears on its lakeside hill, is a disappointingly character-less village when you get there. To be fair, early spring with no action is hardly the time to judge it; the lake has shallow bathing and fine sandy beaches, perfect for parents with small children who prefer cool air and open spaces to grilling with other sardines on a packed Riviera beach.

Just before St-Julien, a left turn on to the D955 begins a substantial alternative route to Manosque via Castellane, the Gorges du Verdon, Moustiers-Ste-Marie where a gastro-nomic stopover awaits the discerning traveller (see p.136).

The wild country that Napoleon allegedly passed through

It was a close call. As I had never been to Digne, the departmental capital, I continued on the N202 north up the Verdon valley along the lakeside. St-André-les-Alpes, at the head of the lake, is a centre for *sportifs* of all persua-sions. Messrs J. Raoust or D. Liautaud will take you canyoning or mountaineering on climbs of medium height. The Club Nautique de Castillon teaches wind-surfing and sailing. And, for a truly poetic experience, 'Aerogliss' free-flight school will take you para-gliding. St-André is the para-gliding (parachute) and hang-gliding (wings) centre of Provence, owing to perfect air-current conditions in its basin of hills and flat landing places in emergency. Avoid the lake, though. Landing on a wind-surfer is not popular. Less adventurous *sportifs* will be happier cycling and

horseback riding in the Parc Naturel Régional du Verdon. Or strolling to the Chalet summit (two hours) where you can watch para-gliders take off; along the Route Impériale to Moriez (three hours); or, more strenuously following the mountainous Crêtes des Serres from La Mure village (four hours).

The Fir-Cone Train's track once again ran alongside the N202. Barrême's railway station, apart from its hospitable café-hotel, has a little geological museum with a permanent Exhibition of Fossils, presented by the enterprising Chemins de Fer de la Provence. Sites in the Asse de Cloumanc valley show that it was once covered by a warm tropical sea which was violently disturbed by the rising of the Alps. St-Lions' fossil reef, dating from about 35 million years ago, is a site where coral and sea-urchins flourished.

Thus encouraged, I made an hour's round-trip detour (D119) to the hamlet of St-Jacques, sleuthing the nearby nummilite site. Nummilites are micro-fossils only observable with a magnifying glass (bring your own!). It was an eerily quiet walk with distant views of Digne's hinterland of pre-Alps, the country rough and the vegetation poor. At the site, ten minutes' walk from the village, a flow of lava seemed to have been petrified and smoothed over millions of years. A lunar landscape. Some animal fossils grew to a size still visible to the naked eye, apparently. Not to my naked eye, however. Without a geologist with you as well as a magnifying glass, you must be content with the awe-inspiring reminder of just how long Provence has been around.

More recently – March 1815, to be precise – Napoleon stayed at Barrême, and a plaque on a modest house opposite a willow-tree in the main street marks the spot. His star was in the descendant. After defeat by the Allies and banishment to Elba, he made a brave attempt to re-instate himself. The ex-Emperor followed what is now known as the Route Napoléon from Golfe-Juan, where he landed from Elba to a hostile reception, as far as Grenoble, where he was greeted triumphantly with cries of *Vive l'Empereur!* His secret, mountainous route towards Paris made a gruelling journey: with the easier route to Paris via the Rhône valley rife with enemies, he settled for a secret mountainous route, much of it over rough mule tracks. It took him seven days just to reach Grenoble. 'The Eagle will fly from bell-tower to bell-tower,' declared Napoleon with typical panache, 'until he reaches the towers of Notre Dame.' Triumphant return was short-lived, however. After the glorious Hundred Days, he was defeated at Waterloo and exiled for good – to St Helena where he died.

At Barrême, three rivers Clumanc, Rieux, and Moriez come together to make the Asse, and it was here that I

Forests nestling below the stark Montagne de Coupe range

turned right on to the Route Napoléon (now the N85). Five minutes of its heavier traffic was enough. I even deserted the Fir-Cone Train, whose track ran beside it, to follow what is now considered to be Napoleon's real route from Norante to Digne – up and over the hills. Like an imperial eagle, I swooped right – from a highway fit for an emperor to a country bumpkin of a lane (D20). The wild country that Napoleon allegedly passed through revealed prairies and orchards and forests nestling below the stark Montagne de Coupe range, its grey *barres* marked with strata lines. The hamlet of Chaudon was just a cow house and a couple of cottages. Pines sprouted from curiously coloured rocks – grey, green, mauve, and orange.

Descending from the Col de Corobin (4,034ft/1,230m), which is sometimes closed in winter, I caught further glimpses of cross-hatched strata on strangely shaped rocks, and distant, hazy blue mountains. The Forêt Domaniale de Cousson, recently replanted, looks like virgin forest. Inaugurated by another enterprising country mayor at Chaudon-Norante, the Domaine de la Clappe development includes a little ranch with good-looking horses. This is great walking country, too, its awe-inspiring silence suddenly broken by the whisper of a gentle breeze in fir trees. Then a wooded valley closes in for the approach to Digne's secret back door – and a strange sight it is.

ALEXANDRA AND TORTOISE

Visitors expecting the Baths of Digne-les-Bains to have the architectural splendours of the Pump Room in Bath or the faded elegance of Montecatini Terme in Tuscany will be disappointed. As I came down a quiet, enchanted valley road (D20), a mass of parked cars broke the spell. On my right, senior citizens were to be seen among flower beds and lush verdure, entering and leaving a long modern building with orange and blue trimmings. Pale they arrived, pink they emerged.

The Thermal Establishment, used in its time by such VIPs as Egyptian astronomer Ptolemy and French King Louis XVI, has now become high-tech but retains some of the past glories of social spas. Taking the waters at Digne in the old days, you gambled and danced and cheated on your diet; and, as late as the fifties, the 'Miss Lower Alps' Beauty Contest was held there. People of Alpes de Haute-Provence love their beauty contests: there's even a 'Miss Mule', held annually since 1923 at Seyne-les-Alpes to choose the prettiest mule in the Blanche valley.

Though the present management have incorporated a Belle Epoque-style Salon de Thé, the thermal theme park provides every sort of contemporary therapeutic distraction for its 10,000 visitors a year: guided hikes, Provençal cookery courses, work-outs, chess competitions, even surfing on Internet.

From St-Pancrace's Cliff, hot water springs once bubbled at 42 degrees – highly mineralized and slightly radioactive. Nowadays two wells – one called Dinia after the city's Roman name, the other Ophelia after a Mayor's grand-daughter – provide 11,878 gallons (54,000 litres) an hour. Most popular in autumn, when regulars come for a pre-winter boost, the waters of Dinia benefit those with breathing problems, while Ophelia's sulphurous, chloritic, sodaic, calcic warmth soothes rheumatic pains.

Frankly, I found L'Etablissement Thermal a bit gloomy for a sunny Saturday in Provence. And I have a suspicion Alexandra and Tortoise would have agreed.

Alexandra David-Néel, in spite of her Anglo-Saxon sounding name (most people forget the é) was a courageous Frenchwoman and explorer whose last years were spent at Digne because the surrounding mountains, distantly snow-capped, reminded her of the Himalayas.

Tortoise was the nickname she gave to her companion, secretary and biographer, Marie-Madeleine Peyronnet, who now greeted me at Samten Dzong (Fortress of Meditation), a Tibetan-style house incongruously sitting opposite a Total Service Station in what are now modern Digne suburbs on the Nice road (N85).

'Visitors often ask me where I'm buried,' said Tortoise with a caustic laugh. 'They can't believe I'm still alive, because Alexandra died in 1969. You see, I was only 28 when I joined her, Alexandra was already 91.'

Alexandra David-Néel Foundations's witty and erudite guide was the antithesis of her nickname, given her ironically by Alexandra because of her speedy efficiency. When writing and reading became difficult for the old lady, Tortoise tried to persuade her to wear glasses. 'Get me a stronger light-bulb!' was Alexandra's reply. In the tiny Buddhist temple, Tortoise was careful to emphasize that Alexandra had not been a practising Buddhist but embraced its philosophy of compassion and loving kindness – also its humour – during her travels. A Tibetan Lama had once said to her: 'Naturally, you Westerners know all about motor cars, but how surprising to find one who knows so much about spirituality!'

Opera-singer daughter of a wealthy Norman property developer called David, she married a man called Néel who long-sufferingly accepted her absence on endurance-test voyages to Ceylon, India, Nepal, Burma and China. Her greatest adventure was to penetrate Tibet and its capital Llasa, then a protectorate of the British. For other Westerners, it was a forbidden city. Disguised as a beggar, Alexandra became friendly with Buddhist monks and herself carried out the traditional two-year solitary retreat in a cave. 'Get that damned Frenchwoman out of her cave!' said British officials.' She's letting the side down dreadfully.' She stayed.

ANCIENT DIGNE

Digne-les-Bains, as capital of Alpes de Haute-Provence, has many places more interesting to penetrate other than its thermal baths. The Old Town clusters around St-Jérôme cathedral (1490) with tortuous alleys and steep inclines. An imposing belltower, built a century later, has a typical wrought-iron Provençal casing to let the wind through. A nearby thirteenth-century well is glassed over so you can safely peer into its depths. More impressive than the cathedral is the Romanesque Notre-Dame du Bourg, a short stroll to the outskirts on Bld St-J. de Chrysostome. Its interior has fine, if dilapidated, vaulting.

Return via the moss-covered Grande Fontaine, green and cooling on a hot day, to nineteenth-century Place Gassendi where a vast market takes place on Saturday. Particularly good local products to look out for are goat's cheese and charcuterie from Thoard, essence of lavender from Barras and biological bread from Mallemoisson.

At the Geological Centre, you can find out more about the many prehistoric discoveries in the region. The Departmental Museum, celebrating local achievement, is appropriately situated on Boulevard Gassendi, named like the square for Pierre Gassendi, Dignois of many parts (theologian, physician, mathematician, naturalist, astronomer). With five Gassendis in one, Digne cannot complain of a lack of local celebrities.

TH = Table d'Hôtes (guest house with dinner)
CH = Chambre d'Hôtes (bed and breakfast only)

Annot is between Provence and the Alps and, with no skiing, hotels only open April – October. At L'Avenue, ceiling fans shift the stuffy summer heat of your room, all part of the period charm; the value-for-money restaurant serves delicious prawn raviolis, knuckle of veal with preserved garlic and aubergine lasagne, and fillet of sea bream with puréed celery.

Auberge du Parc at St-André-les-Alpes is a cosy, cheapish stopover sporting boar's heads and a log fire in the restaurant (hare stew and duck breast with *sanguins* mushrooms). Home-cookers will appreciate the little kitchens with the rooms chez Raymonde and Georges Neveu (CH) at Angles, 5 miles (8km) out of town by the N202 and D33.

Digne-les-Bains has a choice for all pockets but no *grande luxe*. Top end is the central Grand Paris in a seventeenth-century monastery with vast rooms and a terrace shaded by plane trees; Jean-Jacques Ricaud's classic country cooking includes saddle of rabbit, filets of wild pigeon and sweetbreads in an orange sauce. Villa Gaïa is a good alternative in a garden on the Nice road (N85) with quieter rooms. Arguably the best bet in town is L'Origan, a restaurant with eight simple rooms, living up to its herby name (oregano) in its cuisine (snail soup with rosemary, soufflé of goat's cheese with *tapenade*, red mullet with chives, stuffed veal, almond cream).

Near Les Mées (south on the D4) Le Mas des Oliviers (CH) is a comfortable modern villa in an olive grove. The Vergers provide three ways of making tea (basket, pot, or bag) and bacon and eggs for breakfast. At Dabisse the Vieux Colombier is good for a nice, slow on-the-road lunch, while *the* overnight stop on the left bank of the Durance is La Fuste (p.146) just beyond Villedieu, providing great country cooking of super fresh products: truffles with garden vegetables, *denti* (a fish of the sea bream family) roasted with juniper and orange with spelt risotto, and spicy fillet of beef *en croûte*.

Great country cooking of super fresh products

Tortoise took us round fascinating memorabilia. 'Her handbags weren't exactly Hermès,' she said, showing us battered bags of every shape and size, an old Ciné Kodak Eight movie camera, camping tables, photographs of Alexandra, sturdy and determined, in Tibetan costume with bearers and pack-animals, tattered passports, an international driving-licence. 'She was driving herself across deserts at 67, at a time when women were considered to be old by 40!' Also, there was a beautifully woven mandala from Southern India and a Tibetan throne with framed photo of the Dalai-Lama who had once visited the house at Digne. Since Alexandra's death at 101, the Foundation has also supported Tibetans in exile.

DIGNE TO LES MÉES

To leave Digne, the quiet D12 branches right off the N85 along the Bléone river's left bank. Smug on my traffic-free backroad, I caught sight of trucks and cars wedded to their Route Napoléon on the other side. Between back road and river was a peaceful, well-designed public park, the banks of its fishing lake planted with baby palm-trees and lavender.

Headed south-west towards the Durance valley, low hills and gentler slopes appeared for the first time since Var. It was strange to travel without mountains. Not dull, just blander: green fields, cows with calves, horses, even a golf course handy for the new homes and fledgling gardens of

Digne commuters. There was an air of solid bourgeois prosperity that I had not encountered since Nice.

The D12 becomes the D8 by which I crossed the Bléone to take a look at Malijai château on the right bank. The epitome of Age of Reason architecture, the eighteenth-

century château issues enlightenment from every well-ordered feature. Pale pink austerity outside, inside it indulges in a little elegant flamboyance: Louis XV painted scrolls, shells, cameos, and musical instruments adorn the walls. Hardly fitting for the rugged plight of Napoleon who spent a night there as guest of the owner Adrien Noguier, while a loyal officer galloped ahead to see if it was safe to continue to Sisteron, the next town north.

Beyond Malijai, the Bléone joins the Durance. The second river of Provence after the Rhône, the Durance at this confluence flows south along a dramatically wide, fertile valley. Suddenly, to my left on the D4, appeared the valley's most singular rock formations, Les Pénitents des Mées. Rising over 300 feet (90m) along the left-bank's forested hills, each bare, pointed reddish rock resembles a hooded penitent.

A nice legend surrounds The Penitents. In the ninth century, Saracens from North Africa occupied the valley's eastern slopes. Local barons attacked and defeated them, and among prisoners at the castle of Les Mées were seven scantily clad, voluptuous Moorish houris. One look at such desirable beauty and even the monks were hard put to keep their vows of chastity; so over-excited did they become that their Prior could only save them from sin by turning them to stone. The rocks are both suitably penitential and appropriately phallic.

DANGER DURANCE!

'I've learned to mistrust the Durance' is the wise counsel of Nicole Bertrand whose book-and-stationery shop at Les Mées was fatally flooded in 1994 when years of effort were wiped out in a matter of minutes. It was not all bad news, though. 'We owe everything to the Durance – rich soil, beautiful countryside, and stones to build our houses with. She certainly holds us to ransom for it!' In prehistoric times, diluvian rains alternating with glacial ice gave the Penitents their shape. In the eighteenth century, the stalwart men of Les Mées built a tunnel through the rocks to divert the Combe (a tributary of the Durance) torrents which regularly flooded the town – to little effect. Trial by water was nothing new.

It was Palm Sunday. A service was being held outside the church, priest and congregation carrying local sprigs of olive instead of palm leaves. It had an unintentionally pagan symbolism: olive-branches for peace with the town's river. Meanwhile, on the sleepy village square under the plane-trees, men of little faith played *boules*, men of a different faith gathered in groups to gossip in Arabic. Mahgrébins congregate in the cafés because there's work to be found in the vast, agro-industrial fruit and cereal farms of the valley.

To appreciate the Durance's dangers, I decided to get a bird's-eye view of it. Outside the village, a steep path zigzags through Aleppo pines, juniper bushes and *garrigue*. The sun was high, the warm air scented with thyme and pine. On such an unseasonably hot day, I wouldn't have been surprised to hear the first cicada in spring, but it was too early in the year for even a tentative chirrup. The cicada is the emblematic winged insect of Provence, its song the anthem of the south. *Fai pas bon travaia quand la cigalo canta,* say the Provençals. It's not good to work when the cicada sings, because it's too hot. A fable of La Fontaine has the improvident cicada doing nothing but sing all summer and not providing for winter. The reverse is true: the *tsrk-tsrk* of the male rubbing his thorax is an energetic serenade to attract the female; after resisting him quite a while, the seduced female perforates a branch to hide her eggs. But that was for later in the year ...

Mopping sweat from my eyes, I focused on The Penitents' pointed peaks as they stood in line between me and La Durance below. 'Bitch of a river! I hate her,' declared Madame de Sévigné, the witty and acerbic seventeenth-century letter writer. Old Father Thames and Ole Man River can be difficult at times, but La Durance is capriciously feminine. From these magnificent heights, on such a glorious day, she seemed to be in the best of moods. It was a good place to ponder her maverick life.

Temperamental, schizophrenic Durance separates from herself into wayward reaches which rejoin, separate again,

Les Pénitents – each bare, pointed rock resembles a hooded penitent

A bird's eye view of La Durance from Les Pénitents

rejoin, so you never know quite which part of her is going where. Pebbly, scrubby islands lie in between. On just such an island Aurélie, the baker's equally wayward wife, and her Piedmontese shepherd, Dominique, had their passionate idyll in Marcel Pagnol's screen version of Jean Giono's story *La Femme du Boulanger.* Making love on a Durance island must have been very uncomfortable. No wonder Aurélie returned to her baker.

When snows melted on the High Alps and spring rains added to the hazard, the Durance was a wild beast whose roar was like the end of the world. 'When she flooded,' wrote Giono, 'it began with a distant silence stretching to the furthest easterly horizon as though someone were holding their breath. Then the thunder began ...' The 1960 Serre-Ponçon dam helped considerably – though not entirely, as 1994's floods proved – to tame the wild beast. But tame a wild beast and part of her dies. Less water

means less fish; eels have completely disappeared. For fishermen, it's a disaster area. Yet some fauna have diversified with the lack of flooding. Herons and cormorants flourish, as do migratory birds. Like so much of progress, it's both good and bad.

Pondering the river's duality, I descended between the pitted limestone rocks and razor-sharp summits of the Penitents, with tantalizing glimpses of the valley's fields and wooded hills above the right bank. They reminded me of a great hotel-restaurant La Bonne Etape just over the river at Château-Arnoux; and Ganagobie, an exquisite tenth-century priory hidden in the woods on top of the escarpment. I decided to make it an alternative route for those who, hopefully, follow in my footsteps (see page 148),

Continuing south on the D4, I stopped at Dabisse to join the browsers and bargain hunters at an animated *brocante* (flea market), when my eye was once again attracted to the hills on the other side of the valley. What was that enticing little perched village catching the morning sun? Returning to the car, I looked at my map. Lurs.

It was hard to associate so charmingly situated a village with such a bloody event as the Drummond murders, which happened in the valley below Lurs in August 1952. This was the darker side of Provence, redolent of peasant intrigue and violence. Doubt has often been cast about the guilt of farmer Gaston Dominici, convicted murderer of Sir Jack Drummond, a British dietician, his wife and 12-year-old daughter, Elizabeth, at their camp site by the main Manosque–Digne road.

The Drummonds went to the nearby Dominici farm for a bucket of water. Later, Gaston was worried that he had left an irrigation sluice-gate open near the Drummond camp site and, carrying an old American army rifle, went to check. He was drunk. When Gaston made advances to Lady Drummond, Sir Jack went to her defence. In the struggle, the gun went off. Sir Jack was killed and, fearing that there were witnesses, Gaston shot Lady Drummond and battered Elizabeth with the rifle. She later died of the wounds.

That was the official story.

Attending the grim trial in Digne, Jean Giono later wrote a book based on his belief that Gaston was not the murderer. It was simply not in the character of an old Provençal patriarch, whatever he might do to a treacherous neighbour, to murder innocent campers in cold blood. With Giono's penchant for classical Greek tragedy, Gaston and his two sons, Gustave and Clovis, were perhaps trapped inexorably in a plot by the sons to plant a crime on an ageing, irresponsible, dictatorial head of the family to get rid of him.

Whatever the truth, one thing I do know for certain. In 1948, I myself had camped under the stars by the Durance river at Orgon with nothing to fear but mosquitoes. I would never do so again. The Drummond murders gave impromptu camping a bad name, wherever in the world and however bright the stars.

Manosque's medieval
Porte Saunerie

DABISSE TO MANOSQUE

As I continued south on the D4, the alluvial plain of the Durance valley was a carpet of blossom. Apples, pears, peaches and nectarines alternate with wheat and maize; fields are watered by jets pumped from the depths of the much-plundered water table. On either side of the road, row after row of fruit trees were trained to grow on special supports with an an ingenious anti-frost device. When a late frost threatens spring buds, trees are sprinkled with water before the frost strikes and the frozen capsules protect the buds with heat – like mini igloos.

Oraison is a bustling plain town, centre of the surrounding farming community. Handsome wrought-iron balconies adorn its main street; especially fine is the one above the Maison de la Presse-Tabac. After Oraison, the busy D4 became narrower and quieter, as I wiggled up and down again for a short, very pretty stretch of the Parc Naturel Régional du Verdon on the edge of the valley. It was a relief to drive through woods and valleys and meadows again after all that dauntingly efficient large-scale agriculture. Villedieu's unexploited countryside reveals a hotel-restaurant of rare quality. Run by the Jourdan-Bucaille family, La Fuste is an upmarket auberge with flower-and-vegetable garden, almond trees and backdrop of wooded hills (see page 142).

After a right-turn on to the D907 just beyond La Fuste, I bridged the Durance, with a sidelong glance at her ugly

The citadel hill, Forcalquier

Another tempting alternative route follows the right bank of the Durance where three considerable treats are worth the heavier traffic.

At Malijai, you get back on the N85 (Route Napoléon) and cross the Durance at Château-Arnoux where the Gleize family create gastronomic marvels of local products at La Bonne Etape. Since I first went to the famous hotel-restaurant in 1986 and tasted such delicacies as duck with lavender honey and courgette flowers flavoured with herbs from the hotel garden, they have started A Goût du Jour, a value-for-money bistrot next door to the grand restaurant. The bistrot is the baby of Jany Gleize, son of Pierre and Arlette. In a particularly relaxed ambiance, you're regaled with anchovy fillets marinated in fennel, rabbit with savoury, veal roasted with thyme, and a creamy strawberry tart.

Thus replete, proceed south on the N96 to the right-turn (D30) to Ganagobie. The lane winds up from the valley to the Ganagobie plateau through lush woods, providing welcome shade in summer from the Durance's relentless glare. The tenth-century priory, founded by the monks of Cluny in Burgundy, is one of the unmissable Romanesque sites in Provence. Although only Notre-Dame church of the rich architectural ensemble is open to the public, the cloisters are visitable by special arrangement. Early Benedictine austerity relaxes later with a magnificent stone-carved portal showing Christ and the Apostles, a rich mosaic floor, and zodiacal wild beasts on a frieze round the altar. From the belvedere at the end of the wide, leafy Monks' Alley, the aerial view across the Durance stretches to the Plateau de Valensole and pre-Alps beyond Digne.

Lurs – the third treat on the Durance's right bank – is reached by backtracking on the D30, turning right just before the main N96, and climbing to the perched village. Jutting out on a spur, Lurs is blessed with views over Durance olive groves one way, the wheatfields of Forcalquier the other. A village of great charm, it particularly attracts artisans and artists; at the end of August *Les Rencontrers de Lurs*, an annual seminar founded by distinguished typographer Maximilien Vox, reunites professionals of various graphic arts. A lovely Provençal family restaurant, La Bello Visto, serves *petits gris de Provence* snails, lamb grilled with thyme and honey, and goat's cheese in puff pastry.

Continue down from the village, turn left onto the D12 and almost immediately right onto the N96 to join the main route at Manosque.

bed, pebbly and rambling and shallow. Then, crossing Autoroute A51 and the N96 with relief at all that traffic avoided, I found myself face to face with Manosque's medieval Porte Saunerie, one of the finest gateways in Provence. Its Romanesque gallery topped by turrets with sturdy castellation led to a very special section of my journey.

GIONO COUNTRY

When I first encountered his great talent in 1985, Manosque-born writer Jean Giono was comparatively unknown to English readers; even in France, Giono's popularity was not as widespread as Marcel Pagnol's. Ten years later, the centenary of both authors' births, the writing-tables had turned and it was Giono who stole the limelight. Critics and public welcomed a revaluation of his mythic, vanished, peasant Provence of the uplands. Now you can't open a tourist brochure or magazine article without its mandatory Giono quotes.

Giono grew up before the First World War when peasant society still prospered. At No. 14 Grande Rue in the Old Town, I found his childhood house and plaque declaring 'with the magic of his romantic creations he honoured his native town where he lived all his life and died'. He needed no other. Although Pagnol tried to persuade him to go to Paris to work on screen adaptations of his work, Giono never did. And, of the two authors, his is the more authentic voice.

His father, an artisan of Piedmontese origin, gave him an intensive course in the sensuality of nature – flora, fauna, and human – and a solid grounding in the Classics. Giono's writing is never nostalgic; he hated that hankering for illusory good old days. Equally, he hated the greed of modern Provence, the shimmering images of petro-

chemical plants round the Etang de Berre and the Riviera's 'open-air whorehouse'. Giono, 'the joyful pessimist', was his own man, an original, his Provence a tableau of invention, neither past nor present, timeless, anarchic, deeply physical. His conmen, craftsmen, clowns, aristos, murderers, peasants, prostitutes, dreamers live round their days and years with inevitability, a noble fatalism.

The Giono family, in every generation, was close-knit. At St-Sauveur church a baptism echoed it. In the darkened nave, it was like a Dutch painting: the priest lighting candles for children to hold, while a guitarist sang and the mother with baby had family grouped intimately round her. Giono's descriptions of Manosque have the same intimacy:

This beautiful round breast is a hill; its ancient soil supports nothing but dark orchards ... There was an alley of elms. They had been there for God knows how long. (*Manosque des plateaux*)

The church's particularly beautiful bell-tower is typically Provençal with a wrought-iron casing to let the mistral and other winds howl through; solid spires were always blown down.

If I had to give advice, it would be to see the countryside in bad weather, for example the third or fourth day of a winter mistral with still five or six days to blow. Nothing is more beautiful than the sky. If you want azure, that's real azure. It's not at all the colour of total relaxation as you imagined. (*Provence*)

Passions for the sensualist Giono were like the elements, sparing no force to make themselves felt. You lived with the strongest wind and the brightest blue like passionate love or hate. They were part of life's true riches.

I climbed the Montée des Vraies Richesses, the street leading to Mont d'Or, 'the beautiful round breast' of a hill where Giono had his home. Opposite a modern block of flats, Résidence Jean-Giono, literary pilgrims follow a short alley to the house with copious library and quiet study at Lou Paraïs (Paradise). The garden is filled with palm and chestnut trees, and the music of a fountain to inspire him. There he would sit, pipe in hand, straw hat at rakish angle, gazing out over his town, his Durance, replete from a lunch of his favourite recipes. Red mullet with *tapenade*, steak with anchovy sauce, gratin of fennel, peaches in red wine.

Our days are like fruit and it's our role to consume them, to taste them slowly or voraciously according to our nature, to profit by whatever they contain, to make of them our spiritual flesh and our soul, to live. Life has no other meaning but that. (*L'Eau Vie*)

Life-affirming as Giono was, a sinister reminder of the darker side of Provence he so often expressed was there, right on his doorstep. In a kitchen garden opposite 'Paradise', someone had ghoulishly suspended a pop-eyed doll on a string to scare away the birds. When the fruit of life turned sour, was not that often the fate of peasants – like Ugolin in Pagnol's *Manon des Sources* – hanging themselves from beams in a barn or a branch of an olive tree?

To make the most of Giono's Manosque, it's best to come on a Friday when Lou Paraïs is visitable in the afternoon and you can also go to the Fondation Jean-Giono which has a permanent audio-visual exhibition entitled 'Jean Giono or The Immobile Traveller'.

Leaving the Durance valley on the D5, a climb through a sprawl of Manosque suburbs leads to Col de la Mont d'Imbert (1,938ft/590m) at the eastern end of the Lubéron range. The Forêt Domaniale de Pélicier, with its little road twisting through pine woods, was wild country again after the comparative sophistication of Manosque and the Durance valley. Planted romantically on a plateau of green fields, the fourteenth-century village of Dauphin revealed an artisanal bakery reminiscent of Aimable's in *La Femme du Boulanger*. Large, round *pains de campagne* are baked in its wood-fired ovens.

He said: 'Pour in the flour.' And he saw how beautiful his flour was. There they were, the two of them, leaning over their work as though over something living. (*Les Vraies Richesses*)

Outside the bakery, in a bower of flowers, I ate a *fougasse d'olive* – ' fretwork' olive bread – with a refreshing cold beer; the bakery is also the village shop and café.

Just after Dauphin, the D5 joins the D13 for a left-turn to Mane. Mane is one of those lesser-known villages that rewards a quick whip-round or longer stay for its sturdy stone citadel lording it over the rest of the village; Saint-André church which has a particularly good Christmas *crèche provençale*; and grandly Gothic sixteenth-century merchants' houses with sumptuous carved wood doors and mullion windows. Mane is also notable as the junction with the lethal N100, a beast of a road, which I was happy to leave quickly for the Prieuré de Salagon.

The priory, one of the most remarkable architectural ensembles of Upper Provence, is the region's ethnological conservatory, an intriguing museum-in-the-country. Once the site of a modest Roman agricultural villa, the buildings beautifully blend Romanesque and Renaissance, preparing one for the heady mixture of aromatic plants in the surrounding gardens. A medieval garden displays plants existing before the discovery of the New World.

Mane – its sturdy stone citadel lording it over the village

Elsewhere, sights and smells evoked in countless Giono tales titillate the eye and nose – mint, sage, artemesia, hysop, santolina, simples for health, herbs for the kitchen, even a magic garden for the brews of witches and wizards. I learned how beneficial lavender was for migraine, giddiness, 'flu, indigestion, vertigo and rheumatism; the Romans used it as a detergent. Now, however, lavender could be as synthetic as the earnest announcement that 'The Minister of Culture wishes to create an ethnopole of this ethno-botanical site.' Giono would turn in his grave at this technospeak invading the French language.

The N100 brought me to Forcalquier, one of my favourite small market towns and a great centre for exploring Giono country. Winding my way up through the alleys of the Old Town, which is clustered cosily round a former castle site of the Counts of Provence, I reached the top of the citadel hill and yet another majestic panorama without people. Only one person, in fact, was visible – and then only in my mind's eye. Jean Giono. Slowly turning my head, I took in *his* snow-capped Montagne de Lure ('a newly liberated mountain, only just emerging from the Flood'), distant Southern Alps, Durance valley, eastern Lubéron in wispy cloud, *garrigue* sloping up towards invisible Banon and Le Contadour. The early morning air was crisp and bracing, sharpening my senses for the taste and smell of the Monday market just setting up in Place Bourguet. Forcalquier's town

At the top of Forcalquier's citadel hill

centre manages to contain Notre-Dame-du-Marché cathedral, Bourguet café, Visitandines cinema-in-a-convent, Hôtel des Deux Lions and Régusse wine shop within two minutes walking distance of each other. It was a hive of activity. Bearded men, more like artists than market gardeners, were selling *culture biologique* (bio products) watercress, carrots, beetroot and eggs near the Renaissance fountain of Place St-Michel. Restaurant Le Lapin Tant Pis, hidden in a tunnel behind the church, announced *Slow Food içi* – Here We Take Time To Eat. Another notice said 'Please don't urinate against this wall.' An earthy, gutsy town, Forcalquier is modern in outlook and traditional in ambience.

'Traditional farming is dying,' said Gilles Pourcin, my young host at Le Paradis, a comfortable B&B in his old farmhouse on the outskirts of town. 'When I was a kid, everything my parents gave me was home grown: chickens, rabbits, lamb, milk, vegetables, fruit. Now two school friends of mine who inherited their parents' farm find the best profit is in Cavaillon melons and tulip bulbs which they sell to Holland! Thank God for the eco people. At least, they have some respect for the soil.'

In summer, when lavender and sunflowers bloom, and olive groves 'make immense, silent, dark temples', today's Giono country does still look like Provence is supposed to look. Prosperous, too. Villages long deserted show signs of life in the most remote places. To find them, you head out

LAVENDER

Nowhere in Provence is lavender more evident than Alpes de Haute-Provence – around Digne, on the Plateau de Valensole, and between Forcalquier and the Montagne de Lure, spreading over on to the Albion Plateau (Vaucluse).

From the same family of aromatic plants as thyme, it's traditionally used for scenting a bath, feeding bees (hence lavender honey) and providing fragrance to newly-washed linen. Of the cultivated lavender today, the 'pure' is *lavendula angustifolia* flourishing above 2,000 feet (609m), while *lavandin* is the 'hybrid' grown more easily lower down. You need 225 acres (91 hectares) of 'pure' lavender to yield 1 ton (1.016 tonne) of essence, whereas 1 ton of 'hybrid' essence needs only 34 acres (14 hectares). The better quality is used for more expensive cosmetics and medications, but toilet water, oil, soap and bags bought in a Provençal market will almost certainly contain the 'hybrid'.

A vast lavender field

The harvest, largely mechanized since the seventies, happens in high summer when heat makes oil rise up the stem. At the distillery, cut and dried stems are packed into a steam alembic to continue the oil's extraction, followed by a cooling and condensation process. The distilled essence is the basis for all lavender products. You can even cook with it.

of Forcalquier on the D16 to Sigonce famous for its seventeenth-century Château de Bel-Air. The little road winds first through perfect grazing country – admittedly, with nothing grazing on it – then follows a tougher terrain of holm-oak, little pines dotted about grey shale, and streams that dry up in summer under the merciless sun. Once dependent on its lime and lignite mine, Sigonce is a typical old backwoods village with a new life. This is largely because Nicole Audibert's Bar-Tabac displays the welcom-

ing sign *'bistrot de pays'* (country pub) by the bead-curtains of her entrance, indicating that she belongs to a local association of village cafés known for their special conviviality and facilities. A bespectacled redhead with a good strong arm for pulling draft beer for thirsty hikers, Nicole told me: 'Some tourists are fed up with everything plastic and televisions blaring away. *Chez moi* they can actually hear themselves talk and pick up a few tips from my locals about where to go and what to see. Also, now there are no village shops, it's nice to find somewhere you can buy a few basics.' Nicole provides camping gas, confectionery, bread, newspapers, postcards, stamps, cigarettes and sandwiches in summer.

The D16 joins the D951 at Cruis, where the Bar des Alpes de Provence is another *'bistrot de pays'*. Patron Daniel Clémente, like Nicole, also acts as local tourist office with information and sells souvenirs: herb liqueurs and peach wine from Forcalquier's famous distillery, olive oil, *santons,* tee shirts, guide books. Along my route, I was to find other *'bistrot de pays'* signs at St-Etienne-les-Orgues, Ongles and Banon. At Revest-du-Bion, a handsome couple, Michel and Véronique Faraud, even served a simple midday *plat du jour* (dish of the day) which could be typical up-country spelt soup or daube, all the tastier for simmering for a few days. Some of the 15 establishments, I'm told, even cash traveller's cheques.

Continuing on the D951 across a rolling plateau with big *bastides*, I came to St-Etienne-les-Orgues, once a village that prospered not from organs (as the name suggests) but from herbal medicine. A particularly pleasant, pretty village, it is the centre for Montagne de Lure, one of Giono's favourite walks among the sheep and shepherds of its deserted slopes. 'Immobile Traveller' was a misnomer – he just limited his parameters to the Provence he had invented. He particularly loved the wildness of Lure with its variety of vegetation according to height and exposure to weather: heathland, grassy slopes, distinct woods of oak, pine, fir or beech. In autumn the mountain is a blaze of gold. At other times of year, great crows and eagles soar over the crests, vipers wait for the unwary, violets, juniper and narcissus grow wild. It is – or was – a naturalist's paradise. Heracles hedge nettle, one of the rarest plants in France, is threatened by afforestation of grassland.

A round-trip detour on the D113 led up the mountain through a cedar forest, first to the Benedictine abbey of Notre-Dame de Lure where the monks could pursue their hill-country tasks as shepherds and foresters; then, to the Signale de Lure (5,989ft/1,825m) where another panorama without people takes in the Cevennes hills across the Rhône valley, the craggy Vercors to the north, and to the south – on a very clear day – the Mediterranean.

Wild, open country continues on the D951 and its merging with the D950 to Banon. At its best in July and August, the landscape is dotted with little lavender distilleries whose smoking chimneys at harvest time fill the air with a warm fragrance that floats through an open car window. There is an exhilaration we can share with Giono's characters Gédemus and Arsule in *Regain.*

Finally, we'll reach the plateau, its surface shaved clean by a sharp plane of a wind; we'll trot a short quarter of an hour and, in a gentle fold where the earth has sunk beneath the weight of a convent and fifty houses, we'll discover Banon.

Medieval Banon is famous for its goat's cheese wrapped in chestnut leaves, but for better or worse *banon* is now also made elsewhere (rather like *brie* in Somerset!). Eating it on the spot may be folkloric but it somehow tastes better. Banon's timeless stack of red-roofs rises to a handsome fortified gateway at the top of the town. With the portcullis down, hot oil and stones could be poured on the troops of a baron from the next fiefdom.

Giono, an ardent pacifist, would not have approved. At the western end of Montagne de Lure, in 1935, he set up a kind of avant-garde hippie commune at Le Contadour, dedicated to living the simple, pastoral life. Shortly after the climb out of Banon on the D951, a right-turn to Le Contadour (D5) leads through wild, gorse-covered high-

Banon, famous for
its goat's cheese
wrapped in chestnut
leaves

TH = Table d'Hôtes (guest house with dinner)
CH = Chambre d'Hôtes (bed and breakfast only)

Near Notre-Dame-de-Romiger church in Manosque's Old Town, Hôtel Peyrache has no pretensions but much character with flowery wallpaper in the rooms and an entry-phone like a private house. Also serving just breakfast, Le Provence has the advantage of a swimming pool for the dog days of summer.

Great value-for-money is Dominque Bucaille where one of La Fuste's owners masterminds *ceps*-in-chicken-broth risotto, spit-roasted meat and fish flavoured with Provençal herbs, and caramelized figs. Le Lubéron is an honest bistrot serving

grilled pigeon with rosemary; or to make a change from herbs, spicy Asiatic dishes with local ingredients are stylishly served at Viet Nam.

When visiting the Salagon Priory near Mane, lunch in the garden of La Reine Rose is a simple pleasure with such classics as *loup de mer* with fennel and grilled pigeon. Also a classic French stopover is Les Deux Lions, in Forcalquier:

warm welcome, cosy bed, good food and tolerable church bells. A little way out of town (towards Niozelles on the N00) Auberge Charembeau's medium-priced eighteenth-century farmhouse has a swimming pool and some rooms with kitchen. In the shadow of the citadel, Gilles Pourcin's simpler farmhouse, Le Paradis (CH), is thoroughly recommended (see p.152).

Forcalquier also has two *sympa* restaurants, reasonably priced: jazz-fan Bernard Lebailly's La Tourette (local nut wine apéritif, coquille St-Jacques salad, steak with three-pepper sauce, pine nut tart); and Gérard Vives' vaulted, cosy Le Lapin Tant Pis (white or black truffles, mozarella mille-feuilles with sun-dried tomatoes, daube of Camargue bull, sour cherry soup with liquorice ice cream).

The village inn at Cruis, Auberge de l'Abbaye, offers big, well-furnished rooms in Provençal style and basic food (fricassé of rabbit with olives, leg of lamb with almonds) on the terrace.

Giono country near Forcalquier

lands first to Redortiers, a romantic wreck of village with just a tower and an archway on a weed-covered hillock. Inhabited as late as the nineteenth century, its desertion in the flight from the land inspired Giono's *Regain.* In this romantic tale, a hard-working peasant couple put the village on its feet again. Sadly, life does not always mirror art, and Le Contadour's commune was an honourable failure. Inspired by Giono's convivial anarchy, its arty back-to-nature members should have read his books more closely to understand the tragic self-destruct of many back-country Provençal communities, dependent solely on the land. Giono's complex contradictions made him the great, human writer that he was – a man of questions, not answers.

On a plateau rolling as the sea, everything disappears in the troughs of waves. You barely have time to turn round: farm, village and tree sink and other things emerge. Just beyond the birch-trees, the road climbs up and, at the end of an avenue of trees, a blue mountain appears ... (*Provence III*)

In just such a landscape, even a five-hour walk is easy-going compared to ploughing a field by hand. At the end of the D5 I left the car at Le Contadour, a hamlet where once sheep from the transhumance were counted, and began walking towards the crest. I passed Ferme-Auberge Les Tinettes, a simple sturdy farmhouse in a dip of the vale, seemingly at the end of the world. The only place to eat for miles, its chickens, geese and guinea fowl make delicious dishes to feed hungry walkers.

I crossed a vast lavender field where, at harvest-time even in these mechanized days, you occasionally see harvesters cutting with a billhook and carrying the cut lavender in bundles across their shoulders. A path through a forest of young Norway pines led to a beautiful dry-stone sheepfold at Terres du Roux. Known as *jas* from the Provençal verb *se jasser* (to lie down), sheepfolds like this still shelter sleeping sheep and shepherds beneath their sturdy vaults. Stones must be an exact fit, with no mortar, an intricate technique handed down by craftsman since the eighteenth century. Giono knew from his shepherd friends how tough a task it was. 'With these raw stones ... you needed the hand of God to intercede from the very beginning' (*Que ma joie demeure*). Now, climbing further into Giono's mythic, magic Provence, I approached another sheepfold on the Plateau des Fraches – ruined, arcaded and ghostly. It put me in mind of *Crésus*, Giono's brilliant 1960 debut as film director, in which Fernandel as a shepherd finds buried treasure in this very sheepfold.

At the Crête de Larran summit (4,519ft/1,377m), there was another mind-blowing view of places by now familiar – Mont Ventoux, Ste-Baume, Mercantour. And, below to the north, the Jabron valley where the hussar rode his horse in *Le Hussard sur le toit* (The Hussar on the Roof), which was also recently turned into a film. From that apotheosis of the walk, a short distance along the Lure's crest led to the descent back to Les Tinettes. I had been travelling 'on a high rise of land, like a raft lost in an ocean full of sky'.

I returned from Le Contadour a different way, branching right off the D5 on to the tiny, ravishing C1 back to the D950. Leaving Giono country at Revest-du-Bion, it struck me that the skills and hardships of a real French peasant were as remote from a writer's normal experience as Le Contadour from the worldly pleasures of Manosque. All the more credit to Jean Giono that he so convincingly portrayed them.

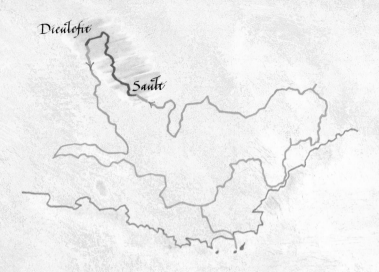

Diculefit

Sault

Chapter 7

THE WILD SIDE

DRÔME PROVENÇAL

To watch the slow motion kaleidescope of mists in a valley like the Bentrix (far right), separating and reforming; to feel the warmth of the sun break through and catch sight of a lunar landscape of blue-grey marl in the Vallée de l'Ennuye (above right); to discover that those bells you heard clinking and clonking belong to a herd of golden-eyed goats in an apricot orchard like the one near La Bonté (below right). These are special Drômois pleasures.

SAULT TO BUIS-LES-BARONNIES

My last *départment*, Drôme, was the wildest. Why 'Drôme Provençale', people wonder? Because Drôme, as a whole, belongs to the Rhône-Alpes regional group, not to Provence–Alpes–Côtes-d'Azur. Its southern area, however, has a distinctly Mediterranean climate and vegetation; who, driving south from Paris on the Autoroute du Soleil, does not remember kissing the clouds goodbye at Montélimar and heading into the clear, azur dome of the Rhône plain? It offers the first taste of Provence: roadside signs for garlic and honey on sale, vineyards and fields of lavender and sunflowers, villages with plane-tree shaded squares, fountains and old men playing boules.

From Revest-du-Bion, my last village in Alpes de Haute-Provence, I passed through a slither of Vaucluse to reach Drôme. Between the solitude of Montagne de Lure and the Plateau de Vaucluse, the D950 suddenly puffed itself up into a wide, major highway constructed for army vehicles at Plan d'Albion's former secret missile base.

Sault's secret weapon is nothing more lethal than nougat. The worst that can happen is losing a tooth or two. André Boyer recently celebrated the centenary of the family nougat-making business begun by grandfather Ernest, a Sault *pâtissier*. 'Call us artisanal – forget that industrial stuff from you-know-where,' he laughed, taking a gentle swipe at Montélimar, capital of industrial nougat. 'We use lavender honey and almonds grown around Sault. And the very purest and most natural bourbon vanilla.' I was impressed by his *torrefacteur*, an ancient oven for grilling almonds. 'If they're too grilled or the sugar's not crystal-lized enough, we chuck 'em away. No regrets. Quality's the best publicity.'

Not just Chez Boyer, I have always found good things in Le Pays de Sault, a UNESCO World Heritage site. Hikes and rides take one through golden miles of open country, past beekeepers working carefully at their hives, fields of spelt, and maybe a family of wild boar – to be kept at a safe distance. Black woodpecker and red partridge are among the many species of rare birds occasionally spotted. The Gorges de la Nesque – long, deep, green and cool – plunge west down to the Carpentras plain. And peaceful Sault itself (out-of-season), on a rocky spur overlooking the eastern slopes of Mont Ventoux, is a pleasant place to relax after a hard day's hike. On a crisp winter's day some of the best game dishes of the region – wild boar, kid, veni-son – are to be had Chez Signoret, as good for local gossip as for its reasonably priced food.

On the D942 out of Sault, Mont Ventoux seen from this height (2,492ft/760m) seems less like a massive whale-back rising from the sea, more like a modest dolphin. Descending through yet more lavender fields, of which only the very blasé or hay-fever sufferers get tired, I came upon Aurel, one of those photogenic hill villages that take your breath away when you find them suddenly round a

André Boyer of the family
nougat-making business, Sault

Aurel, a favourite subject of painters

Montbrun-les-Bains, an oasis in rocky, arid countryside

Rolling panoramas from Brantes to Buis-les-Baronnies

bend. On the footpath from Montagne de Lure to Mont Ventoux, Aurel is a favourite subject of artists – and no wonder, with all that lavender around. In July, you can't move for travel magazine photographers.

A little further down, a defile led off the plateau, and the D942 changed to the D542 as I crossed the Vaucluse – Drôme border. The first call was to Montbrun-les-Bains. Continuing on the D542, a short detour led to this extraordinary watering-place whose town lies – or, more accurately, stands up – extended along a steep hillside like an elaborate frieze. Near the confluence of Anary and Toulourenc rivers, lush green fields surround it, an oasis in arid, rocky countryside. Place du Grand Soleil, on top of the town, is well-named and has the best viewpoint – of Mont Ventoux's north face. After my descent to the valley, the mountain's chameleon aspect had changed once again; from here, it was a white-capped Everest among bleak, bare foothills. The fourteenth-century castle, once big enough for two hundred men and horses, is now a ruin. Its Catholic warlord, Charles Dupuy-Montbrun, departed for Geneva to bring his wayward sister, who had become a Calvinist, back to the Faith. It was she, however, who converted him, and he became one of the great Calvinist leaders of the Wars of Religion, massacring Catholics who would not renounce their faith in village after village of the Baronnies hills. God was on nobody's side during the French Renaissance; organized religion's bigotry and cruelty were at their most repellent.

Compared to liquid lead and skull-breaking rocks pouring from the machicolation at the Tour de l'Horloge's fortified gateway, a covering in mud at the spa would be a pleasure. Air baths, enemas, underwater massage and body-toning ungents were also available. And while you soothe away aches and pains in 37 degree water, rich in sulphur and magnesium, your children play on the swings and slides. Designed for the younger stressed-out set, this boutique spa is one of the VillégiaTherm chain which here provides slick modernity in a medieval setting.

Alternative therapy is to be found with a Montbrun botanist, Alain Tessier, expert on the healing properties of Drôme plants. Sometimes he'll take two hours to search 500 yards (457m) because there's so much to see, touch and smell. 'Lavender, of course, is best of all,' Alain claims,

La Charette Bleue

EATING OUT AND OVERNIGHT IN DRÔME

TH = Table d'Hôtes (guest house with dinner)
CH = Chambre d'Hôtes (bed and breakfast only)

Drôme is mainly for the simpler treats of Provence. Make the most of Hostellerie du Val de Sault (Vaucluse) before crossing the border: deep in lavender country, 11 rooms, pool and garden, plus Yves Gattechaut's innovative lamb carpaccio with lavender vinegar and other market-fresh exotica. Great value for money. An earthier choice is Chez Signoret in Sault (see p.160).

Near Montbrun-les-Bains, horse-trekkers (and others) overnight gastronomically at La Honas (TH), a seventeenth-century farm at Rochette-de-Buis. Between Brantes and Buis, just off the D72 (by the D526) is La Clue at Plaisians, where mainly locals tuck into brawn terrine, blanquette of kid and quince sorbet.

For an important tourist centre, Buis-les-Baronnies leaves you, like Oliver, asking for more. Hungry travellers head for La Fourchette in the arcaded market place (see p.170) or Le Grill au Four à Pain (The Bread Oven Grill) for its lamb terrine with spelt taboulé and other herb-scented delicacies. Best place to stay is the Dominican convent (cheap and reasonably cheerful) or just out of town, Sous L'Olivier, with balconies over-looking river and mountain and a sauna to tone you up after hikes.

A welcome taste of Italy (northern) is to be had at Ste-Jalle's La Cantinetta (see p.174) where Roberto di Mascio serves mouth-watering *antipasti* (including *bresaola* ham), home-made ravioli and Barbera wine. At Tarendol-Bellecombe you order the night before Chez Marilou, where Marilou entertains you royally in her village house. Ferme-Auberge Les Garelles (TH) has simple rooms, good farm cooking and horses to ride.

La Charette Bleue (see p.179) is a more upmarket roadside restaurant at La Bonté on the D94 (guinea fowl with preserved lemons and olives), while the Cormonts at Le Petit Caveau, Nyons, serve seriously good food and wine (rabbit preserved in thyme and olive oil, scallops and *girolles* mushrooms sautéed in garlic). You can overnight quietly and comfortably in a Nyons olive grove at La Picholine, but

l'Ormeraie (CH)'s two rooms with terrace overlooking the Eygues valley are a bit more personal, thanks to the welcome of your hostess, Véronique.

If night is falling in the wilds of Montagne de la Lance, Hameau de Valouse (TH) is a convenient hamlet lovingly restored and converted into a hotel. The comparative sophistication of Dieulefit begins with Auberge les Brises, a hotel-restaurant serving goose breast with Vesc honey and raspberry vinegar and crême brulée with thyme on its shady terrace; a close second but without rooms, La Barigoule, serves mussels stuffed with almonds, and roast *sandre* with goat's cheese sauce and rosemary.

Guinea fowl with preserved lemon and olives

'both as an antiseptic and stimulant.' His colleague, Françoise Richez, accompanies a theme walk 'Herbes de la Saint-Jean' from June to July, instructing you in magic herbs around the Toulourenc valley and the occult Mont Ventoux itself. 'Sage and artemesia capture the moon's rays,' declares Françoise, 'while St John's wort and camomile get their strength from the sun. At the summer solstice, the plants are at their maximum power.' That, apparently, is the best time to mix a love potion.

I wanted to know more. Returning on the D542 to the junction with the D72, I turned right into the Toulourenc valley, one of the prettiest in Provence. It runs lush and green in the shadow of Mont Ventoux's north face, back into another slither of Vaucluse where the D40 branches left. My first stop was Savoillan, a hamlet just off the road across the river. A nearby botanical pathway enlightens one about Drôme's rich variety of plant life with such Shakespearean-sounding exotica as madderwort, laburnum, spurge and hawthorn. Some cure you, others kill you; like mushrooms, you have to know your medicinal plants (see page 169).

In its lower reaches, the Toulourenc makes an exhilarating adventure between the end of June and beginning of September. Put on rubber-shoes and wade waist-deep, hopping from rock to rock, swimming through deliciously cool rock pools. Whole families go, babies on their parents' shoulders, children swimming along and grandparents doing their best to keep up. It's a good idea to share the trip with friends, come in two cars, and leave one at the end (Pont de Veaux on the D242), then drive to the start (St-Léger-du-Ventoux on the D40) where you leave the second car. This saves a spectacular but quite rough two-hour hike along the top of the canyon to get there. The river walk takes three hours downstream.

From Savoillan, I crossed the Toulourenc back to the

The Toulourenc valley, Mont Ventoux's north face

D40 and returned to a left-turn on the D136 for the short hill road from the valley to Brantes, a village so spectacularly well-preserved it really has to be visited out of season. Crowds invade it – why wouldn't they? Good restoration and a healthy disdain for boutiques selling mock-artisanal trash are evident all along its pedestrians-only pathways and cobbled steps. Walking these unstructured thoroughfares, it's hard not to meander into someone's garden, but nobody seems to mind. Flower-filled, terraced plots abound, some with baby palm trees. Suddenly I found myself blocked by sheets, newly washed and sweet-smelling as they dried on a line; unwittingly I had wandered into Madame's welcoming back yard. Kindly, she put me back on course to La Poterne.

La Poterne is an hospitable café and arts centre, with a terrace overlooking Ventoux. Lizard-like, I relaxed over perfectly made Earl Grey tea with two kinds of home-made cake, chestnut and olive. Olive *cake*? It was an old recipe, the young owner told me; I took a piece wrapped in silver foil for Sheila to taste. Like the enterprising young couple who run La Poterne, Brantes is laidback yet original – a species of village becoming sadly extinct in the more touristy parts of Provence.

Brantes lulls you into a specially relaxed state of mind. Dozey, even. Badly parked at the entrance of the village, the Panda was blocking an articulated truck negotiating a hairpin bend. In my haste to move my car, I left camera and olive cake on the roof. The truck-driver jumped out of his cab, and handed them to me. 'I'm not in that much of a hurry!' he said. We discussed the merits of the olive cake, until someone on the hill behind his truck, gave a tentative honk. No one is rushed at Brantes.

The D136 joined the D41 just above Brantes, where I turned left to Buis-les-Baronnies. Back in Drôme, the road became the D72 winding over green-grey hills with rolling

Brantes lulls you into a specially relaxed state of mind

panoramas stretching for ever into the distance. Apricot orchards and lime trees relieved the darker schist and shaley outcrops. After crossing the Ouvèze river, which I had already crossed on this journey further downstream at St-Marcellin's Roman bridge, I turned right on the D5 (Route des Princes d'Orange). For more than 60 miles (100km), the road links Orange with the Lower Alps, and was probably the route Hannibal took with his elephants and 60,000 men when he crossed the Alps in 218 BC. From the fourteenth to eighteenth centuries, it served the House of Orange-Nassau, ancestors of the present Dutch royal family, whose Provençal real estate was inconveniently separated by hills between Orange and Eyguians. Today, it is an enchanting run through Les Baronnies, some of the wildest hill country of Drôme. It is at its best in October, when apricot and cherry trees turn red amid the golds, browns and greens of the valley's autumn tints.

LIME BLOSSOM FAIR

Ten minutes' drive up the Ouvèze on the D5, I came to Buis-les-Baronnies, the area's main town and tourist centre which, off-season, seems like a faraway place with a long-ago story to tell. Around AD 1000 nobody much bothered with these savage lands until Percipia, a formidable lady by all accounts, annexed them for her son Ribert who became the first baron. Other barons, not to be outdone, created fiefdoms left, right and centre, and the defensive mountains became known as Les Baronnies. The highest is Le Duffre (5,762ft/1,756m).

Buis, joint capital of the Baronnies with Nyons, nestles comfortably in their foothills, at the confluence of Ouvèze and Menon. And once a year, under a great plane tree, you will see a singular sight – the weighing of lime flowers in vast jute sacks called *bourras*. On the first Wednesday of July, producers come for the Lime Blossom Fair. *Tilleul* is a popular tea in France, and three-quarters of its harvest traditionally comes from Buis. Insomniacs, neurotics, asthmatics and fractious children find that it gives them a good night's sleep. It also cleans the blood and purges the body of toxins, and is good for the heart, arteries, liver and lungs. No wonder it is known, according to Maurice Messegué in Mon Herbier de Santé, as *La Tisane du Bonheur*.

Ironically, today's lime blossom is creating sleepless nights for its producers. Its history is one of wax and wane. In the nineteenth century, after phylloxera killed off vines in the region, enterprising farmers turned to lime blossom as a productive crop. Its heady, erotic perfume pervades long avenues and courtyards, anywhere and everywhere the lime tree grows. For the ten days' harvest, a family can pick about 89 pounds (40kg) a day. Like feathers, 2 pounds (1kg) of lime blossom is bulky and the going rate is only 65 francs for 2 pounds (1kg). Competition from China and Poland is fierce, and the producers of Drôme are fighting to stay in the market. For the moment, Buis is still hanging in there as the European capital of lime blossom.

A hill town in a southern climate, Buis's popularity was evident from a full car park on the Esplanade, though it was only the first week in April. As Easter arrivals stocked up second homes and camping cars for the holiday, an old man in a white cap, impervious to us *étrangers*, was giving two grandchildren a lesson in *pétanque*. Brave, goose-pimpled shorts-wearers strolled beneath the still bare plane trees of Boulevard Aristide Briand, while a café on the corner of Place de Verdun, its terrace shaded with a profusion of dazzling blue wisteria, was doing brisk business in the afternoon sun. Place du Marché, discreetly tucked away from the tourist beat, is quieter – except at the vibrant Wednesday market when stalls spread under

'Whoever has sage in their garden doesn't need a doctor' is an old Provençal saying. Students use it before exams, as do ageing actors having trouble remembering their lines. Its tonic qualities help anaemia, hypertension, impotence and depression. Not that such

The old Ursuline convent, Buis-les-Baronnies

urban ills are prevalent in Les Baronnies. Yet nowhere is more prolific in sage and other healing herbs: even its capital has a botanical name, Buis (box), and is famous for its lime-blossom fair (see p.168).

For the summer solstice of St-John, people of Les Baronnies hang a mixed bunch of St-John's wort, lavender, rosemary and sage by their front door. It stays there the whole year and brings good health. A herb tea was always considered a cure for most minor ailments. And if an evil

spirit won't go away, try burning a few herbs in the fireplace; the smoke smells so good, they can't stand it!

Rosemary is not only for remembrance but keeping your dreams sweet, your rheumatic pains at a distance, your wounds quickly healed and your partner amorous. Savory is known locally as *pèbre d'aï* (donkey's pepper)

because, besides being a delicious flavouring for a stew, it encourages a lazy donkey to mate. Thyme, both wild and cultivated, helps climbers with a touch of vertigo, gourmets with indigestion, beekepers with a buzzing in the ears, children with pink eye.

Hangovers, migraine, sore throats, bad breath, piles, jaundice ... there's not an ailment that doesn't have a herb to help magic it away. And that other Provençal standby, garlic, is alleged – among its many therapeutic properties – to be a preventative against cancer. For more information consult Alain Tessier at Montbrun-les-Bains (04.75.28.87.69) and Françoise Richiez at Buis-les-Baronnies (04.75.28.04.59).

the fifteenth-century arcades; now, with the place to myself and a fountain, I pondered the menu of a restaurant that had been recommended, La Fourchette, for local lamb *confit* with herbs, tomatoes, garlic and Nyons olive oil, rabbit civet, aubergine *mousse* and prunes soaked in lime blossom tea.

In a first-floor window, as though posing for my camera, an old lady had all the town's pigeons to tea on her window-sill. 'They're my friends. I do this all the time,' she said, whacking one off her head. 'Get off! What d'you take me for? A bird's nest?' The party was over. She clapped her hands and off they flew till tomorrow, same time.

Buis is a far cry from the painstakingly and expensively restored village museums of Gordes or Tourettes-sur-Loup. Away from the main street's well-tended bourgeois houses shaded by the great plane trees, the Old Town of Buis is the Havana of Drôme, romantic dilapidation run riot. Malodorous alleys compete with each other for stairways leading nowhere, blocked fountains, medieval walls patched with modern cement and gaping roofs. Happily, there are oases of loving care and attention. A handsome Dominican convent has had its first going-over since the sixteenth century. The beautifully restored façade of the old Ursuline convent contains a Renaissance carved-wood door that alone would be worth a detour. And the rue du Planet house of the Catelan brothers, nineteenth-century archeologists, has a fine Louis XIV front-door with an elegant staircase beyond – even if the period windows are patched with plastic.

No wonder Jean Giono 'invented' Buis-les-Baronnies as the home of his 'Saint-Jérôme-de-Buis', businessman, womanizer, sage of the human heart and artist supreme.

In one solitary street (they all are, but this one especially: it didn't unfreeze all winter), between two crumbling houses adorned with archways, mullion windows and embellished lintels, a door opened and revealed a passage at the end of which you arrived at a little courtyard, three square metres, all covered in moss. (*Noé* III)

Giono may have invented it, but I bet you could still find St-Jérôme's house somewhere in Buis today.

BUIS-LES-BARONNIES TO STE-JALLE

The D546 (Route des Princes d'Orange) leads out of town and passes almost immediately through the Gorges d'Ubrieux, a short defile where the outcrops of the Ouvèze valley close in. As you approach, they seem about to crush you and you wonder how the hell Hannibal's elephants squeezed through. Evidence of their passage this way occurs in a nearby cave drawing clearly identifiable as an elephant. Who else but Hannibal had elephants around here? No doubt, like the bathers of summer, they enjoyed a dip in the bracing fresh water.

After crossing the Ouvèze, I immediately turned off the Route des Princes d'Orange to climb yet another pass (D108) – and I was still not tired of them. The Col d'Ey (2,355ft/718m) was short and sweet, its zigzag rise taking me through olive groves and apricot orchards. Beyond the entrance to a nudist camp, Mont Ventoux stretched out long and languid with a single white breast. At the head of the pass, a squirrel ran across my path.

From the top, a panorama of Les Baronnies gives a chance to ponder Drôme Provençale's particular fortune as a stronghold of nature. One of the least populated areas of France, Les Baronnies do not have to be designated a Parc Naturel Régional because they are already protected by absence of human spoilers. Hunters are few on the ground, sheep graze without fear of wolves, and there are

Les Baronnies hills, the frontier between
Provence and the Alps

CH. = Château
DOM. = Domaine

Coteaux des Baronnies has vineyards more than 2,000 feet (609m) above sea level. At Dom. la Rosière (see p.174), stunningly situated overlooking the Ennuye valley, Serge Liotaud and son have only been making their *vin de pays* for twenty years. They follow the increasing fashion for calling a wine by its *cépage* (grape varietal), quite unlike traditionally blended Côtes du Rhône: Syrah (taste of raspberries), Gamay (normally a Loire and Beaujolais grape) and Cuvée Traditionelle (slightly more Côtes du Rhône-ish with *grenache*, *cinsault*, *syrah* and *gamay*). The '97 Merlot (ripe blackcurrants) is particularly good. White Chardonnay and Viognier are also available for tasting.

Down at Ste-Jalle, Serge's brothers Dominique and Jean-Yves Liotaud at Dom. du Rieu Frais are his only rivals, specializing in a woody Cabernet-Sauvignon, a grape varietal more usually associated with Bordeaux. In these sunny hills, the classic red has more of the full-bodied quality of Australian, Californian and Chilean

Cabernets. Their '95 is particularly well-balanced.

Where Nyons stands guard at the exit from the Baronnies hills to the Rhône valley, Côtes du Rhône comes on to the scene again (see p.177). La Nyonsaise is a highly reputable *cave coopérative* with a '95 red matured in oak barrels particularly fresh and tasty with barbecued lamb or country sausage from the Baronnies. Serious wine-lovers should extend the Nyons detour by a 10 mile (16km) round trip west to Vinsobres whose name 'Sober Wines' does not preclude it being one of the strongest Côtes du Rhône villages. Taste Denis Vinson's spicy '97 white at Dom. du Moulin, and Dom. Jaume's fruitful '96 red. The village alone is worth the effort.

Back on my route, vineyards began again on the plain where an early Christian saint, Paul Tricastin, gave his name to the Coteaux de Tricastin *appellation*. Its reliable red wine is usually lighter than Côtes du Rhône. Try St-Pantaléon-les-Vignes' summery red, drunk a little chilled instead of rosé; or, slightly superior, the '96 red produced at Dom. St-Luc, a fine eighteenth-century farm at La Baume-de-Transit (D142 from Valréas). Also look out for Dom. de Grangeneuve, pride of the Bour sisters, on wine lists.

Also off my route but on most wine lists, Clairette de Die is Drôme's much appreciated sparkling wine (dry or semi-dry), better value than many supermarket champagnes at double the price.

miles and miles of isolated paths for adventurous walkers and mountain-bikers and horseback riders to get lost in – as they frequently do. It is a twin-faceted country: the crest of Montagne de Raton is said to be the frontier between two worlds – Provence and the Alps. Les Baronnies have the best of both worlds.

I looked down on the Vallée de L'Ennuye below, more basin than valley, refreshingly green after so much aridity. The Drôme hills and mountains are poorer, craggier, more violent than the Alps, yet their very wildness is their appeal. To watch the slow motion kaleidoscope of mists in a valley, sepa-rating and reforming; to be enveloped in swirling, humid greyness which becomes translucent; to feel the warmth of the sun breaking through and to catch sight of Mont Angèle's

Stone-carved portal, Ste-Jalle church

pearly, milky whiteness; to discover that those bells you heard clinking and clonking beyond the gloom belong to a herd of golden-eyed goats – these are special Drômois pleasures.

Nature responds to the double influence of Provence and Alps. Homely birds we don't often hear or see in Vaucluse, because of the pesticides and savage chopping of trees for industrial agriculture, mix with more exotic predators: blackbirds, jays, wrens, bullfinches, martens and kingfishers share the air with Royal eagles, sparrow-hawks and falcons. As well as Provençal plants already mentioned, you can find cornel (wild cherry), blue chicory and mullein (yellow flowers). In winter, hellebore with its

green flowers grows beneath high-flying wild vultures, a species once wiped out by hunters and now returning. In spring, wild orchids, peonies and lilies celebrate the return of the migratory hoopoe and black kite. Summer's dryness brings hordes of butterflies – everywhere the hot air is filled with tortoiseshell, painted lady, Bristol blue, swal-low-tail and countless others. Autumnal humidity nurtures rare Caesar's mushroom and Royal agaric with its orange cap, said to have the best taste of all mushrooms but also to be the most threatened. So we are asked not to pick it, and Drôme Provençale requests these things seriously.

Another vanished species has returned to Les Baronnies: the vine. On my way down to Ste-Jalle, I stopped at

Domaine La Rosière. The vineyards, planted as recently as 1972, are dramatically spread over the high hillside (2,230ft/680m). Serge Liotaud, black moustache, baseball cap and jeans, greeted me like a long-lost friend, though I'd never bought wine there before. His excellently made *vins de pays* were reasonably priced, with a light, sunny taste of the hills.

THE LAST SHANGRI-LA

A lot of places claim to be The Last Shangri-La: Ladakh, Sikkim, Bhutan. If there was a competition, I would reckon Vau d'Ennueo to be a strong contender. Vallée de l'Ennuye in French, this beautifully unspoiled basin in a circus of hills is about as far from *ennui* as it could be. Six miles (10km) long by four miles (6km) wide, the centre of the basin reveals a lunar landscape of blue-grey marl. A kaleidoscope of colours enchants the eye as you drive past: a golden wheat field, a pubescent pine forest, a vivid green prairie, a line of poplars, a lavender field, an orchard of apricot trees, the stark grey *barres* of its sacred hill, Mont Vanige which takes its name from an early pagan god worshipped by the valley's first inhabitants.

The valley was not always so peaceable. As the bread basket of the Baronnies, it was much fought over, particularly in the Wars of Religion when the very parfit Catholic knight Faulque-Thollon-de-Ste-Jalle, who eschewed massacres as unfair play, was constantly hassled by the Protestant convert, Charles Dupuy-Montbrun, whose foul play I have already described. Four villages guarded four passes, as they still do. And the chief town, Ste-Jalle, controlled the strategically important outlet of the Ennuye river where it flows down to join the Eygues, the valley's easiest point of access from the rest of the Baronnies.

Ste-Jalle was the starting point. An easy stroll took me uphill to the Chapelle des Pénitents Blancs, a small seventeenth-century gem with a painted frieze and unusual mezzanine. It had clouded over. The château stood like a medieval baron's home, silhouetted against a backdrop of clouds scudding across bleak hills. Even somewhere as small as Ste-Jalle can have you lost in its warren of tunnels and alleys, then suddenly you come upon somewhere you recognize. In my case, naturally, a restaurant. La Cantinetta's Italian cuisine and wine, in an old Provençal village house with secret garden, has pilgrims coming from far and wide.

Eleventh-century Notre-Dame de Beauver church is the pride of the Baronnies, a perfect Romanesque ensemble notable for a rare stone-carved portal with symbolic figures (violin-player, pilgrim-shepherd, cock). Like the chapel, the church was open. With its open-door policy, unlike many bigger towns, Ste-Jalle does its saint proud; I was to find the same at all the valley's churches.

Left at the church, the narrow D568 serpents steeply up the northern hillside to Le Poët-Sigallat. Balanced delicately on its ridge, this enchantingly unspoiled one-street village was semi-ruined – until recently. Pioneer restorers, like the weatherbeaten Frenchwoman who greeted me from her battered bike, do the job simply but sturdily, with patches of virgin garden to enjoy the staggering all-round views. High above, little white shapes turned out to be hang-gliders ready to take off – in better weather. To the east, a spectacular rocky gully was slashed diagonally across a hillside.

The D568A (signposted Rémuzat) ran past young white oaks and a black lunar landscape in the valley below, until I joined the D162, the road down from Col de Subeyran. The pass is famous for its mushrooms (*grissets, bolets des pins, lactaires*) and guarded by the village of Tarendol. Here, Dutch trekkers in garish rain-gear were setting off

Vallée de l'Ennuye, a kaleidescope of colours

Dany and Noël Aubert raise shaggy angora goats

for a 'moon' walk through the black marl. I passed horse-back riders getting mounted at the Ferme-Auberge des Garelles, as I descended on the D162 to Bellecombe.

It had begun to rain. Tumps of black marl remind you that this Drômois 'Jurassic Park' was once – 35 million years ago – buried deep beneath a warm sea. On the other side of Bellecombe (beautiful vale), the gentler aspect of apricot and pine trees seemed to belong to another planet.

Shortly after a tunnel of plane trees at St-Sauveur-Gouvernet (left off the D162 to the D510), guardian of the Col de Peyruergue, I turned right on the D64, the quiet poplar-lined road alongside the Ennuye river, then left on the D162 to Bésignan. At the eighteenth-century mill house near the turn, Dany and Noël Aubert raise shaggy angora goats for mohair and the making of goat's cheese. With children, it's fun to visit at evening milking time. I passed a very local-looking lavender distillery, yet in the hamlet of Bésignan there were only Belgian or German cars. The

unpretentious stone houses had been lovingly restored. A German gone native got out of a beat-up station wagon, proudly showing me the lamp he'd picked up at a flea market, then disappeared into his workshop to fix it up.

The D162 climbed to the Col d'Ey on the south side of the valley where I'd entered it yesterday, then the D108 swept down and off left on the D528 to Rochebrune, another one-street village but more sophisticated than Le Poët-Sigallat. *Restanques* (terraced orchards and gardens) fell away from the village, with a cornucopia of blossom set off against the grey shale opposite. The main street was newly paved. Its tiny church was well-restored and redecorated with over-bright frescoes and ceilings.

Backtracking on the D528, I followed the branch-left signpost 'Chemin de Ste-Jalle' which turned out to be a dirt track down to a stream swollen by the rain. At a farm, a sodden girl was shoveling manure on to a truck. Vines spread from one side of the road, apricot trees from the other. A tractor driver greeted me while I was having a pee, neither of us the least embarrassed. And, a minute or two later, rejoining the D108 I came full circle back to Ste-Jalle.

In that one small basin of Drôme, the delicate Provençal balance between second home owners, short-term tourists, and local producers seemed to be just right.

STE-JALLE TO ROUSSET-LES-VIGNES

I continued on the D64 down the Ennuye valley alongside the vineyards of its second winery, Domaine du Rieu Frais. By the riverside village of Curnier, at the confluence of Ennuye and Eygues (spelt Aigues in Vaucluse), I turned left on the main Nyons-Serre road (D94). Eygues and Ouvèze run parallel with each other through the Baronnies, between similar limestone ridges with grey bluffs and jagged outcrops, patches of black, sandy marl

Before or after shopping for olives, oil and soap at Ramade's fragrantly scented old olive mill, Nyons itself is fun to explore. Not for those who panic about getting lost, though: the labyrinthine alleys of its medieval town could have a Minotaur safely trapped, but there's always a helpful Nyonsais who knows the way back to your car parked in the Place de la Libération.

When the last of the barons of the Baronnies lost control of Nyons to the French King Louis XI in 1352, the town prospered under the commercial enterprises of Lombard and Jewish immigrants, resulting in many of the fine façades and sculpted doorways visible today. Place des Arcades, entered by Porte Saint-Jacques gateway, housed many of the town's grandees. Interior courtyards and little gardens appear mysteriously beyond tunnels, apparent dead ends reveal steps leading to the *quartier des forts* (quarter of fortresses) on its hill. From St-Vincent and St-Césaire church, the easier circular rue des Petits Forts leads to the round tower of the ruined Château des Dauphins. Descending by the rue des Grands Forts, you pass the still inhabited twelfth-century Château des Montauban.

The ensemble of Nyons, including the elusive Randonne tower, is best seen from the other side of the river. A sturdy medieval single-arched bridge, wrongly called Roman, crosses the river which is spelt Eygues in Drôme from the Ligurian word for thunder and Aigues in Vaucluse from the Provençal word for water. Despite Nyons's cheerful motto *l'ensouleiado tou l'an* (sunshine all year), it can thunder and rain both sides of the border.

and orchards of fruit-trees. A hard-soft country which can be gloomy at the bottom of valleys in the depths of winter.

From La Bonté, where I planned to head back up into the hills, Nyons is an easy, worthwhile detour (see above). Every bit as important an olive centre as Les Baux, its February and July olive festivals in the Place des Arcades are famous; also its ancient olive-oil mills owned by Ramade and Dozol-Autrand. Known as Little Nice, even boasting its own Promenade des Anglais, it is the most southerly and Provençal of Drôme towns and blessed with a microclimate which attracts retirees to settle there. Occasionally, the Pontias – a vile cold wind – comes whistling down the Eygues to besmirch the town's windless reputation, and in 1956 and 1985 killer frosts wiped out entire olive groves. The Thursday market rivals nearby Vaison-la-Romaine's for size and animation; you'll see some of the same faces behind stalls but others come from more outlandish parts of Drôme where small farms unbelievably still thrive.

At La Bonté on the D94 is a favourite country restaurant, La Charette Bleue, which has a particularly understanding *patronne*. One Sunday, we had walked with friends to lunch there from Mirabel-aux-Baronnies, taking a short cut – 15 miles (24km) of amazing views along the mountain crests. Not unsurprisingly, it took us a little longer than we had imagined. We arrived at 2.30p.m., just as the kitchens were closing and with no time to change from mud-caked boots and splattered jeans. Yet we were treated to goat's cheese ravioli and roast leg of Drômois lamb with garlic sauce as calmly as if we'd arrived on the dot of twelve, like the rest of the Sunday lunchers.

From the D94 I turned right to Condorcet and began to climb up the Bentrix valley. The D70 must be one of the most unspoiled back roads in Drôme, leading as it does to deserted uplands where the sigh of a breeze and the buzz of bees are the only sounds to disturb a roadside siesta after a summer picnic of the Ennuye valley's goat's cheese, wine and apricots. To the west was the Montagne de la Lance (4,388ft/1,337m), to the east Montagne d'Angèle (5,267ft/1,605m). From near our house we see Angèle in the colder months, the smooth, feminine curve of its summit covered in snow like an iced cake. Now it was raining so hard I could hardly see the road. In spring and autumn, diluvian rains veil the view, but never for long.

The first village on the D70 announces itself as 'Condorcet, 200 children' but you'd be hard put to it to find one under the age of forty. The euphemism for its tiny population is a reflection of the flight from enchanted countryside and crumbling villages, leaving them more or less by-passed. Except, of course, for aficionados of eccentric buildings like Condorcet's 1881 mish-mash of a church, built for its sixteen inhabited houses. And trout-fishers, content to ponder the crystalline water of the Bentrix while waiting for a catch. And honey-lovers at Christine and Hubert Poquet's L'Apiarium (on D94), tasting chestnut, pine, and lavender honey, all distinguishable by their different colours.

Higher up, soon after St-Ferréol, the valley gets lusher and greener until suddenly the Bentrix plunges into a narrow gorge, Le Défilé de Trente-Pas (The Defile of Thirty Steps). The steps are not meant to help us explore the gorge, but for the stream to tumble down in its descent towards its confluence with the Eygues. Unfortunately, although it's a *site classé* (classified beauty spot), there's nowhere to stop for photo opportunities. Perhaps because the local tourist board don't want you bopped on the head by the occasional fall of stones. Off to the left, just before the gorge, the alternative D130 takes you closer to Montagne de la Lance via Teyssières, famous for its goats during transhumance, to La Paillette. On that narrow, sinuous, magical hill road, the sign to the Hameau de Valouse's auberge makes many a traveller sigh with relief. In such wild country, amenities tend to be sparse and eccentric – like the Naturist Equestrian Centre where nudes on horseback are alleged to be seen lolloping over hill and dale, though I have personally never encountered any.

Still higher on the D70, big old farms sold specially aged goat's cheese (*picodon*); orchards and meadows covered the slopes; and the valley was opening up towards a watershed plateau. From there the Veysanne stream flows one way down to the Lez, while the Roubion follows another valley to the Rhône where all tributaries eventually end. At Crupies, I was at the most northerly point of my circuit: a typical little Drômois hamlet, not more than a cluster of houses surrounding a simple, workaday church. Turning south on the D330 down the Veysanne valley, I came to La Paillette, a beautifully restored village with an artisanal baker. A four-mile (6km) detour (D538) takes you to the Protestant town of Dieulefit, famous for its pottery.

The Bentrix valley, leading to deserted uplands

Descending towards the Rhône plain near Rousset-les-Vignes

Less than a mile from La Paillette, Montjoux has a big eighteenth-century *manoir* as centre-piece of its stack of tightly packed houses and a bridge over the stream where the Veysanne joins the Lez. Prairies full of wild spring flowers began an expansion of the countryside as I turned left on the D538, descending towards the Rhône plain along the western flanks of Montagne de la Lance's lengthy swell. To my right, on the other side of the Lez, the so-called Château d'Alençon is in fact a typically extensive Drômois *bastide*, a once fortified farm now, much of it, in ruins.

From Béconne, you can easily climb La Lance, zigzagging gently up a forest track to pasture land inhabited by tinkling cows and the occasional shepherd's donkey. Climbers to the top are rewarded by a doubtful panorama of the Rhône valley with the apocalyptic steam belching from the chimneys of Pierrelatte's nuclear power station. On a still day, a sickly, greenish strip of pollution hangs over the valley's industrial middle, 12 miles (20km) away, and you're glad to be here and not there.

Back on the plain, I continued by the D538 to Montbrison-sur-Lez, passing a plantation of truffle oaks, a speciality of the region. Spring was more advanced than in the hills, vegetation a more vivid green. The rain had stopped. The wet landscape looked pin new and glistening, as the clouds cleared from the hill tops and patches of blue expanded to a sudden explosion of sunlight. The rain storm receded as quickly as it arrived, and for a while its blackness was a dramatic background to sunlit hills.

I stopped for a look at the Romanesque Chapelle Ste-Anne at La Pégue. There was also a particularly good Archeological Museum, specializing in prehistorical artefacts. Le Donjon hotel, more in tune with our own times, displayed a friendly sign: *Acceuil Motards* (Bikers Welcome). Often, they're not.

Rousset-les-Vignes made a fine culmination to my Drôme journey. An architecturally distinguished hillside village, commanding a fine view of the plain, Rousset attracted fifteenth-century refugees from the lower village of St-Pantaléon-les-Vignes, fleeing itinerant bandits. Its ramparts and château offered protection for the body, the twelfth-century priory for the soul. The priory's stunning façade, redone in Renaissance times, is a masterpiece. Its mullion windows, wrought-iron balcony, *oeil-de-boeuf*, and stone carvings are typical of features to be seen all over the village, superbly endowed for its size. Down a sinuous back street, friends live in a fine silk merchants' house with the date '1697' carved in stone over the front door. It was a strange feeling to be still on my travels, yet so near home.

Rousset-les-Vignes priory's stunning Renaissance façade

The Enclave des Papes, a small island of Vaucluse dropped into Drôme.

Chapter 8

HOME STRETCH

ENCLAVE DES PAPES

ROUSSET-LES-VIGNES TO VALRÉAS

A winding country lane (D620 becoming the D197) carried me in a matter of minutes down on to the plain, and back into the Enclave des Papes. Let me explain this strange name. The final few miles of my journey took me through a small island of Vaucluse dropped into Drôme, the only one of its kind in France. In 1317, while it was still part of Le Dauphiné which only became French in 1349, the Dauphin sold four small towns – Valréas, Visan, Richerenches and

Grillon – to Pope John XXII as cool summer retreats for his sweating cardinals in Avignon. The wine was good, the air fresh, the girls pretty. What more could a cardinal want? After the Revolution, when Comtat Venaissin (the papal lands) became part of France as the *département* of Vaucluse in 1791, the people of those four formerly papal *communes* became Drômois. However anti-clerical their heads, their hearts had a nostalgic attachment to their papal past and, after vigorous protest, their little Vauclusian island was granted them in 1793. And that's how we lapsed Anglicans come to live in an 'enclave of popes'.

The Coronne river meanders through a rich plain set against a backdrop of the first serious hills between the Rhône and the Alps, sprinkled with snow in winter. In high summer the yellow of sunflowers, the purple of lavender, and the green of vineyards create an unforgettable tapestry in the fields around the Enclave's capital, Valréas. For us, living nearby, a town for all seasons.

HOME-TOWN

How do you tour a home town? What fresh, objective eye can observe its well-known sights, familiar faces? Valréas revisited was something of a challenge. A voyage round its people, I decided, could be the only way to make it different. The antecedents of Marcel Pagnol, the best known of Provençal writers, hailed from Valréas; yet the town is a long way north of Marseilles, where his best work was set, and I never met people less Pagnolesque. However much true spirit of place Pagnol manages to pack into his work, he is often criticized for caricaturizing Provençals. Valréas has no stage Provençals that I've met. Easy laughers, yes, but not given to excess, either amorous or violent, even on high days and holidays. They never put on a show for the benefit of visitors.

Valréas's Grand Hotel is the haunt of local businessmen who couldn't care less about Pagnol's antecedents – or Pagnol, for that matter. Just as long as the *patron*, who makes something of a club of his hotel, keeps the good food and wine coming. Same story at Aux Délices de Provence, a much newer Old Town bistrot which enchants a conservative clientèle with such innovations as fish *tartare* with three kinds of salmon. And at Mastignac, our favourite B&B and family home of Madame de Précigout, furniture and pictures look as though they go back to the popes. Valréas has no fashionable cafés. Events are as much for locals as visitors. Fun fairs, bric-a-brac sales, food and wine celebrations, concerts in convents and open-air theatre are on a less ambitious scale than bigger Provençal towns, and sometimes the better for it. More real.

A circular avenue, shaded by ancient plane-trees, circumscribes the Old Town. For one night in August, the whole Cours smells as if it has been doused in essence of lavender. Carnival floats composed of thousands of bundles of lavender parade in the Corso de Lavande, led by strapping, mini-skirted drum majorettes. Now that the jolly cardinals are gone, there's not much for the girls to do after the parade but sit together in a café; tales of what goes in on in their caravans may be just wishful thinking.

Every year, on 23 June, candles are lit in the windows of tall houses surrounding Place Pie. It is the big night of the year, La Nuit du Petit St-Jean. Suddenly, amid much medieval pageantry, trumpets sound and the doors of Notre Dame de Nazareth cathedral burst open. A five-year-old boy rides out on a white horse to be crowned 'king' of the town for a year. This is no commercialized come-on to attract tourists; it is an entire town partaking, down to the last costume-stitch, in a 450-year-old ceremony which was revived in 1954. Symbolizing the Lamb of God and Eternal Youth triumphant, the 'king' is traditionally chosen from among the poorest children in town.

Only too recently many children were candidates. Unemployment in Valréas was badly aggravated by the closing of one of its cardboard-box factories. The workers occupied the factory and protestors took to the streets. Then, by some miracle, the factory was bought by enterprising newcomers and flourished in the upswing of the French economy. Cardboard packaging is the traditional Valréas industry and, apart from delicious artisanal chocolates produced by Jef Challier, its *only* industry. There is an excellent Musée de Cartonnage et de l'Imprimerie, displaying much humour and ingenuity in the design of packaging since its nineteenth-century heyday.

Valréas has a history of hard times. On 12 June 1944, at the corner of Avenue du Maréchal-Foch and Cours Jean-Jaurès, 53 hostages were shot by the Nazis during the Resistance. A moving plaque commemorates them. At my table beneath the huge mirrors of the retro Café de la Paix, just across the avenue, it struck me how easy it is, in such a peaceful southern town, to forget the sacrifices that made it possible to be sitting there comfortably drinking coffee, and for the little Saturday market to go on – with the eternal zest of its fruit and veg sellers, of the old man with fresh eggs and a few sprigs of thyme for sale, of the sausage lady who never has change.

Place Cardinal-Maury, where the regular Wednesday market is held, is named for a *bon vivant* Valréas cardinal who also gave his name to *Boeuf à la mode du Cardinal Maury*. In 1801, he sent his recipe to his nephew, Louis, a canon at Rome, clearly about to entertain some Very Important Clerics. He gave excellent advice about the cooking of *daubes* in general: 'One should barely hear the liquid laughing.' You hear much laughter in the market. If there are complaints, they are lightly expressed. Cathy and André Jehannin bring free-range ducks, chickens and

rabbits from Bouvières, one of the far-back Drôme villages I'd just been through.

'Foxes!' said André, wrapping my duck. 'I have to sit up all night with my gun sometimes. We really should start hunting them – like you British!' I told him fox-hunting might soon be banned in Britain; he looked incredulous. A purer shade of Green was the lady at the pizza stall, concerned about Man changing the course of river beds and causing floods, rooting up trees and creating mudslides. 'Michel de Nostradamus has prophesied that a catastrophe will destroy half the world in the 1990s.' It was already 1999. 'And where will Provence be then?' I asked. 'Naturally, in the other half,' she laughed, handing me my sizzling hot pizza.

Upbeat Valréassians are not hard to find. It just takes a little time. They have plenty of it for you, and you are expected to have plenty in return. Quiet, practical, reserved, they get the job done with the miniumum of fuss. One Sunday, *garagiste* Couston, who kept our ancient Volvo on the road, left his gardening to mend a snapped accelerator cable; he and my wife talked roses afterwards. Dufrien came personally after shutting his electronics shop to replace our on-the-blink VCR; when I thanked him, he said, 'We've known each other since I sold you the old one, and it gives us a chance to have a whisky together!' Pellerey, at the stationery shop, goes slowly and methodically about finding me exactly the right ball-point pen for my spidery writing; Madame Pellerey, his mother, gets in a muddle photocopying a manuscript, with much licking of thumbs and adjusting paper, doubtful mutterings and quick shrugs of incomprehension, but never, never does it defeat or panic her.

When Bron had the hardware store, he showed us how to vitrify a wooden floor, giving it a glossy, hard surface. Eydoux, 81-year-old master carpenter now departed, taught me how to install a flight of wooden steps; I can hardly bang a nail in straight normally, but Eydoux worked miracles with his apprentice.

At Lire et Ecrire, Jacques and Marie-Claire Bussat's bookshop, they always had time to talk books as well as sell them; now they have retired, we have switched loyalties to Arcanes, another friendly bookshop, where coffee is offered round a big table on Saturday mornings. Children going up in the world, thanks to books or technological skills, make Valréassian parents proud. Plumber Merlin's daughter, Valérie, practised her English with us when at school; she became an English and German interpreter, and is now married to a German banker. A master plasterer's daughter, Muriel, went to friends in London as an au pair; her sights were on higher things. 'I love England,' she later told us in accentless, only slightly hesitant English. 'I hope to get a job as a lab assistant. But you need perfect English – for Internet.' She is now a lab assistant in Huntingdon.

Valréas, for all its problems, seems to combine the best of forward-looking Provence with its traditional values. I could not think of a nicer home-town to come back to.

VALRÉAS TO LA COSTE

The back road home (D191 signposted St-Maurice-sur-Eygues) is only a few minutes longer than the main road – and much more agreeable. So why do I never take it? Today was an exception. I had to end up as unhurriedly as I'd begun.

On the Route de St-Marcellin I climbed up out of the town via a gently sloping hill. Valréas, on its own hillock, looks as solid from afar as from within. The lane curved through golden vineyards, past Domaine des Grands Devers belonging to Renée and René Sinard, among our top wine-makers. Their house was like a Breughel when I first bought wine there twenty years ago – ducks, geese and manure everywhere, dilapidated buildings; now it is a well-restored *mas* with a smartened-up winery where you can not only buy wine but stay the night. Renée Sinard's home-made jams are competition for the velvety wines.

I crossed the Hérin river for the last set of s-bends, winding up to the top of my ridge. Turning right on the unnumbered road past Domaine de Coste Chaude, I saw our Swiss neighbour Marianne talking to her vineyard workers. She looked askance at the Panda, mud-splattered as from a Monte-Carlo Rally. 'How was your one-man rally? Where did you go?' she asked. 'On slow roads to Nice,' I replied. 'And back via the Alps.' '*C'est pahhh vraiyyy!*' she exclaimed as though I'd said Khatmandu. But it was true, although it did seem a bit of dream.

Sentimentally, I thought of Dorothy waking up at the end of *The Wizard of Oz* to find there was no place like home. And my Yellow Brick Road had not had a phony wizard at the end of it. Whatever aggressions of modern man might contrive to spoil it, Provence along the way had delivered genuine magic.

On my journey, I had been on back roads more spectacular and hills higher than these, among thicker trees and more exotic vegetation. Right now, right where I was had its own enchantment, whatever winds might howl or thunder roar. In the roundness of our days, the year was moving on. The grass of our lawn was greener than when I left, the wild irises yellow on the banks. And before long I would be sitting under a pergola of vines, watching the grapes ripen. And later still, our dessert would hang in lush clusters among the green shade above my head, and all I had to do was reach up a lazy hand and pick.

Itinerary and Tourist Offices

NOTES

1. Distances below are given in **miles** with kilometres in parentheses.
2. Detours and alternative routes are not counted in total distance.
3. *Département* names in parenthesis indicate change of road number at border crossings, e.g. D223 (Var).
4. A local tourist office (*office de tourisme* or *syndicat d'initiatives*) will probably be of more help than a guidebook for up-to-the-minute information about sites, museums and places to eat, stay and play. They will make reservations for you too. English is spoken at most tourist offices.

The Michelin maps which cover the tour are:
> Marseille-Toulon-Nice (84)
> Montélimar-Avignon-Digne (81)
> Carcassonne-Montepellier-Nîmes (83)

CHAPTER 2 VAUCLUSE

Place/Roads/Mileage/Miles (km)

La Coste–Villedieu D191, D94, D20, D75, D7 **9** (14)
Villedieu–Vaison D94, D51 **5** (8)
Vaison–Entrechaux D938, D151,C3, D13 **4** (6)
Entrechaux–Malaucène D13, D938 **4** (6)
Mont Ventoux detour D974 round trip **26** (42)
Malaucène–Suzette D90 **5** (8)
Suzette–Beaumes D90 **5** (8)
Beaumes–Caromb D21 **5** (8)
Caromb–Carpentras D13, D974 **5** (8)
Carpentras–Mazan D942 **4** (6)
Mazan–St-Didier D1, D5, D4a, D39 **3** (5)
St-Didier–Venasque D28 **3** (5)
Venasque–Murs D4 **8** (13)
Murs–Sénanque Abbey D15, D244, D177 **6** (10)
Sénanque–Gordes D177 **3** (5)
Gordes–Roussillon D102, D2, D102, D169 **5** (8)
Roussillon–Goult D105, D104 **4** (6)
Goult–Lumières D145 **1** (1.6)
Lumières–Bonnieux D106, 'bike road' to Pont Julien, D149 **8** (13)
Bonnieux–Buoux D36, D232, D943, D232 **7** (11)
Buoux–Lourmarin D113, D943 **8** (13)
Lourmarin–Cadenet D943 **3** (5)

Total mileage in Vaucluse **105** (170)

VAUCLUSE TOURIST OFFICES

Place/Address/Tel./Fax

Vaison-la-Romaine, pl. Chanoine Sautel. 04.90.36.02.11; 04.90.28.76.04
Malaucène, pl. Mairie. 04.90.65.22.59; 04.90.65.22.59
Beaumes-de-Venise, Cours Jean-Jaurès. 04.90.62.94.39; 04.90.62.94.39
Caromb, pl. Eglise. 04.90.62.36.21; 04.90.62.40.28
Carpentras, 170 ave. Jean-Jaurés. 04.90.63.00.78; 04.90.60.41.02
Mazan, 83 pl. 8 Mai. 04.90.69.74.27; 04.90.69.66.31
Venasque, Grande-Rue. 04.90.66.11.66; 04.90.66.11.66
Gordes, pl. du Château. 04.90.72.02.75; 04.90.72.04.32
Roussillon, pl. de la Poste. 04.90.05.60.25; 04.90.05.60.25
Bonnieux, 7 pl. Carnot. 04.90.75.91.90; 04.90.75.92.94
Lourmarin, 8 ave. Ph. de Girard. 04.90.68.10.77; 04.90.68.10.77
Cadenet, 11 pl. Tambour d'Arcole. 04.90.68.38.21; 04.90.68.38.21

CHAPTER 3 BOUCHES-DU-RHÔNE

Place/Roads/Mileage/Miles (km)

Cadenet–Silvercane D943, D561, D561A **5** (8)
Silvercane–Orgon D561A, D561, N7 **16** (26)
Orgon–Eygalières D24B **5** (8)
Eygalières–St-Rémy D74A, D99 **9** (14)
St-Rémy–Le Trévallon C138 **4** (6)
Le Trévallon-Arles C138, D99, D32, N570 **14** (23)
Arles-Le Paradou N570, D17 **9** (14)
Les Baux detour D78D, D78F round trip **9** (14)
Le Paradou–Mouriès D17 **6** (10)
Mouriès–Salon D24, D25, D569, D17 **19** (30)
Salon–Lambesc D572, D15 **10** (16)
Lambesc–Rognes D66 via Caire–Val **6** (10)
Rognes–Aix D543, D15, D14C, D14 **12** (20)
Aix–Vauvenargues D10 **11** (18)

Total mileage in Bouches-du-Rhône **126** (203)

BOUCHES-DU-RHÔNE TOURIST OFFICES

Place/Address/Tel./Fax

La Roque-d'Anthéron, Cours Foch. 04.42.50.58.63; 04.42.50.42.59
St-Rémy-de-Provence, pl. Jean-Jaurès. 04.90.92.05.22; 04.90.92.38.52
Les Baux-de-Provence, 'Post Tenebras Lux'. 04.90.54.34.39; 04.90.54.51.15
Arleses, pl. Charles-de-Gaulle. 04.90.18.41.20; 04.90.18.41.29
Fontvielle, 5 r. Marcel-Honorat. 04.90.54.67.49; 04.90.54.69.82
Maussane, pl. de l'Eglise. 04.90.54.52.04; 04.90.53.39.44
Mouriès, 2 r. Temple. 04.90.47.56.58; 04.90.47.54.87
Eyguières, pl. Hôtel-de-Ville. 04.90.59.82.44; 04.90.59.89.07
Salon-de-Provence, 56 Cours Gimon. 04.90.56.27.60; 04.90.56.77.09
Rognes, 5 pl. de la Fontaine. 04.42.50.13.36; 04.42.50.12.36
Aix-en-Provence, 2 pl. du Gén.-de-Gaulle. 04.42.16.11.61; 04.42.16.11.62
Trets, 32 ave. Jean-Jaurès. 04.42.37.55.40; 04.42.37.55.40

CHAPTER 4 VAR

Place/Roads/Mileage/Miles (km)

Vauvenargues–Trets D10, D223 (Var), D23, D6E
  (B-du-R) **18** (29)
Trets–Ste-Baumes D12, D85 (Var), D480, D80, D95
  22 (35)
Ste-Baume-Forcalqueiret D95, D64, D554 **19** (31)
Forcalqueiret–Le Lavandou (round trip) D43, D12,
  D14, N98, D42bis **80** (129) then unnumbered
  roads as described
Forcalqueiret-Le Thoronet D15, D13, D79 **18** (29)
Le Thoronet–Lorgues D79, D17, D562 **10** (16)
Lorgues–Flayosc D562, then a lane via Sauve-Clare
  5 (8)
Flayosc–Ampus D557, D57, D49 **10** (16)
Ampus–Bargemon D51, D955, D19 **14** (23)
Bargemon–Fayence D19 **16** (26)
Fayence-Fréjus D563, D4, N7 **20** (32)
Fréjus–Cap du Dramont N98 **5** (8)
Dramont–La Napoule N98 (Corniche de l'Esterel)
  15 (24)

Total mileage in Var **252** (406)

VAR TOURIST OFFICES

Place/Address/Tel./Fax

St-Zacharie, pl. Victoire. 04.42.32.63.28;
  04.42.72.97.63
Plan d'Aups/Ste-Baume, pl. Hôtel-de-Ville.
  04.42.62.57.57; 04.42.62.55.24
La Roquebrussane, 15 r. Clemenceau. 04.94.86.82.11
Bormes-les-Mimosa, 1 pl. Gambetta. 04.94.01.38.38;
  04.94.01.38.39
Le Lavandou, Quai Gabriel-Péri. 04.94.71.00.61;
  04.94.64.73.79
Cabasse, la mairie. 04.94.80.22.14
Le Thoronet, 8 r. des Trois-Ormeaux.
  04.94.60.10.94; 04.94.60.10.57
Lorgues, pl. Antrechaus. 04.94.73.92.37;
  04.94.67.67.61
Flayosc, pl. Pied Barri. 04.94.70.41.31;
  04.94.70.47.91
Bargemon, r. Pasteur. 04.94.47.81.73; 04.94.47.81.73
Seillans, Le Valat. 04.94.76.85.91; 04.94.76.84.45
Fayence, pl. Léon-Roux. 04.94.76.20.08;
  04.94.84.71.86

Fréjus, 325 r. Jean-Jaurès. 04.94.51.83.83;
  04.94.51.00.26
Agay, bld. de la Plage. 04.94.82.01.85; 04.94.82.74.20

CHAPTER 5 ALPES-MARITIMES

Place/Roads/Mileage/Miles (km)

La Napoule–Mandelieu D92, N7 **2** (3.2)
Mandelieu–Auribeau D92, D138, D509 **11** (18)
Auribeau–Grasse D509, D9, N85 **6** (10)
Grasse–Vence (via Gorges du Loup) D2085, D3, D6,
  D2210 **25** (40)

Alternative art museum circuit:

Grasse–Valbonne D2085, D3 **6** *(10)*
Valbonne–Antibes D3, D103, D35 **10** *(16)*
Antibes–Biot N7, D4 **5** *(8)*
Biot–Cagnes-sur-Mer D4 return, N7 **8** *(13)*
Cagnes–St-Paul-de-Vence D107, D7 **5** *(8)*
St-Paul–Vence D2 **3** *(5)*
Vence–St-Jeannet D2210 **5** (8)
St-Jeannet–Nice D2210, N202, D514, D414, D914
  20 (32)
Nice–Falicon D14, D214 **8** (13)
Falicon–Tourette-Levens D214, D19 **3** (5)
Tourette–Contes D19, D815, D15 **10** (16)
Contes–Coaraze D15 **6** (10)
Coaraze–Col St-Roch D15 **9** (14)
Col St-Roch–La Bollène D2566, D70 **17** (27)
La Bollène–Roquebillière-Vieux D70, D2565 **5** (8)
Roquebillière–St-Martin D2565 **6** (10)
St-Martin–Lac du Boréon D2565, D89 **6** (10)
(Parc du Mercantour)
Lac du Boréon–St-Dalmas D89 return, D2565 **10** (16)
St-Dalmas–Rimplas D2565, D66 **6** (10)
Rimplas–Roure D66 return, D2565, D2205, D30,
  D130 **15** (24)
Roure–Roubion D130 return, D30 **8** (13)
Roubion–Col de la Couillole D30 **4** (6)
La Couillole–Beuil D30 **5** (8)
Beuil–Valberg D28 **5** (8)
Valberg–Gorges de Daluis D28, D2202 **11** (18)

Total mileage in Alpes-Maritimes **203** (327)

ALPES-MARITIMES TOURIST OFFICES

Place/Address/Tel./Fax

Théoule-sur-Mer, 1 bld. de la Corniche-d'Or.
  04.93.49.28.28; 04.93.49.00.04
La Napoule, ave. Henry-Clews. 04.93.49.14.39;
  04.93.93.64.66
Auribeau-sur-Siagne, la mairie. 04.92.60.20.20;
  04.93.60.93.07
Grasse, palais des Congrès. 04.93.36.66.66;
  04.93.36.86.36
Gourdon, pl. Victoria. 04.93.09.68.25;
  04.93.09.40.21
Le Bar-sur-Loup, pl. Francis-Paulet. 04.93.42.72.210;
  4.93.42.92.60
Alternative route Grasse-Vence:
Valbonne, 11 ave. St-Roch. 04.93.12.34.50;
  04.93.12.34.57
Antibes, 11 pl. du Gén.-de-Gaulle. 04.92.90.53.05;
  04.92.90.53.01
Biot, pl. de la Chapelle. 04.93.65.05.85;
  04.93.65.70.96
Cagnes-sur Mer, 6 bd. de Maréchal-Juin.
  04.93.20.61.64; 04.93.20.52.63
St-Paul-de-Vence, 2 r. Grande. 04.93.32.86.95;
  04.93.32.60.27
Vence, 8 pl du Grand-Jardin. 04.93.58.06.38;
  04.93.58.91.81
St-Jeannet, 8 r. Soucare. 04.93.24.73.83;
  04.93.24.89.11
Nice, 5 prom. des Anglais. 04.92.14.48.00;
  04.92.14.48.03
Contes, pl. Albert-Ollivier. 04.93.79.13.99
Coaraze, pl. Alexandre Mari. 04.93.79.37.47;
  04.93.79.31.73
Roquebillière, 26 ave. Corniglion-Molinier.
  04.93.03.51.60
St-Martin-Vésubie, pl. Félix-Faure. 04.93.03.21.28;
  04.93.03.21.28
St-Sauveur-sur-Tinée, la mairie. 04.93.02.00.22;
  04.93.02.05.20
Beuil, quartier du Pissai-Re. 04.93.02.32.58;
  04.93.02.33.72
Valberg, 4 pl. Quartier. 04.93.23.24.25;
  04.93.02.05.20
Guillaumes village 04.93.05.52.2304.93.05.54.75

CHAPTER 6 ALPES DE HAUTE-PROVENCE

Place/Roads/Mileage/Miles (km)

Gorges de Daluis–Annot D2202, N202, D908 **15** (24)
Annot–St-Julien D908 return, N202 **13** (21)
Alternative route via Moustiers Ste-Marie:
St-Julien-Castellane D955 **8** (13)
Castellane–Moustiers D952, D23 (Gorges du Verdon)
40 (64)
Moustiers–Valensole D952, D6 **18** (29)
Valensole–Manosque D6, D907 **21** (34)
St-Julien–St-André N202 **5** (8)
St-André–Barrême N202 **9** (14)
St-Jacques detour D119 round trip **5** (8)
Barrême-Digne N85, D20 **20** (32)
Digne–Malijai N85, D12, D8 **15** (24)
Malijai–Les Mées D4 **4** (6)
Les Mées–Manosque D4, D907 **25** (40)
Alternative route via Durance right bank:
Malijai–Château-Arnoux N85 **4** (6)
Ch-Arnoux–Ganagobie N96, D30 **12** (20)
Ganagobie–Lurs D30 return, then to Lurs **5** (8)
Lurs–Manosque D462, D12, N96 **14** (23)
Manosque–Dauphin D5 **7** (11)
Dauphin–Salagon Priory D13, N100 **5** (8)
Salagon–Forqualquier N100 **2** (3.2)
Forqualquier–Sigonce D16 **6** (10)
Sigonce–Cruis D16 **7** (11)
Cruis–St-Etienne-les-Orgues D951 **6** (10)
Montagne de Lure detour D113 round trip **16** (26)
St-Etienne–Banon D951, D950 **13** (21)
Banon–Le Contadour D950, D5 **8** (13)
Le Contadour–Sault D5 return, C1, D950 (Vaucluse)
16 (26)

Total mileage in Alpes de Haute-Provence **176** (283)

ALPES DE HAUTE-PROVENCE TOURIST OFFICES

Place/Address/Tel./Fax

Annot, bd. St-Pierre. 04.92.83.23.03; 04.92.83.32.82
Alternative route St-Julien-Manosque:
Castellane, r. Nationale. 04.92.83.61.14;
04.92.83.76.89
Moustiers-Ste-Marie, r. Bourgade. 04.92.74.67.84;
04.92.74.60.65
Riez, 4 allée Louis-Gardio. l04.92.77.99.09;
04.92.77.09.08

Valensole, pl. Héros de la Resistance. 04.92.74.90.02
St-André-les-Alpes, pl. Marcel-Pastorelli
04.92.89.02.39; 04.92.77.76.23
Digne-les-Bains, pl. Tampinet. 04.92.36.62.62;
04.92.32.27.24
Alternative route Malijai-Manosque:
Château-Arnoux, ferme de Fort-Robert.
04.92.64.02.64; 04.92.62.60.67
Lurs, village. 04.92.79.10.20
Les Mées, 21 bd République. 04.92.34.36.38;
04.92.34.36.38
Oraison, allée Léon-Masse. 04.92.78.60.80;
04.92.79.89.01
Manosque, pl. du Docteur P.-Joubert.
04.92.72.16.00; 04.92.72.58.98
Forcalquier, 8 pl. du Bourguet. 04.92.75.10.02;
04.92.75.26.76
St-Etienne-les-Orgues, pl. Mairie. 04.92.73.02.57;
04.92.73.00.32
Banon, pl. République. 04.92.73.36.67

CHAPTER 7 DRÔME PROVENÇALE

Place/Roads/Mileage/Miles (km)

Sault–Montbrun D942 (Vaucluse), D542 (Drôme)
10 (16)
Montbrun–Brantes D542 return, D72, D40
(Vaucluse), D136 **8** (13)
Brantes–Buis D136, D41,D72 (Drôme), D5 **11** (18)
Buis–Ste-Jalle D546, D108 **9** (14)
Ennuye valley circuit D568, D568A, D162, D510,
D64 **12** (20)
D162, D108, D528
Ste-Jalle–La Bonté D64, D94 **6** (10)
Nyons detour D94 round trip **9** (14)
La Bonté–St-Ferréo lD70 **6** (10)
Alternative route via Teyssières:
St-Ferréol–La Paillette D70, D130 **11** (18)
St-Ferréol–Crupies D70 **10** (16)
Crupies–La Paillette D330 **8** (13)
Dieulefit detourD130, D538 round trip **6** (10)
La Paillette–Montjoux D330 **1** (1.6)
Montjoux–La Pégue D330, D538 **10** (16)
La Pégue–Rousset D538 **3** (5)

Total mileage in Drôme Provençale **94** (151)

DRÔME PROVENÇALE TOURIST OFFICES

Place/Address/Tel./Fax

Sault (Vaucluse) ave. de la Promenade
04.90.64.01.2104.90.64.15.03
Montbrun-les-Bains L'Autin 04.75.28.82.49
Buis-les-Baronniespl. du Quinconce 04.75.28.04.59
Nyonspl. Libération 04.75.26.10.3504.75.26.10.57
Dieulefit1 pl. de l'Abbé-Magnet 04.75.46.42.49

CHAPTER 8 ENCLAVE DES PAPES

Place/Roads/Mileage/Miles (km)

Rousset–Valréas D620, D197 (Vaucluse) **4** (6)
Valréas–La Coste D19 **16** (10)

Total mileage in Enclave des Papes **10** (16)

Total mileage **966** (1,555)

ENCLAVE DES PAPES TOURIST OFFICE

Place/Address/Tel./.Fax

Valréas, pl. A.-Briand. 04.90.35.04.71; 04.90.35.04.71

Suggested Reading

Mary Blume, *Côte d'Azur: Inventing The French Riviera*
Dirk Bogarde,
    A Period of Adjustment
    Jericho
Henri Bosco,
    L'Ane Culotte
    Le Jardin d'hyacinthe
Colette, *Earthly Paradise*
    Belles saisons
    Paysages et portraits
    Bella-Vista
Alphonse Daudet, *Letters from my Windmill*
Lawrence Durrell,
    Monsieur
    Livia
    Spirit of Place
    The Plant-Magic Man
Scott Fitzgerald, *Tender is the Night*
Lady Fortescue, *Perfume from Provence*
Jean Giono,
    Que ma Joie demeure
    Ennémonde
    Provence (l'eau vive)
    Regain
    Rondeurs des Jours
    Jean le Bleu
    Notes sur l'affaire Dominici
Victor Hugo, *Provence*
Henry James, *A Little Tour in France*
Rudyard Kipling, *Souvenirs of France*
Guy de Maupassant, *Chroniques inédites*

Marie Mauron, *Quand la Provence nous est contée*
Peter Mayle,
    A Year in Provence
    Toujours Provence
    Encore Provence
Jacques Médecin, *La Cuisine du Comté de Nice*
Mistral, *Mireille*
Julian and Carey More,
    Views from a French Farmhouse
    A Taste of Provence
    Pagnol's Provence
Friedrich Nietsche, *Le Gai savoir*
Marcel Pagnol,
    The Marseilles Trilogy (Fanny,
    Marius,César)
    La Gloire de mon père
    Le Château de ma mère
    Manon des Sources
    Jean de Florette
    La Femme de Boulanger (based on Jean Giono story)
Petrarch, *L'Ascension du Mont Ventoux*
J-B. Reboul, *La Cuisine Provençale*
Tobias Smollett, *Travels through France and Italy*
Stendhal, *Mémoires d'un Touriste*
Patricia Wells, *At Home in Provence*
Lawrence Wylie, *A Village in Vaucluse*
Arthur Young, *Travels in France*
Emile Zola, *La Fortune des Rougon*

Also see the letters of Marquise de Sévigné, Paul Cézanne and Vincent Van Gogh

Index